W9-BKQ-685

THE MONEY BUBBLE

What To Do Before It Pops

by
James Turk and John Rubino

Published by DollarCollapse Press
[www.dollarcollapse.com]

Articles by James Turk can be found on his company's website:
www.goldmoney.com

Articles by John Rubino can be found at www.dollarcollapse.com

The information contained herein has been compiled from sources believed to be reliable, but no representation or warranty, express or implied, is made by the authors, their affiliates, representatives or any other person as to its accuracy, completeness or correctness.

All opinions and estimates reflect the writers' judgment at the time of writing, are subject to change without notice and are provided in good faith but without legal responsibility. To the full extent permitted by law neither the authors nor any of their affiliates, representatives, nor any other person, accepts any liability whatsoever for any direct, indirect or consequential loss arising from any use of the information contained herein. Before making an investment decision, please consider whether this information is appropriate to your objectives and consult a trusted advisor.

This book may not be reproduced, distributed or published without the prior consent of the authors.

Copyright © 2013 James Turk and John Rubino
All rights reserved.

ISBN (Print): 978-1-62217-034-0

"The secret of freedom lies in educating people, whereas the secret of tyranny is in keeping them ignorant." – Robespierre

TABLE OF CONTENTS

TABLE OF FIGURES

A NOTE FROM THE AUTHORS

In 2004 we co-wrote a book called *"The Coming Collapse of the Dollar and How to Profit From It,"* and at the time our biggest worry was that the global financial system – led by the US dollar – would implode before we could get the book to market.

As it turned out we were right about many particulars: Wall Street nearly collapsed in 2008 with the bursting of the housing bubble; banks, mortgage companies and home builders were terrific short sale candidates; and gold and silver rose for the next eight years. But the dollar itself – and the global financial system which it dominates – have survived. In fact, by deploying a set of previously-only-theoretical monetary policies, borrowing unprecedented amounts of money and, to put it bluntly, lying about the true state of their economies and financial commitments, the US, Europe, and Japan have managed to not only avoid a monetary collapse but to prolong the "Money Bubble" that has been inflating for the past four decades.

Think of it as a "meta-bubble," a framework within which other, smaller financial bubbles (junk bonds, tech stocks, housing) have emerged and then burst. Its extraordinary – and very dangerous – nature will be covered in some detail in later chapters, so for now suffice it to say that by adopting currencies that circulate by government decree, or fiat (hence "fiat currencies"), without the backing of tangible forms of money like gold and silver, the developed world has managed to amass debts that make a period of chaos virtually certain. And because the Money Bubble involves the world's major currencies rather than just a discrete asset class like houses or tech stocks, its bursting will be both far more devastating for the unprepared and far more profitable for those able to understand it and act accordingly. Our goal is to usher you into that small but happy second group.

But first, a few notes about this book:

It's Full of New Material

The general structure is similar to that of *"The Coming Collapse of the Dollar..."* but thanks to the eventfulness of the past decade, the content is mostly new. We've recently been writing and speaking about quantitative easing, interest rate swaps, government gold price manipulation, the euro's fatal flaws, the hidden debts of the major economies, the state of the gold/silver mining business and much else, and are happy to be able to present these topics – each fascinating in its own right – in one volume.

The small amount of material that does appear in both books is generally background necessary to introduce new readers to concepts like the nature of money and to put today's world into historical context. We buzz through these sections, however, and encourage those who crave a deeper understanding of how the current mess was made to check out some of the excellent books on monetary history and theory that are available in most bookstores and the huge online library at Mises.org.

It Presents a Range of Possible Scenarios

The end game – the destruction of the major fiat currencies – is inevitable. But how the world gets from here to there is inherently unknowable. So rather than predict a single path, we outline a number of possibilities with names like "crack-up boom," "currency war," "catastrophic failure," and even "cyber-war" and "debt jubilee." Each is a fascinating, plausible narrative in its own right, but none are sure things. Think of them as different lenses through which to view the unfolding crisis, each offering a unique perspective which adds to one's understanding without claiming to predict exactly how the coming monetary events will unfold.

It Repeats Itself Occasionally

Because we're telling the same story from a number of different perspectives, there is occasional overlap that requires the same events to be recounted several times. Central bank reaction to the crash of 2008, for instance, is a crucial part of many different scenarios and reappears frequently. Ditto for the story of what the big commercial banks did with all the money they received from their central banks, as well as our admiration for the Austrian School of economics. Because the context is different for each repetition we're hoping that readers won't find this too annoying.

It Is Self-Published

For years, James has been pointing out that technology has given authors the ability to create and publish professional-quality books in a fraction of the time previously required within the traditional agent-publisher-bookstore model. No need to negotiate over foreign rights, wrangle with inexperienced editors, water down controversial statements to satisfy corporate sensibilities, or stew for months while the publisher converts edited manuscript into physical books and finally ships them to stores. The writer is now in control.

It took John a while to grasp this new reality, but eventually he came around. *"The Money Bubble"* was written in Microsoft Word and – with invaluable help from our friends at publishing consultancy WaveCloud – turned into paperback and e-books in a total of five months rather than the eight or more it would have taken via the traditional route. As a result, we've been a lot less anxious about *this* bubble bursting before we finish writing about it – though we still expect it to burst soon.

It Is an Investment Book

Don't be put off by all the references to monetary policy and historical trends and cataclysmic crashes. That's just us setting the table for the actual meal, which consists of a broad look at portfolio management followed by a series of investment strategies that will, if things play out as we expect, offer a chance at massive, life-changing profits – or, depending on your objectives and temperament, the peace of mind that comes from understanding what's happening and being able to protect yourself and your family.

It Emphasizes Gold

Because we view fiat (i.e., government created and controlled) currencies as the root cause of the financial world's many problems, we see the failure of these currencies and their replacement with something better as both inevitable and imminent. Because gold was humanity's money of choice for the 3,000 years prior to 1971 – during which time it worked very well – we think it will be central to the coming transition. Society will simply go back to tried-and-true money, on terms that are extremely favorable to those who own gold today.

It Contains Some Perhaps-Unfamiliar Terminology, Including:

- **The printing press.** Until very recently currency existed primarily as actual pieces of paper, run off on a government printing press. Today, of course, most currency exists as bits in computer databases ready to be spent with plastic cards. But commentators still refer to the "printing press" when discussing central bank money creation activities. We do the same, both from habit and because the term is a great piece of shorthand for a much more complex process. So when the term appears here, it refers to currency creation in general, whether electronically or physically.

- **Gold's exchange rate**. An old Chinese proverb says wisdom begins with calling things by their right name. In the financial media, gold is generally presented as having a "price," but this is incorrect, because gold is not a consumable commodity like oil or eggs. Gold is money, and since we don't talk about the *price* of euros or yen, but instead discuss their "exchange rate," in this book we treat gold in the same way, as in "gold's exchange rate to the dollar was $1,323 on October 31. To the euro it was €973."

- **Ounces versus grams.** In the US, the most familiar measurement of gold is the troy ounce. This convention is a historical legacy of the British Empire, in which the gold standard and gold itself played central roles. But these days most of the world, including the U.K., is on the metric system, and gold's weight is expressed using the gram, which is about 1/31 of a troy ounce (31.1034 grams per troy ounce, to be precise). So while we stick with ounces to avoid confusion, we also give the equivalent measurement in "goldgrams," as in "$1,323/oz. ($42.54/gg)."

It Glosses Over Some Topics That Are Explained Later

In the early chapters, for the sake of moving things along we occasionally toss out assertions like "according to the government's somewhat deceptive accounting methods" without further explanation. That's because we cover it in a later chapter and don't want to bog down the narrative with complex material that is repeated elsewhere. We'll generally include a "(to be explained in Chapter xx)" to indicate that more information is coming, and in the meantime ask for the benefit of the doubt.

Its Treatment of Those Deceptive Government Statistics Is a Bit Inconsistent

In Chapter 6 we explain how the statistics emanating from the US and elsewhere are being systematically distorted to hide the true weakness of the major fiat currencies and the general state of the economy. But in other chapters we cite government statistics to illustrate various points. To avoid having to repeat a disclaimer every time we mention a statistic, we'll just say it here: Each time you see an official government number, there is an unspoken but implied assertion that it's probably fictitious, but is being cited because even the distorted version backs up whatever point we're making.

It Was Written During a Period of Accelerating Change

Because things are moving so quickly, any present-tense statement risks being made false or obsolete by subsequent events. So we repeatedly qualify facts and figures with "as this is written…" or "as of late 2013." We apologize in advance to readers who, by the end of the book, are annoyed by these qualifiers.

It Is Neither Anti-American nor Anti-Government

We are decidedly critical of the foreign and domestic policies of many governments, particularly the United

States. But we but have no desire for America to fail, suffer, or decline in any way. John is an American citizen and plans to remain so, while James lives in Europe but enjoys summer holidays in the mountains of New Hampshire. Our problem is with how the ability to create money out of thin air has corrupted what was once a society based on free individuals living self-directed lives without undue fear of governmental power. The right to "life, liberty and the pursuit of happiness" is rapidly being eroded by endless interventions abroad and pervasive surveillance, regulation, and coercion at home – and as you'll see in Chapter 11, the growing threat of government confiscation of private assets. Sadly, most Americans are passively allowing it to happen. So every once in a while our frustration peeks through in our writing.

It Is Ultimately Optimistic

Extremely hard, chaotic times are coming. But they will pass. And the period that follows will be amazing, as a wide range of breakthrough technologies coalesce to give our grandkids a rich, free, clean world. In the meantime, as the old saying goes, crisis equals opportunity.

> *"The Chinese symbol for crisis...is actually a combination of two symbols: the symbol for danger and the symbol for opportunity. The danger is what everybody sees; the opportunity is never quite so obvious as the danger, but it's always there."*
>
> *– Doug Casey*

INTRODUCTION

THE LONG WAVE VERSUS THE PRINTING PRESS

Today's world of rising debt and ever-greater financial instability certainly feels like uncharted territory. But that's only because we humans have such short life spans. From a historical perspective, what's happening is depressingly familiar. Over the centuries dozens if not hundreds of societies have borrowed too much and then, wittingly or not, destroyed the currency in which their debts were denominated. In most cases this play has consisted of three acts: excessive borrowing, "blow-off" inflationary bubble, and catastrophic economic crash. And every few generations, most major countries stage a new version, with different actors but the same general story line.

Several "Long Wave" theories claim to account for these recurring cycles, and while each has its own unique take on the process, all begin with the assumption that we are emotional creatures with limited, selective memories. As a result we are, as Spanish-American philosopher George Santayana famously observed, condemned to repeat the past because we don't remember it.

In fact, for as long as there have been money and markets, societies have been passing through the same sequence of cultural moods, beginning with anxious conservatism in the aftermath of hard times, followed by cautious optimism and finally – as the original "depression-era" generation is replaced by its memory-impaired grandkids – let-it-all-hang-out financial excess. A horrendous debt-driven economic crash (or its geopolitical/ military equivalent) then resets the cycle.

The fascinating thing about these theories is that while each employs a unique set of indicators to trace society's progress through these recurring cultural/psychological /financial cycles, they've all reached the same conclusion: The modern world is toast. Or it should be by now. Virtually all Long Wave theories conclude that the expansion that began after World War II has ended, and that nearly the entire world – which is now interlinked to an unprecedented extent by technology and common mistakes – should be deep in a 1930's-style, capital "D" depression.

To illustrate the point, here's a quick overview of three well-known Long Wave theories:

Kondratieff Wave

During the 1920s, Russian economist Nicolai Kondratieff studied historical trends in commodity prices and identified a recurring four-part, six-decade pattern of expansion, stagnation, recession and collapse. This insight burnished his professional reputation but alarmed the Soviet Union's leaders, whose Marxist theology envisioned a linear world moving from capitalist oppression to workers' paradise rather than a cyclical one. They had Kondratieff imprisoned and eventually shot.

His work, however, lives on, and over the ensuing decades his four stages gained seasonal names – spring, summer, autumn and winter – with summer being a time of fast growth in incomes and asset prices, autumn a period of post-boom "stagflation," and winter a debt-induced crash.

The most recent cycle began after World War II and (should have) peaked in the late 1990s.

Elliott Wave

In the 1930s, retired businessman Ralph Nelson Elliott noticed repeating five-part wave patterns in seemingly-unrelated markets. Elliott's intellectual successor, Yale

University psychology graduate and former Merrill Lynch technical analyst Robert Prechter, has popularized and refined this analytical lens via his *Elliott Wave Theorist* newsletter and best-selling books *At the Crest of the Tidal Wave* and *Conquer the Crash.*

Economics, says Prechter, is more about psychology than finance. And psychology – as expressed in popular culture and international relations as well as stock and real estate prices – evolves through Elliott's predictable five-wave pattern. In an interesting twist, he notes that these patterns are fractals that recur on different scales. Decade-long cycles constitute one leg of 50-year "supercycles," which are in turn single legs of several-century "grand supercycles," and so on. Today's world, alas, is at the end of a *"millennium cycle"* that began in the late 1700s, encompassed numerous smaller cycles – such as the one running from World War II to the present – and peaked in 2007. The resulting crash, says Prechter, will be commensurate with the length of the millennium cycle – and should be well under way by now.

The Fourth Turning

Historian William Strauss and economist Neil Howe, in their 1997 bestseller *The Fourth Turning,* detail research that they believe explains how successive generations are shaped by and in turn shape the society in which they come of age. Space considerations prevent us from delving too deeply into their fascinating theory, except to say that Strauss and Howe place today's world at the end of a long cycle, which is a very bad place to be:

> "Around the year 2005 [give or take a few years], a sudden spark will catalyze a Crisis mood. Remnants of the old social order will disintegrate. Political and economic trust will

implode. Real hardship will beset the land, with severe distress that could involve questions of class, race, nation and empire…Sometime before the year 2025, America will pass through a great gate in history, commensurate with the American Revolution, Civil War, and twin emergencies of the Great Depression and World War II…The risk of catastrophe will be very high. The nation could erupt into insurrection or civil violence, crack up geographically, or succumb to authoritarian rule."

ENTER THE PRINTING PRESS

This has without doubt been an interesting decade, but nothing like the Mad Max scenarios one might conjure up after reading the above. So has Long Wave analysis failed? No. It has, however, encountered something new: an unlimited monetary printing press that allows governments to manipulate markets on an unprecedented scale. Long Wave theories are derived from history and until very recently, most money was sound – that is, based on gold and/or silver, tangible assets that existed in limited supply. When debts rose to debilitating levels, borrowers were unable to acquire enough (scarce) money to pay off their loans and defaulted en masse, causing the depressions that generally followed extended booms. Past governments couldn't derail this process because they couldn't make more gold.

They still can't make more gold. But over the past 40 years they've convinced their citizens that paper, un-backed by anything real, is the same thing. Today's central banks can create as much new fiat currency (banknotes or its electronic equivalent) as they choose, and the global economy continues to accept it as money. This widespread and systemic gullibility allowed the US government to more than double its already-excessive national debt between 2007 and 2013. And it is allowing Europe to, in effect, move much of the debt of Greece, Spain and Portugal onto Germany's balance sheet without setting off a financial panic or revolt. *And* it is enabling the Japanese government to borrow more, as a percent of its economy, than any other major country in history. None of this profligacy would have been possible in a sound-money environment.

But this monetary orgy hasn't suspended the economic laws described by Long Wave theories. On the contrary, it has *amplified* those laws. By delaying the end of the cycle, the fiat currency printing press has allowed the world to accumulate another $20 or so trillion of debt (much more if you count unfunded pension liabilities and derivatives and other such obligations – see Chapters 4 and 5), which will make the coming liquidation that much more painful.

So the question becomes one of timing. At what moment and under what circumstances will a critical mass of people realize that more currency does not equal more wealth? That is unknowable, because a global financial system of this complexity is inherently unstable and unpredictable. Instead of a machine that reacts in a linear fashion to inputs and stresses, a modern financial system is like a weather front that can suddenly morph from tropical depression to Category 5 hurricane, or a snow-covered mountainside that is perfectly stable until a snowflake lands on just the right spot to set off an avalanche (more on the instability of complex systems is coming in Chapter 13).

Which snowflake will set off the global financial avalanche can't be predicted in advance. But there are dozens of candidates. A broad Middle East war could send the price of oil soaring. The eurozone could begin to fragment, as peripheral countries like Greece and Spain realize that they can't live under the same monetary regime as Germany. A major bank's derivatives book could blow up. Interest rates could spike, setting off a death spiral in government finances and/or the implosion of the leveraged speculating community. The list goes on. And on.

Whatever the proximate cause, the bursting of this latest, greatest bubble, will lead to the mass-realization that un-backed fiat currency, created in unlimited quantities by over-indebted governments, is not money in the true sense of that word, and government bonds and bills denominated in fiat currency are certainly not the "risk-free" assets that investors have been led to believe. Eventually individuals, businesses and creditor nations will begin to convert these currencies and financial assets into real assets at whatever price is prevailing. Inflation will spread from isolated niches like US stocks and Chinese real estate to virtually everything.

Ludwig von Mises, a pioneer in the Austrian School of economics, called this sudden loss of faith in a fiat currency a "crack-up boom," and historically it has spelled the end of the currency in question. Since today's fiat currency regime is global, the transition – the crack-up boom – will be global as well. The list of victims will range from the people holding the ruined fiat currency to the *concept* of fiat currency itself. The idea that government can be trusted to create currency out of 'thin air' – a process that describes the essence of fiat currency – will be laid to rest, and the world will return to some form of sound money.

During this monetary phase-change, traditional methods of diversifying among financial assets will no longer protect your wealth. Stocks will gyrate wildly, formerly-safe bonds will plunge along with the currencies in which they're denominated, and paper cash, whether under the mattress or in a bank account, will trend towards zero as its purchasing power evaporates.

On the other hand, some assets will soar in price and some strategies will work beautifully in this environment. The chapters that follow will show you how to both survive this transition and profit greatly from it.

Brief Digression: You Know It's a Bubble When...

As long as there have been markets there have been bubbles. During the Tulip Bulb Mania in 17th century Holland, a single bulb could reportedly be exchanged for twelve acres of land. And since that time asset bubbles have sprung up regularly in market economies around the world. For some fascinating background and insight into past market manias, we recommend Charles Mackay's classic Extraordinary Popular Delusions and the Madness Of Crowds.

But simply labeling a market a "bubble" doesn't really shed much light on why it, as opposed to some other popular and pricey sector, is worthy of special attention. So here we'll define the term and show how it applies (boy does it ever) to today's fiat currencies.

An asset class is in a bubble when:

1) Its price rises far beyond what rational analysis would have deemed reasonable just a few years before.

2) Individuals in the market begin making apparently easy money doing things that experts used to find difficult. Think day-traders and house-flippers in, respectively, the dot-com and housing bubbles.

3) Tried-and true business practices are replaced with "innovations" that in more rational times would be seen as harebrained ideas at best or scams and cons at worst: Focusing on "eyeballs" rather than earnings when valuing tech stocks, for instance, or eschewing conforming loans in favor of liar loans and interest-only mortgages.

4) They can be identified fairly early in their life-cycles, but tend to go on longer than reasonable analysts expect. In 2004's The Coming Collapse of the Dollar *we wrote, "By virtually every measure, today's housing market is a classic financial bubble." We were right, but the housing bubble didn't burst for three more years. If this pattern holds, our prediction of the Money Bubble's imminent demise might also be a bit premature.*

5) As a bubble forms, a unique mantra emerges to justify its excesses. During the real estate bubble, for instance, the idea that "home prices only go up" became the conventional 'wisdom,' even though logic or a cursory analysis of historical prices could have proved it wrong.

Today's fiat currencies emphatically meet the above bubble criteria. The prices of government bonds denominated in euro, yen and dollars have risen to extraordinary levels (which is the same as saying interest rates have been forced to extraordinarily-low levels). And befitting its size and scope, this bubble is rationalized with two popular mantras: the sovereign debt of countries with a printing press is "risk-free," and those same governments can use their printing presses to control interest rates and boost asset prices – forever.

Where in lesser bubbles individuals make fortunes doing things that the pros used to find hard, in the Money Bubble it is countries that are able to finance (through borrowing and money printing) extremely generous entitlements programs and/or aggressive foreign military adventures, something only financially rock-solid superpowers used to be able to manage. As for tried-and-true business practices being supplanted by "innovations," consider the fact that no major country balances its budget any more, while all engage in historically-unprecedented deficit spending and money printing. Viewed through this lens, quantitative easing is sub-prime lending on a global scale.

Bubbles have one other salient trait: They usually go out with a bang. Virtually every major bubble in financial history has popped rather than deflated gradually. And the Money Bubble, as the biggest of them all, will put its predecessors to shame in that regard.

PART I:
HOW WE GOT HERE

CHAPTER 1

THE PAPER MONEY EXPERIMENT

"Paper money has had the effect in your State that it ever will have, to ruin commerce, oppress the honest, and open a door to every species of fraud and injustice."

– George Washington, 1787

Money matters, and not just in the "more is better" sense. A society is shaped to a surprising degree by the thing it chooses to use as money, and the first half of this book is a chronicle of how the world's most powerful countries chose badly, making perhaps the worst series of monetary mistakes in history and creating the conditions for chaos in the years to come.

But first let's consider money itself, what it is and is not.

It is not, for instance, the root of all evil, nor is it a shared hallucination. It is simply a tool that enables individuals and societies to accomplish certain things. And to accomplish any given task, the right tool yields the best results. A carpenter can hammer nails with a rock – or his shoe or his forehead. But give him a well-balanced hammer and the house he builds is more likely to be a comfortable home. For a society, the right money enhances stability, prosperity, honesty and harmony, while the wrong money does the opposite.

The ideal form of money is:

- A communication medium that allows buyers and sellers to convey ideas about value in an understandable way.

- A "store of purchasing power" that allows its owner to delay consumption by holding wealth not immediately needed for spending in a form that can be converted to a comparable amount of useful things later on. To ensure that a money's purchasing power is stable over long periods of time, its supply should be very slow-growing and predictable.

- A medium of exchange that can be easily identified and moved from buyer to seller (regardless of whether or not they are in close proximity) to enable them to transact for goods and services. That is, each unit of money must be identical, light enough to be carried, and easily and safely transferable.

- A tangible asset to eliminate payment risk (this is the least familiar aspect of money, so we'll spend a bit more time explaining it). The underlying principle of all commerce is that goods and services pay for goods and services. So a shopkeeper accepting a fiat currency in payment has not actually "extinguished" the transaction until he uses that fiat currency to purchase some other good or service. In the interim he faces "counterparty risk," the danger that the purchasing power of his pieces of paper will decline due to inflation or devaluation, be lost in a bank failure, or be repudiated and replaced with some new paper currency of lesser value. In other words, fiat currency is in effect an IOU, the value of which depends on someone else – in this case the government – keeping its promises. Gold and silver coins, in contrast, are tangible assets that don't depend on government for their value. When our hypothetical merchant accepts such coins in return for goods, the transaction is extinguished because real goods have been exchanged for real goods.

Any money that meets all of the above criteria is considered "sound."

"Currency," meanwhile, is the form money takes when it circulates. But it is not always money itself. When paper is printed to represent the gold or silver in a government's vaults, that paper is not money but a "money substitute." It can be spent and even saved as if it was metal, but the two are not identical. We'll expand on the differences between money and currency in later chapters.

The earliest societies operated without money, instead relying on barter, i.e., the direct trade of one kind of good or service for another. If one of our distant ancestors needed a beaver pelt, they would simply take some arrowheads or other tradable goods to a local trapper and work out a deal.

Barter is fine for a society where only a few things are made and exchanged. But it becomes hopelessly time-consuming as societies grow more complex. Consider the challenge a barter-based society would present for, say, a speech therapist in need of a new motherboard for her computer. Unless someone at the computer store has a lisp, she's in for a harrowing day of multi-party negotiating that might never result in a working computer.

So eventually, in order to smooth the process of transacting and saving, every society has ended up designating something with an agreed-upon value to serve as money. Over the centuries numerous things have been auditioned for this role, including livestock, slaves, rocks, seashells and tea leaves, to name just a few. All had major (obvious in retrospect) flaws, and eventually the early world settled upon bits of metal that could be turned into identical coins and were easy to carry around. By the time of the Ancient Greeks, gold, silver and sometimes copper coins were generally accepted as money.

Metal coins performed exceptionally well, enabling people to communicate and transact efficiently. And as a store of purchasing power, gold and silver excelled. The same ounce (31 grams) of gold that bought a good-quality toga in ancient Rome will buy a nice business suit today. In more recent times, the prices of oil and wheat and most other things, when expressed in gold, have been remarkably stable.

But this store-of-purchasing-power function – dependent as it is on a limited supply of monetary metals – is actually a drawback for governments in need of resources to fight wars and maintain the support of powerful constituents. So every so often a country decides to replace gold and silver with a more plentiful and easily-manipulated substitute. In other words, they choose political expediency over stability, and adopt "unsound" money.

The result, in every recorded case, has been the same: Released from the discipline of a limited money supply, government goes a bit wild, creating so much new currency that its value evaporates. After a period of chaos, the traumatized society has – in every single case – returned to some form of sound money.

Here are a few of history's more interesting experiments with unsound money:

Rome Floods the Empire with Copper

The Roman Empire, which two millennia ago ruled its world in much the same way that the US recently ruled this one, used three metals as money: copper for small change, and relatively-scarce gold and silver for larger denominations. The denarius, the most commonly used coin of the time, was pure silver in the first century AD. But the pressures of running a far-flung empire while placating "the people" led to steadily-rising government spending. Successive emperors addressed this mounting budgetary pressure the dishonest way – by mixing cheap, plentiful copper into their silver coins. By around AD100, the denarius contained 85 percent silver. By 218 the figure was 43 percent and by 244, only 0.05 percent. As its character changed, the denarius lost its ability to communicate ideas of value and preserve the purchasing power of savings. Romans, as their money became increasingly impaired, found it harder to figure out what things should cost and began to doubt the future value of their savings. They began to convert coins into tangible goods, whatever the cost.

Emperor Diocletian (284 - 305) responded to the resulting price instability with one of the earliest attempts at price controls, mandating not only that merchants charge the same amount for goods as in previous years, but that sons of merchants, on pain of death, stay in the business even if inflation had made it unprofitable. The empire collapsed not long after.

China Invents Paper Currency

In the 11th century China experienced a copper shortage, replaced that metal in its coins with iron, and then began over-issuing those coins, causing them to plunge in value. It then switched to paper notes which were initially exchangeable for gold, silver or silk. This went well for a while. When Marco Polo visited China in 1269, he wrote: "You might say that [Kublai Khan, China's emperor] has the secret of alchemy in perfection…the Khan causes every year to be made such a vast quantity of this money, which costs him nothing, that it must equal in amount all the treasure of the world."

Soon, alas, the supply of paper became unmanageable and the currency collapsed, wiping out the savings of a whole generation and leading to a period of chaos before a return to sound money could be achieved in 1455 – under a different dynasty. (We're oversimplifying a hugely complex era but are comfortable stating that, as with Rome, a mismanaged currency contributed to the eventual fall of the empire.)

France Makes the Same Mistake Twice

1716. Its treasury strained by a series of wars and a spendthrift monarch, France turned its finances over to a Scottish adventurer named John Law, who proceeded to introduce a paper currency and to print a lot of it. At first, this rising currency supply made everyone feel richer, and Law was hailed as a hero. But as more and more paper notes were printed, bubbles formed in France's real estate and stock markets (look up the Mississippi Bubble for details), while prices of most other things began to rise at an accelerating rate. Instability ensued, followed by a widespread collapse in asset prices. By 1721 the country was devastated, and Law was an outcast.

1789. Soon after the French Revolution, the new government began issuing paper notes, called assignats, which were supposedly backed by lands then being confiscated from the Catholic Church. But paper issuance quickly outstripped land seizures and inflation soared. A notably bloody period of chaos ensued, followed by the rise of Napoleon and nearly twenty years of pan-European war.

The American Colonies Try Paper – and Get Hyperinflation

During the American War of Independence, the colonies needed equipment and supplies to defend themselves against the British Empire. The Continental Congress responded by creating a new paper currency with the promise that after the war the notes would be paid off with tax revenues. The war lasted longer than expected, far too many "continentals" were created, and the currency's value evaporated. In 1779 $100 worth of gold or silver coins would buy $2,600 face value of continentals. Two years later the same coins bought $16,800 of continentals. Within another two years continentals had become worthless, wiping out many of the soldiers and other patriots who believed their government's promises. For decades thereafter Americans referred to items of little value as "not worth a continental."

Weimar Germany Defines Modern Hyperinflation

After World War I the winners, led by France and Great Britain, imposed onerous reparations payments on the loser, Germany. Overwhelmed by what was in effect a massive national debt, the government (known as "Weimar" for the city in which it was constituted) began printing ever-greater quantities of paper marks in the hope of generating growth and trade and thus much-needed tax revenues. Instead it got hyperinflation, and the world got compelling images of Germans carrying wheelbarrows full of cash to the grocery store and burning stacks of bills to keep warm. In 1919, 12 marks were worth one dollar. By 1921 the dollar bought 57 marks and by October 1923 *170 billion*. Here again, the savings of a generation was wiped out, setting the stage for a dictator – in this case Hitler – to take power.

A FIAT CURRENCY WORLD

Past episodes of unsound money were local affairs conducted in a generally sound-money world. Even when an entity the size of Rome inflated away its copper coinage, gold and silver still circulated internally (mainly in the hands of the rich) and continued to function as money both within and without the empire. In other words, there was still sound money for those who could afford it.

But since 1971, when President Nixon decided to, in his words, "suspend temporarily the convertibility of the dollar into gold," every major country has been asking citizens to accept fiat currency and to trust that their government will manage it wisely enough for it to both function as a medium of exchange and retain purchasing power over time.

Based on the results of past fiat currency experiments, an observer might predict that today's governments would react to this freedom from the constraint of a limited money supply by spending far more than they receive in taxes and borrowing/printing whatever it takes to cover the difference. Our hypothetical observer might also predict that today's world would be heavily-indebted and prone to booms and busts of ever-rising amplitude.

The observer would be right. Nearly every major government is doing exactly what past printing press owners have done, but – thanks to modern technology and globalization – they're doing it on a scale that has never before been attempted. So this time around, the entire global financial system finds itself drifting inexorably toward the chaos that has claimed all previous fiat currencies.

CHAPTER 2

THE SAME RESPONSE TO EVERY CRISIS

"Insanity is doing the same thing over and over again and expecting different results."

– Albert Einstein

Now let's jump to the near-present, with an overview of how the US brought the global financial system to the brink of dissolution in 2008. To state the theme up front: When armed with a printing press, a nation tends to respond to every problem in the same, politically-expedient way by throwing newly-created money at it. But as with any other form of addiction, the dosage has to keep rising to produce the same result – until the level becomes fatal.

DIFFERENT LEADERS, SAME DEBT

To most Americans, the 1980s and 1990s were very different decades, with leaders who implemented different policies in pursuit of unique goals – and got very dissimilar results. But that, as it turns out, was mostly an illusion. When viewed from a suitable distance and through the right lens, those two decades form one long period of excessive debt accumulation.

With his 1980 election, conservative Republican Ronald Reagan set about reversing what he saw as an American economic and geopolitical decline brought about by expanding government and rising taxes. He cut taxes aggressively, increased military spending and began flexing the American empire's muscles around the world. Growth ensued, but (since one thing even the Great Communicator could not cut was fast-growing entitlement programs) spending outstripped tax revenues and federal deficits soared.

When Bill Clinton was elected in 1992, he raised taxes and cut military spending and – due in part to a deadlock with a Republican-controlled congress – authorized little new domestic spending. This restraint, combined with the capital gains generated by the tech stock bubble of the late 1990s, caused government revenues to actually exceed its (reported) spending for a while, giving the impression that its debt problems were solved. But this conclusion is only possible if the focus is solely on government debt. Zoom out to total societal debt – that is, government debt plus mortgages, credit cards, business loans etc. – and the US actually borrowed more during the 1990s than the 1980s.

Figure 2.1: Total US Debt, 1980–1999

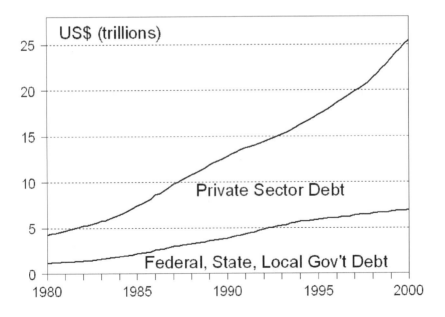

The surprising profligacy of the 1990s illustrates an important point about public finances, which is that there are several ways to cover the costs of rising government spending. One is to raise taxes, which is honest but difficult because it is both visible and guaranteed to enrage important constituencies. The second is to borrow the excess, which is less obvious and therefore more frequently chosen by leaders who can get away with it. That was the 1980s.

The third strategy is to encourage the private sector to do the borrowing. For a sense of how this works, pretend for a moment that the availability of cheap mortgage financing convinces you to build your dream house. Your decision creates jobs for carpenters, plumbers, bankers and furniture makers, all of whom pay taxes on their new income. The government takes in more revenue and therefore needs to borrow less. *But total societal debt rises by just as much as if the government borrowed that money instead of you.*

This strategy is even harder for most people to understand than deficit spending. And even when understood it's hard to dislike because initially it feels great. Individuals find jobs and credit plentiful while the value of their homes and investments soar. Politicians can point to falling deficits as proof of their responsible stewardship. And businesspeople are energized by dreams of commercial empires built with other peoples' money.

That, in a nutshell, was the 1990s, as the Federal Reserve repeatedly cut interest rates and encouraged home buying and corporate empire building – just as the Internet was emerging as that generation's Next Big Thing. So hundreds of billions of dollars were borrowed to lay fiber optic cable and consolidate media empires and fund the start-up of eBay and Amazon and countless other dot-coms

– and then to bid their shares into the stratosphere. The taxable income thus generated balanced the government's books, at least under Washington's questionable accounting methods, while sending the country's total debt soaring. But because so many of the uses to which these borrowed funds were put turned out to be unwise or unprofitable, debt ended up growing faster than productive assets. This "malinvestment" left the country poorer than it would have been had the money never been borrowed.

Meanwhile, excessive currency creation by central and commercial banks (see Chapter 15 for an explanation of how they do this) tends to produce a torrent of "hot" money that surges from one part of the globe to another – causing localized debt bubbles that eventually pop and destabilize the victim countries. And it emboldens leveraged speculators like hedge funds and Wall Street investment banks to take ever-larger chances – some of which also eventually blow up. The government then responds with its only remaining tool: the printing press. And because each infusion of new currency leaves the system more indebted, the amplitude of the succeeding booms and busts tends to rise. Here's a timeline of smaller crises leading up to the big one of 2008:

1994: Mexican Bailout

During the early 1990s Mexico pegged its currency, the peso, to the US dollar while running big deficits and borrowing aggressively. Then a series of problems arose more-or-less simultaneously: a banking corruption scandal ensnared some top leaders and their families, the price of oil (Mexico's biggest export) fell, an armed rebellion gained traction and a major presidential candidate was assassinated.

In many ways it was business as usual for a developing Latin American country of the era. But then the hot money that had been flowing into Mexico's dollar-pegged economy began to flow back out. Foreign exchange reserves dwindled (i.e., the government began to run out of money), and it became clear to all that the peso would have to be devalued.

Large US banks including Goldman Sachs and Citigroup were owners of billions of dollars of Mexican bonds which would plunge in value in the event of a default or major devaluation. So President Clinton proposed that Congress bail Mexico out directly. When Congress balked, US Treasury Secretary (and former Goldman Sachs co-chairman) Robert Rubin simply gave Mexico $20 billion of currency swaps and loan guarantees from the Exchange Stabilization Fund, a Treasury account that as Treasury Secretary he controlled, in effect bailing out his former employer and the other major banks. Mexico stabilized and the crisis subsided – but a lesson was learned: When big US banks are threatened, the money will be found to protect them.

Brief Digression: *The Mexican bailout was a seminal moment in America's descent into financial decadence because it effectively removed downside risk from Wall Street's calculus. Capitalism – in theory and previously in practice – was very much a carrot-and-stick philosophy. Succeed (primarily through hard work and creativity) and the result was extraordinary wealth. Fail and all was lost. By exaggerating the stakes in this way, free markets unleash the energies of a wide range of would-be entrepreneurs who generate the "creative destruction" that typifies a dynamic, rapidly-progressing modern society. But eliminate the downside risk and the system is perverted.*

The Mexican bailout taught managers of global banks that they couldn't lose. In taking extreme risks by, for instance, lending aggressively to weak borrowers or creating and selling exotic and untested financial instruments, they could generate massive fees in the short run, which would translate into gigantic year-end bonuses and soaring stock prices. And if they failed the government would bail them out with taxpayers' money, allow them to keep their jobs and remain, for the most part, rich and powerful. This government guarantee came to be known as the "Greenspan put," after the Federal Reserve chairman who repeatedly injected liquidity into the system to support asset prices, thereby bailing out pretty much every major bank in sight. And it created a system in which, as Nobel laureate economist Joseph Stiglitz famously put it, profit is privatized and risk is socialized.

1997: Asian Contagion

By the mid-1990s hot money was pouring out of the US and into the "Asian Tigers," up-and-coming countries like Korea and Thailand that were replicating Japan's export-driven growth model. But too much of a monetary good thing leads to bad decisions, and the productivity of new investments had been falling for a while. Then China devalued its currency and the US raised interest rates in response to an "irrationally exuberant" stock market. The dollar rose strongly and hot money started pouring out of the Asian Tigers and into suddenly-higher-yielding US bonds. The Tigers' economies began to implode.

Here again, much of the money at risk was owed to large US banks, and the response was swift. The International Monetary Fund (using mostly American capital) began a multi-billion dollar bailout of the Asian economies, while the US Federal Reserve reversed course and cut interest rates to lower the value of the dollar and reduce bank borrowing costs. The panic subsided within a few months.

1998: LTCM Implodes

Long-Term Capital Management (LTCM) was a hedge fund (an unregulated investment company) that had been founded by a star bond trader and stocked with Nobel Prize-winning mathematicians and economists. Banks were in awe of this lineup and – armed with very cheap, plentiful money from the Federal Reserve – competed to finance LTCM's strategies. Without going into excessive detail, suffice it to say that using unprecedented leverage, LTCM made a global bet on stability in the bond markets. Then Russia defaulted on its debt, producing exactly the opposite result. LTCM's trades blew up, and since a range of large banks had lent it over one hundred billion dollars, the global financial system was suddenly threatened.

The Federal Reserve convened a meeting of Wall Street banks, organized a bailout of LTCM, and once again cut short-term interest rates. The crisis was averted and Fed chair Alan Greenspan and Treasury bureaucrats Robert Rubin and Larry Summers ended up on the cover of TIME magazine. By this time the "Greenspan put" was widely seen as official government policy.

2000: The Tech Bubble Bursts

The tidal wave of liquidity unleashed by Washington's response to the past decade's crises poured into US tech stocks. In one final spasm in late 1999 and early 2000, the NASDAQ, the market where big tech names traded, doubled from its already grossly-overvalued level of a year earlier. Then, finally, it crashed.

Figure 2.2: NASDAQ, 1990–2002

So much money had been bet on so many unworkable business plans and ridiculously-overvalued stocks that trillions of dollars simply evaporated from Americans' nest eggs and bank balance sheets. A recession was unavoidable, and a Depression was very possible – right on schedule from a Long Wave Theory point of view. So the Fed once again cut interest rates.

Then came the World Trade Center attacks of September 11 2001, which threatened to terrify consumers into becoming savers, thus depressing the economy even further. And the Fed, as if the past few crises were just warm-ups, opened the floodgates. It cut interest rates dramatically and made it clear to all concerned that it was there to backstop the economy with easy money.

Figure 2.3: Yield on 3-Month Treasury Bill, 1990-2003

The government ramped up spending, especially on the military, and the federal deficit, so recently in a relative decline, soared to several hundred billion dollars annually. In effect, the US combined strategies 2 and 3 mentioned at the beginning of this chapter, with the government both borrowing record amounts of money and encouraging the private sector to do the same.

It took a while, but the massive infusion of credit set off yet another bubble, this one in housing. Home prices soared, banks offered mortgages to virtually anyone and then packaged the increasingly low-quality loans into mortgage backed bonds and sold them – and derivatives based on them – to institutions around the world. Ratings agencies like Standard & Poor's and Moody's – which in a truly amazing conflict of interest, get paid by the issuers of these bonds – gave triple-A ratings to pretty much everything that came their way, often without even looking at the underlying mortgages. Homeowners began using their houses like ATMs, extracting cash via home equity credit lines and using the proceeds to buy cars, vacations and more houses. And last but not least the share prices of home builders, big banks, mortgage lenders, and virtually everyone else associated with the housing business soared to record levels, taking the overall stock market along for the ride. An epic bubble had been blown, on the back of an equally epic increase in total system-wide debt.

Figure 2.4: Total US Debt, 2000–2007

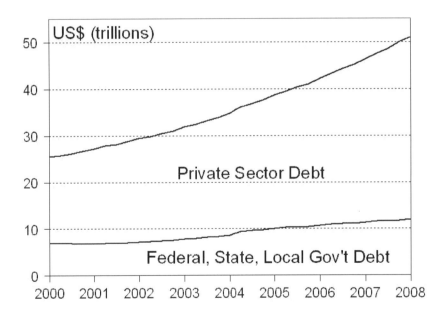

Then *this* bubble burst, creating a financial crisis in 2008 that could very well have decimated the global financial system. We certainly thought that the end of the fiat money era had arrived, and forecast as much in *The*

Coming Collapse of the Dollar. But we were wrong. As it turned out the experiment had one more, truly-extraordinary surprise in store.

CHAPTER 3

BATTLING THE GREAT RECESSION: MORE POWERFUL WEAPONS, MUCH BIGGER MISTAKES

"The money rate can, indeed, be kept artificially low only by continuous new injections of currency or bank credit in place of real savings. This can create the illusion of more capital just as the addition of water can create the illusion of more milk. But it is a policy of continuous inflation. It is obviously a process involving cumulative danger."

– Henry Hazlitt

By 2007, the entire US economy was one big financial bubble. Home prices were soaring while some broad stock market indexes were back above their dot-com mania peak, this time led by the banks and homebuilders that were feasting on post-9/11 easy money.

This bubble, as most tend to do, lasted longer than many thought possible, expanding to almost ridiculous proportions before finally popping in 2007. First to go was the sub-prime mortgage market, where banks had been lending to virtually anyone with a heartbeat. From there the carnage spread to other kinds of mortgages, then to mortgage backed bonds, credit derivatives and finally to the shares of banks and home builders. With the collapse of venerable Wall Street investment bank Bear Stearns in early 2008, the realization finally dawned that the economy had become dependent on finance, and the financial markets were seizing up. When Lehman Brothers failed just a few months later, the Long Wave was poised to swamp the US economy.

On September 19, 2008, Treasury secretary Hank Paulson (another former Goldman Sachs chairman) informed legislators and a seemingly befuddled President George W. Bush that unless taxpayers bailed out the banks to the tune of *several trillion dollars*, the financial world would end. On October 2, Rep. Brad Sherman (D-Calif.) said on the House floor that "Many of us were told in private conversations that if we voted against this bill on Monday the sky would fall, the market would drop two or three thousand points the first day, another couple of thousand the second day, and a few members were even told that there would be martial law in America if we voted no."

This, in retrospect, was a bluff. The disappearance of Goldman Sachs and half a dozen of its peers wouldn't have changed the number of factories, farms and hospitals in the country, so total real, as opposed to financial wealth would barely have changed. Moving thousands of derivatives traders and investment bankers into useful professions like cab driving, farming or factory work might actually have made the transition to a post-Wall Street world a net plus.

But Congress and the White House caved in to the threats and signed off on the largest taxpayer bailout in history. It was later revealed that the Federal Reserve had gone even further than originally reported, secretly lending big banks around the world nearly $16 trillion. This was by far the most audacious monetary/fiscal experiment in history, all aimed at keeping a moribund system going. But it was just the beginning.

ENTER QUANTITATIVE EASING

When the economy didn't respond to the bank bailout – and the banks remained hobbled by the looming default of trillions of dollars of bad loans and derivatives – the Federal Reserve dusted off a theoretical idea called "quantitative easing," in which the central bank buys bonds on the open market, paying for those securities with newly-created currency. ("Quantitative" refers to the increasing quantity of money, while "easing" refers to reducing interest rates to make cheap capital readily available to banks. This practice is also known as "debt monetization" because it turns debt into circulating currency.)

The goal was two-fold: First, to enable the US government to borrow unprecedented amounts of money and spend it in an attempt to revive the economy. Second, to "recapitalize" the banks, keeping them alive and – hopefully – convincing them to start lending again.

The first quantitative easing, or QE1, program was announced in November 2008, with the purchase of $600 billion of mortgage-backed securities. (This figure seems unremarkable today but at the time was extraordinarily large.) But this liquidity infusion wasn't enough to get the economy moving. Banks were still traumatized and preferred to simply park their extra reserves with the Fed, earning next-to-nothing but incurring no risk. The country seemed to lose interest in lending, borrowing, and spending. As a result, the "velocity of money" – a measure of how often a given dollar, once created, changes hands – continued to plunge from its late 1990s peak.

Figure 3.1: Velocity of Money (M2), 1960–2013

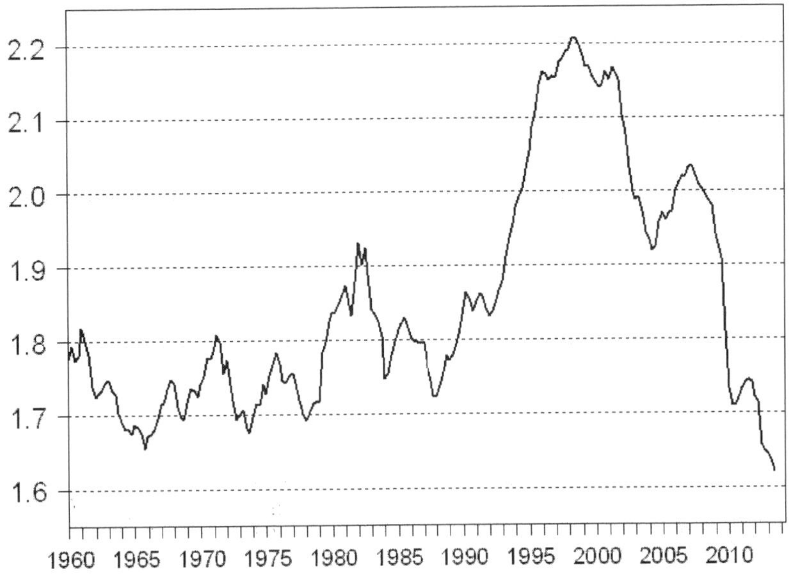

QE2, The Fed Ups the Ante

In November 2010, the Fed unveiled a second round of quantitative easing, dubbed "QE2," that called for the purchase of another $600 billion of Treasury securities by the middle of 2011. But once again, the additional stimulus didn't produce an economy in which banks were happy to lend or consumers and businesses eager to borrow. Growth was slow and unemployment remained above 10 percent – and elections were coming up.

QE3, To Infinity and Beyond

Washington's response was to make QE open-ended. In September 2012 it announced that it would buy $40 billion of bonds per month until its definition of normal life – more debt and spending – resumed. In December 2012 this was raised to $85 billion a month and dubbed "QE-Infinity" because of its indeterminate lifespan.

Zero Interest Rate Policy (ZIRP)

The now-desperate Fed concluded that even lower interest rates were required to energize business investment and home buying. So it pushed short-term rates down to virtually zero, and – in yet another experimental departure from tradition – began targeting its buying at the long-term end of the spectrum in order to force down mortgage and Treasury bond rates (recall that a bond's price and yield move in opposite directions; a higher price equals a lower yield). The Fed had traditionally targeted short-term interest rates and allowed the bond market to set long-term rates, so its new strategy – a near-complete government takeover of the debt markets – was something that had never previously been attempted.

This combination of banks and borrowers having little interest in taking on new loans and the Fed actively trying to make money cheaper extended the decline in interest rates that had been in place since 1980, sending the rates on long-term Treasury bonds, home mortgages and corporate bonds to levels not seen since the 1950s.

Figure 3.2: Yield on Aaa Corporate Bonds, 1950–2013

Taken together, ZIRP, the QEs and the Fed's other departures from tradition and historical precedent have changed the US financial system almost beyond recognition. Figure 3.3 shows the Fed's balance sheet soaring (because of the securities it has purchased from banks) from $850 billion in 2007 to nearly $4 trillion by the end of 2013. The banks, meanwhile, saw a correspondingly huge increase in their reserves, giving them the ability to flood the system with many times this much in new loans (for a sense of how banks turn reserves into loans, see Chapter 15).

Figure 3.3: Federal Reserve, Total Assets, 2003-2013

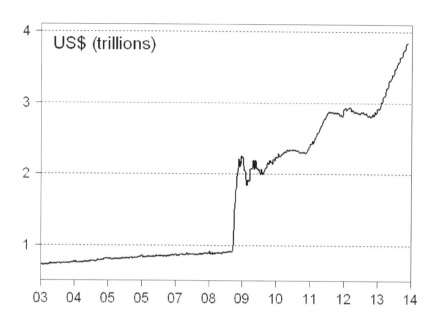

EUROPE AND JAPAN JOIN THE PARTY

So far we've focused on the US because it has been leading the easy money parade. But the US isn't the only country that is monetizing its debt on an unprecedented scale. Europe and Japan in particular are catching up fast.

Japan: Debt, Demographics, Deflation

In the 1990s, Japan suffered through the simultaneous bursting of equity and real estate bubbles and responded (see if this sounds familiar) by borrowing huge amounts of money and propping up its banks and builders.

This strategy worked, in one sense, because Japan's financial sector did not collapse. But disaster avoidance came at a price, which was the creation of a whole generation of "zombie" companies that couldn't function without continued infusions of public money. As a result, one stimulus program followed another, ballooning Japan's public debt to levels that, as both a percent of GDP and of government tax revenues, dwarf those of any other major country. The economy, meanwhile, remained in a kind of twilight, neither growing nor shrinking while the debts continued to mount and domestic deflation (via an increasingly valuable yen and steadily falling real estate prices) made those debts even harder to manage. By 2013 Japan's government owed an amount equal to about 22 times its annual tax revenues, an imbalance far greater than those of other mega-debtors like the US and Greece.

Figure 3.4: Japan Tax Revenue to Sovereign Debt, 2007–2013 (trillions of yen)

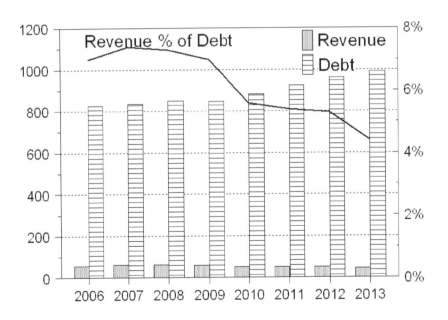

In early 2013, incoming president Shinzo Abe decided to roll the dice and insist that the Bank of Japan (BOJ), their version of the Fed, inject enough cash into the system to produce an inflation rate of at least 2 percent a year. The

BOJ acquiesced, and as this is written in late 2013 has expanded its balance sheet more, in relation to the size of its economy, than has the US Fed.

Figure 3.5: Bank of Japan, Total Assets, 2007–2013

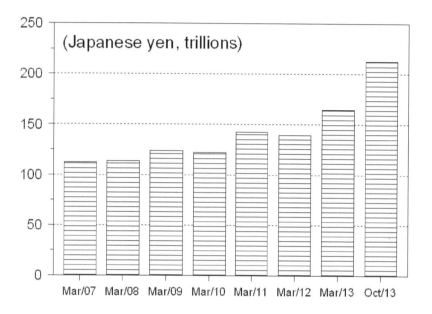

The result was initially quite impressive. The Japanese stock market, anticipating a torrent of new liquidity, soared with the Abe election, while the economy stabilized and even began generating a bit of inflation. But we'll go out on a limb and predict that this, like the other attempts to solve a debt problem with more debt, will fail and an even bigger debt monetization program will commence during 2014.

Europe: The Euro's Fatal Flaw

The 1999 adoption of a common currency, the euro, by 11 European states (subsequently expanded to 17 members) is just the latest stage of a process leading ultimately to an integrated super-state, based on the premise that greater commercial and social interconnectedness would make future wars too disruptive to contemplate. In other words, the intention is understandable and laudable.

But the euro itself has some glaring design flaws, beginning with the assumption that simply imposing the same currency on a group of widely-disparate nations would lead to a cultural convergence around Germanic thrift and efficiency. This convergence would, it was hoped, make low interest rates and cheap loans available across the Continent.

For a while, it seemed to work. The markets initially assumed that all euro-denominated sovereign debt was the same, and by 2004 "peripheral" countries – Portugal, Italy, Ireland, Greece and Spain (the PIIGS, as they've unflatteringly come to be known) – were able to borrow at interest rates comparable to and in some brief cases lower than "core" countries like Germany and France. And borrow they did, but without adopting sound budgetary practices – and in the case of Greece, while falsely reporting the state of government debt and deficits. The result was a wide variety of debt-driven ills, from housing bubbles to soaring deficits to insolvent banks and PIIGS governments. Since the major German and French banks had lent hundreds of billions of euros to the PIIGS, the latter's crises threatened the entire eurozone banking system.

How could something so obvious in retrospect have been allowed to happen? One explanation is that much of the original debt was essentially vendor financing (a business practice in which one company lends money to another to allow the second company to buy the first's products), with Germany and France subsidizing the peripheral countries' purchase of German and French exports. This was pleasant for all concerned, pumping up core countries' trade surpluses and tax revenues while allowing peripheral countries to "boom" without initially-apparent consequence.

Another explanation is that unelected European Union leaders let their egos overrule their judgment. As European Commission president José Manuel Barroso said in 2007, "We are a very special construction unique in the history of mankind...Sometimes I like to compare the EU as a creation to the organization of empire. We have the dimension of empire."

This hubris led European authorities to encourage banks to invest heavily in eurozone government debt on the assumption (now seen to be catastrophically naïve) that such debt was risk- free. As a result, by 2012 the European financial sector was an emergency room full of over-indebted countries and mega-banks that would evaporate if their sovereign debt holdings were priced honestly. Then, ominously, PIIGS interest rates began to rise to levels that would make it impossible for them to service their debts. True to the script, the relatively healthy "core" eurozone countries responded with open-ended bailouts of the PIIGS, in part by pressuring European banks to load up on eurozone sovereign debt.

In 2012 the new head of the European Central Bank (ECB), Italian economist Mario Draghi, announced that, "The ECB is ready to do whatever it takes to preserve the euro. And believe me, it will be enough." The markets interpreted this to mean a European version of QE-Infinity, and interest rates instantly reversed course in anticipation of the new ECB demand to buy PIIGS paper. Spain's 10-year government bond yield, for instance, fell from 7.5 percent to a much more manageable 4 percent. Peripheral country stock markets stabilized and in some cases recovered strongly.

But as with the US and Japan, debt monetization did not produce sustainable economic growth. In late 2013, the average eurozone unemployment rate was a record 12 percent, and twice that in the hardest-hit PIIGS countries. In August 2013, Spain's retail sales fell by 4.2 percent year-over-year, for its 38th *straight month* of annual declines. Greece, despite two large, contentious bailouts in 2011 and 2012, "will probably need another aid package," predicted the head of the European Stability Mechanism (ESM) permanent bailout fund in late 2013. Even Germany, generally seen as the locomotive pulling the weaker eurozone countries, was barely growing.

It appeared that the only thing the past two years' quantitative easing had really accomplished was to make eurozone banks even more dependent on continued easy money. On October 13, 2013 the *Financial Times* reported: "Europe's financial institutions are more exposed to their domestic government bonds than at any time since the eurozone crisis started, reigniting concerns that the fates of sovereign states and their banks are too closely intertwined. Despite official pledges by eurozone authorities to break the "sovereign-bank nexus," government bonds accounted for more than a 10th of Italian banks' total assets at the end of August...up from 6.8 per cent at the beginning of 2012...In Spain the proportion has risen to 9.5 per cent, up from 6.3 per cent over the same period, and in Portugal it has increased to 7.6 per cent from 4.6 per cent."

To sum up, the developed world accumulated too much debt, found the burden intolerable, and began taking extraordinary, unprecedented steps to stop the crisis. Nothing like this has ever been tried on so vast a scale, and by late 2013, the various measures had succeeded in holding at bay the collapse predicted by the Long Wave theories in this book's introduction.

But this was "success" only in the sense that giving an addict another, even bigger shot of heroin succeeds in alleviating withdrawal symptoms – for a while. The underlying problem, the continuing accumulation of debt across the developed world, continues, and, as the next chapter illustrates, is now at levels that can only be called catastrophic.

CHAPTER 4
BANKRUPT GOVERNMENTS

"When national debts have once accumulated to a certain degree, there is scarce, I believe, a single instance of their having been fairly and completely paid. The liberation of the public revenue if it has ever been brought about at all, has always been brought about by a bankruptcy; sometimes by an avowed one but always by a real one, though frequently by a pretended payment."

– Adam Smith, The Wealth of Nations (1776)

When a person buys something, they judge their purchase according to two criteria: how useful it is, and how much it costs. If utility outweighs price, they've received a good deal. Put another way, something is only worth having if you don't overpay for it.

This principle tends to be ignored in the reporting and analysis of most economic statistics, which focus only on headline numbers like GDP growth and employment while failing to mention the borrowing that was required to get those results. As this is written in late 2013, the mainstream consensus is that the past few years' aggressive deficit spending and money creation have been an unqualified success because stock and home prices are up and employment is growing (and of course bank profits are soaring). But when you consider the cost side of the equation – i.e., the new debt that was required to achieve those results – this partial return to normalcy looks less like a triumph of innovative public policy and more like a family maxing out its credit cards to pay the mortgage.

In the US, for example, when the private sector – which had been encouraged to borrow as much as possible for houses, cars, stock speculation, etc., – began to collapse under the weight of its obligations, Washington stepped in, borrowing more between 2002 and 2012 than it had in the two-plus centuries since the days of George Washington.

Figure 4.1: Total US Government Debt, 1950–2013

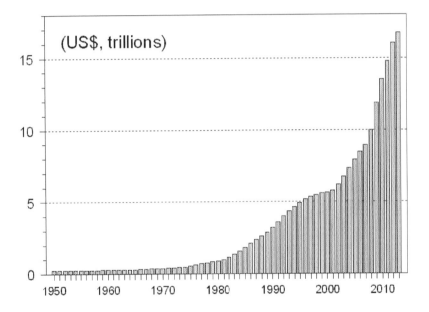

This surge in government borrowing nearly offset the recession-induced decline in private sector debt, leaving total reported debt down only slightly by 2012. Then the private sector began to revive, thanks to historically-low interest rates and the impact of much higher government spending. Home sales and prices took off, which led to a renewed frenzy of mortgage borrowing. Stock prices soared, leading to a surge in margin debt (through which investors borrow against their stocks to buy more stocks), and student loans continued their record climb. The result: private sector debt began once again to rise, taking total debt back to record territory in 2013. If debt was the problem, then by late 2013 it was on the way to becoming an even bigger one.

Figure 4.2: Total US Debt, 2000 – 2013

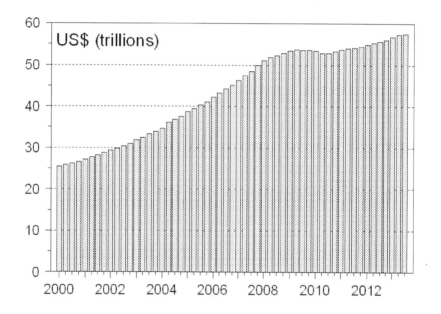

Meanwhile, much of the rest of the world was borrowing as aggressively as the US. The following table shows the increase of indebtedness for several large countries:

Figure 4.3: Increase in Debt, Selected Countries, 2007–2012

Australia	369%
France	132%
Germany	124%
Ireland	219%
Italy	113%
Japan	124%
Russia	231%
Spain	181%
UK	197%
US	147%

AND THAT'S JUST THE TIP OF THE ICEBERG

Based on officially-reported debt, the world is overleveraged and becoming more so. But it turns out that officially-reported debt is just part – and not the biggest part – of the obligations that the modern financial system is creating. Entitlement programs like Social Security and Medicare are accruing future benefit liabilities that, according to prudent business practices, should be addressed by putting aside enough money to cover the net present value of those future obligations. Then those obligations should be recorded according to generally accepted accounting principles (GAAP). A private sector company with a pension plan is legally required to do this, and has to report any underfunding to regulators. But governments exempt themselves from this requirement and simply allow the future obligations to build up with little if any reporting on their true size.

Figure 4.4: Total Federal Obligations: Direct Debt and Other Promises

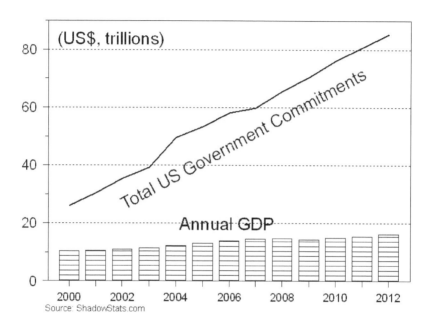

In the US, benefits promised to future recipients of Social Security and Medicare are very real obligations (imagine cutting retirees' health care and then running for re-election), arguably more real than bond interest owed to China or Saudi Arabia. So it makes sense to view them as a form of debt. When these unfunded liabilities are folded into the US federal deficit calculation, the annual figure soars from the $1-plus trillion of recent years to over $6 trillion, while total federal obligations rise from 2.5 times the size of the economy in 2000 to 5.3 times in 2012. As this is written in late 2013, total real US debt comes to about $1.1 million per family of four. And rather than stabilizing, the imbalance continues to grow at an alarming rate. It would be a very different world indeed if the US was reporting $6 trillion annual deficits and federal debt exceeding 500 percent of GDP.

The lesson to be drawn from the past decade? A nation can't grow its way out of debt if growth requires ever-increasing amounts of new borrowing. In that situation debt increases faster than societal wealth until the system becomes unsustainable. Then it collapses.

The US has been getting dramatically less bang for each new borrowed buck in recent years, implying that 1) the strategy of meeting every crisis with new debt has about run its course, and 2) the debt now being taken on will hurt vastly more than it will help, leaving the system far more fragile and prone to new crises. Meanwhile, unfunded liabilities are even higher in Europe, where populations are aging rapidly, pensions are extremely generous, and most governments – like in the US – don't pretend to fund the resulting future obligations. Even Germany, the continent's powerhouse and financial success story, has total debt and unfunded liabilities that exceed 400 percent of GDP.

FAILED STATES, ZOMBIE CITIES
Apparently taking their cue from Washington, US states and localities have spent the past few decades offering ever-more-generous pensions and retiree health benefits to public sector workers, frequently without putting away enough money to cover the resulting obligations. Now yesterday's workers are becoming today's retirees, and in many cases the promised money is not there. But instead of cutting benefits and/or raising taxes, many pension plans are using accounting tricks to hide their problems.

One popular trick is the overly-aggressive return assumption. Assume, for example, that you're running a state teachers' retirement fund. You have a certain amount of money on hand and more coming in each year. Your invested capital will probably earn about 4 percent annually over the next twenty years, but that won't leave you with nearly enough to cover the likely benefit costs. In other words, you're massively underfunded. But raise the return assumption to 8 percent and the magic of compound interest gives you twice as much hypothetical future income, which might spell the difference between being 80 percent funded, which is adequate, and only 40 percent funded, which is catastrophic.

Figure 4.5: 20-Year Asset Growth Under Different Average Annual Return Assumptions

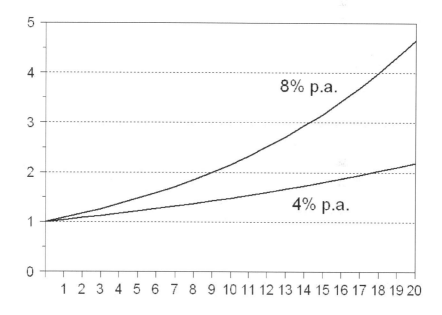

This ploy is common enough to be thought of as standard operating procedure. At the state level, return

assumptions are concentrated around 7.5 percent – 8 percent, which is wildly unrealistic in an environment where 10-year Treasury bonds yield around 2.5 percent. So the gap between what pension funds have and what they claim to have grows wider each year. How wide is it currently? In 2013, Mauldin Economics calculated that under more reasonable return assumptions, state pension plan unfunded liabilities, officially reported at $1 trillion, were actually around $4 trillion.

The other accounting trick is the pension bond, where a state borrows against future pension fund returns and uses the proceeds to expand its investment portfolio. The idea is that by borrowing at 5 percent and investing at 8 percent the fund will be able to add the 3 percent positive spread to its returns. Illinois, arguably the most egregious offender, had $25 billion of pension bonds outstanding in 2013. This is analogous to using margin to speculate in the stock market, in that your future rate of return has to exceed your borrowing rate or it compounds rather than solves your problem.

Both of these props may soon be kicked out from under pension funds. Bond yields are too close to zero to generate significant capital gains going forward, so today's miniscule yields are tomorrow's total fixed income returns. Stocks, meanwhile, have had a huge run in recent years and were, in late 2013, due for a double-digit correction. For pension plans buying equities with borrowed money, the effect of this inevitable loss will be magnified, laying bare the extent of their underfunding.

Zombie Cities

Detroit declared bankruptcy in 2013, and Chicago may not be far behind. Chicago's outstanding debt is $18 billion, but that, it turns out, is less than half the story: In late 2013, bond rating agency Moody's evaluated the city's pension plans using realistic return assumptions and concluded that its true debt was $86.9 billion, its pension plans were 23 percent funded, and its unfunded liabilities were $23 billion. According to Chicago's own annual report, "contributions made by the City to the [Pension] Plans have been lower than the cash outlays of the Plans in recent years. As a result, the Plans have used investment earnings or assets of the Plans to satisfy these cash outlays." In other words, Chicago is not even contributing enough to keep the unfunded liability from growing, as shown in Figure 4.6. Not surprisingly, both Moody's and Standard & Poor's downgraded the city's debt in 2013.

Figure 4.6: City of Chicago Pension Liability, Percent Funded, 2003–2012

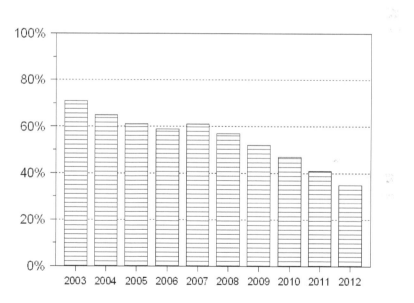

Where the federal government has a printing press and (for a time) effectively unlimited borrowing capacity, a troubled state or city requires a decent bond rating to be able to borrow. As their accounting tricks are exposed and their bond ratings slip towards "junk," Illinois, Chicago and their mismanaged peers will increasingly have to live within their means. And short of default, this can be done only through some combination of higher taxes and reduction in services, both of which scare away the tax base (Chicago lost more than 200,000 residents in the 2000s), making the financial hole even deeper.

Numerous other states and cities find themselves in similar straits, just one garden-variety stock market correction away from a fiscal crisis in which taxpayers suddenly find themselves on the hook for billions more in pension obligations, while supposedly risk-free municipal bonds start trading like junk bonds. Then what? Either the aforementioned Greek-style austerity, default with a lot of broken promises or a federal bailout in which Washington effectively converts pension obligations to Treasury bonds, at taxpayer expense. Given that default is the least attractive option for elected officials, recipients of government services, and municipal bondholders alike, it seems probable that attempts will be made to fix the underfunding and overspending with borrowed money. So total government debt in the US, rather than stabilizing at current levels, is on the verge of another spike.

CHAPTER 5

OVER-LEVERAGED BANKS AND THE DERIVATIVES TIME-BOMB

"An unregulated derivatives market essentially gives Wall Street a way to place hidden taxes on everything in the world."

– Matt Taibbi, Rolling Stone

Amazingly, the liabilities described in the previous chapter aren't the scariest issue facing today's financial world. That distinction belongs to over-the-counter derivatives, unregulated contracts between financial institutions in which each "counterparty" takes one side of a bet on interest rates, currency movements, bond default or pretty much anything else that moves. Because there is no limit on how many contracts can be written on a given bond issue or currency position or whatever, the amount of derivatives that can be created is effectively infinite. As a result, banks and hedge funds now treat this market as a casino, making bets and collecting fees in ever-increasing amounts. The face value of all derivatives outstanding in 2013 was about *$693 trillion dollars, or nearly ten times the size of the entire global economy.*

Why isn't this front-page news? Because banks and hedge funds are frequently on both sides of these bets, and they net out long and short derivatives positions to arrive at a modest-sounding exposure number. So the reported amount of risk – to the extent that such things are reported at all – looks quite modest. This practice explains how the notional, or face value of over-the-counter derivatives can rise from \$99.7 trillion in 2001 to \$693 trillion in 2013 without a corresponding increase in reported financial sector liabilities. When everyone is everyone else's counterparty, net risk doesn't change even while gross risk – the total number of derivatives contracts – soars.

Figure 5.1: Notional Value of Over-The-Counter Derivatives, 2007–2013 (US\$ billions)

	2007	2010	2013
TOTAL WORLDWIDE	507,907	582,655	692,908
Foreign exchange	57,604	62,933	81,025
Interest rates	381,357	478,093	577,269
Equity-linked	9,518	6,868	6,963
Commodities	8,255	3,273	2,727
Credit derivatives	51,095	31,416	24,845
Other derivatives	78	72	78

But recent history proves that actual risk does indeed rise along with the total amount of derivatives. In 2008, money center banks' seemingly-modest net derivatives exposure was revealed to depend on counterparties like Lehman Brothers, Bear Stearns and AIG. When those firms imploded, one side of trillions of dollars of derivatives defaulted, leaving the remaining counterparties suddenly "un-hedged," that is, liable for other contracts without the expected protection from the now-defaulted contracts. The "net" derivatives exposure became irrelevant while the gross number became real, with near-catastrophic consequences for the global financial system.

Now, after coming within days of complete corporate evaporation and only surviving because of an absolutely unprecedented government bail-out, one might think the big banks would recognize that derivatives were bad and dial back their exposure by, say, 99 percent or so. Instead, the lure of those big fees flowing through to the annual bonus pool apparently proved stronger than the lingering memories of 2008, leading the money center banks to keep on writing derivatives at a near-record pace.

The following table compares the assets and derivatives books of some major banks.

Figure 5.2: Notional Value of Derivatives at Major Banks Compared to Total Assets, June 30, 2013 (US$ millions)

	Total Assets	Notional Derivatives	Derivatives as % of Assets
JP Morgan Chase	2,439,494	72,844,543	2986%
Citigroup	1,883,988	61,063,085	3241%
Bank of America	2,125,686	59,041,917	2778%
Morgan Stanley	802,691	49,396,207	6154%
Goldman Sachs	938,611	46,982,118	5005%
Deutsche Bank*	2,653,457	73,320,804	2763%

*December 31, 2012

To give some sense of the magnitude of these derivatives numbers, Deutsche Bank's notional derivatives book is 21 times the size of the German economy.

Gradually, an understanding of the risks posed by derivatives does seem to be creeping into the mainstream. As economist Sheri Markose explained in a recent International Monetary Fund report:

"The global derivatives markets in the post-Lehman period, despite considerable compression of bilateral positions, are unstable, and they can bring about catastrophic failure. Quite simply, a threat of failure to any of the [major banks] is an immediate threat to the others. The network topology where the very high percentage of exposures is concentrated among a few highly interconnected banks implies that they will stand and fall together. This topological fragility of the derivatives markets as risk-sharing institutions has an implicit moral hazard problem that undermines their social usefulness."

PART II: CONSEQUENCES AND SCENARIOS

CHAPTER 6
UNSOUND MONEY = A CORRUPT SOCIETY

"The American Republic will endure until the day Congress discovers that it can bribe the public with the public's money."

– Alexis de Tocqueville

If a single quote can define a book, the following, from economist John Maynard Keynes, comes close to defining this one:

"There is no subtler, no surer means of overturning the existing basis of society than to debauch the currency. The process engages all the hidden forces of economic law on the side of destruction, and does it in a manner which not one man in a million is able to diagnose."

This chapter will uncover some of those "hidden forces of economic law" and show how they've been systematically turning a society based on thrift, industry and transparency into one based on debt, fraud and lies.

The story begins in 1971, when the US broke the formal link between the dollar and gold. Henceforth the dollar was a purely fiat currency which the US could create in infinite quantities. But it was also the world's reserve currency, and therefore in great demand virtually everywhere. In effect, the US found itself in possession of a seemingly unlimited credit card, which it proceeded to max out. Among other things, it built a global military empire, a cradle-to-grave entitlements system, and a consumer society that encouraged individuals to buy whatever they wanted on credit. Debt soared, too much new currency was created, and the value of the dollar began to decline.

At this point the government had a problem, because a depreciating currency makes life hard for voters by raising the cost of living and lowering real investment returns, while straining the federal budget by increasing the cost of inflation-indexed programs like Social Security. Because the victims of such policies tend, rightly, to blame elected officials for their suffering, the federal government now had an incentive to lie about the value of its currency.

Prior to 1980, government statisticians calculated the cost of living by tracking the changes in a fixed basket of goods assembled to represent a constant standard of living. But when the resulting number began to rise at an uncomfortable rate, the formula was, ahem, adjusted, via a series of statistical tools in order to bring the changes into a tolerable range. The new tools include:

- **Hedonic Quality Modeling**, which lowers reported prices to account for changes deemed to be quality improvements. If new cars have airbags and new computers are faster, statisticians shave a bit from their actual prices to reflect the perception that they offer more for the money than previous versions.

- **Substitution**, in which index components that are rising too quickly are replaced with things that are not. In other words, if steak is rising, government statisticians replace it with chicken on the assumption that this is how consumers operate in the real world.

- **Geometric Weighting**, in which rising components are given less relative weight.

- **Homeowners' Equivalent Rent**, which replaces what it actually costs to buy a house with an estimate of what homeowners would have to pay to rent their homes – adjusted hedonically for quality improvements. When home prices are rising faster than rents, as they have been for the past couple of decades, this change lowers the impact of housing on inflation.

Today, after three decades of statistical massaging, the Consumer Price Index (CPI) no longer measures the cost of maintaining a constant standard of living. Instead, it measures the cost of a *declining* standard of living in which consumers are constantly assumed to switch from their first choice to their second or third choices among life's necessities. Meanwhile, because Social Security payments and many other pensions and wage agreements are tied to the CPI, this deliberate understatement of official inflation lowers the real incomes of participants in these programs – in most cases without their knowledge or understanding.

Figure 6.1: Consumer Price Index, Official vs. Pre-1980 Method, 1980–2013

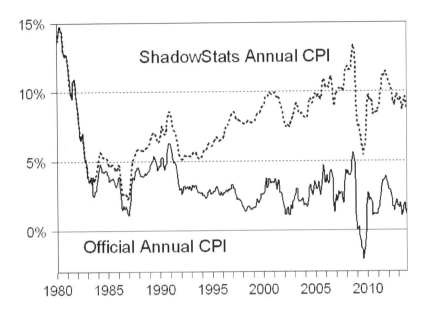

Figure 6.1 illustrates the widening gap between traditional and "modern" inflation measures. The modern inflation rate, represented by the solid line, is modest, painting a picture of a well-run monetary system in which the cost of living is rising only slightly. However, according to calculations performed by John Williams of ShadowStats, if the US had continued to calculate inflation the old way (broken line), the cost of living would be rising at a near-double-digit rate.

And the gap is about to widen with the adoption of a "Chained-CPI" which increases the substitution effect, thus lowering the reported rate of inflation by another 0.3 percentage points annually. In year-end 2013 budget negotiations it was being sold as a politically-expedient (i.e., invisible) way of cutting the deficit by lowering the real purchasing power of future Social Security payments even while they increase in nominal dollar terms.

GDP and Personal Income

Inflation is a crucial part of the calculation of other economic statistics. Gross Domestic Product, for instance, is a measure of the size of the economy, and to calculate it the government compiles raw data from various sectors and then "deflates" the result by its measure of the past year's depreciation of the dollar, to arrive at a "real" inflation-adjusted GDP number. If inflation is high, then the deflator is large and GDP is correspondingly smaller, and vice versa.

By systematically understating inflation, the government systematically overstates GDP. Figure 6.2 shows the difference between GDP as currently reported and GDP as it would have been reported if it had been deflated by a more accurate measure of inflation. Reported GDP (solid line) shows a sharp decline in 2008-2009, followed by a decent recovery. But the other version (broken line), using inflation calculated the pre-1980 way, shows the economy slipping into recession in 2006 – and never recovering. Eight straight years of contraction by the world's largest economy paints a very different picture of the global economy.

Figure 6.2: Annual GDP Growth, Official vs. Privately Calculated, 1980–2013

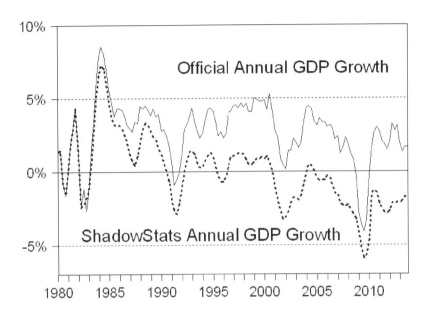

Another statistic that is affected by inflation is Median Household Income, a measure of the average family's financial welfare. Here again, the reported numbers (solid line), adjusted for the government's deceptively low inflation rate, show unspectacular but noticeable gains since the 1960s. The average family, by this measure, is somewhat better off. But adjust the data for inflation calculated the old way (broken line), and incomes are actually lower than they were in the early 1970s.

Figure 6.3: Median Household Income, Official vs. Privately Calculated, 1967–2013

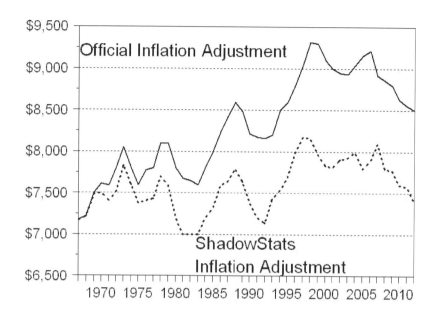

The Deception Spreads Beyond Inflation

Once it got used to lying, Washington found plenty of other statistics in need of a good massage. Unemployment, for instance, was reported in late 2013 at an almost-acceptable 7 percent. But this measure leaves out a few crucial things. Pretend for a moment that you lose your high-paying job and the only thing you can find is a part-time, near-minimum-wage spot at McDonald's. According to the Bureau of Labor Statistics you are now employed and your entry in its database carries just as much weight as did your old high-paying job, even though from your point of view you are grossly underemployed.

Now let's say you lose your McDonald's job and are so discouraged that you give up and stop looking for work. The government then stops counting you as unemployed because you've "left the workforce." You are now one of many, since the labor force participation rate – the percent of able-bodied people who are working – has dropped from 66.4% at the beginning of 2007 to 62.8%, the lowest in decades. And none of you are counted as unemployed.

These omissions have combined to dramatically lower the official unemployment rate. The government itself tracks – but doesn't widely report on – the discrepancy. By starting with the reported unemployment number and adding back people who are involuntarily part-time and who have grown discouraged and left the workforce, it produces the more realistic U.6 unemployment rate showing Figure 6.4. The ShadowStats number, meanwhile, adds long-term discouraged workers to arrive at the most realistic measure, one that shows Great Depression-level unemployment and, importantly, is not declining.

Figure 6.4: Alternative Unemployment Rates, 2007–2013

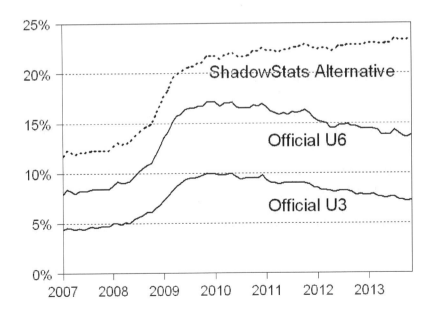

While we're on the subject of employment statistics, in 2009 the *Washington Post* reported that "President Obama has decided to have the director of the U.S. Census Bureau work directly with the White House," to make possible "oversight of the director by senior White House aides." And in November 2013 the *New York Post* reported that Census Bureau analysts, allegedly under orders from superiors, fabricated data that went into unemployment reports leading up to the 2012 presidential election. This apparent politicization of government statistics further highlights the importance of reports prepared by independent, private-sector analysts.

BAD BANKERS DRIVE OUT GOOD BANKERS

An economic concept called Gresham's Law states that bad money drives good money out of circulation when governments impose an exchange rate that makes one equal to the other when in fact they are not. In other words, if paper dollars and silver dollars are both legal tender at face value, most people will spend the paper and keep the silver because paper currency can be printed in infinite quantities by central banks, while silver is rare, cannot be produced with a printing press, and is therefore more likely to retain its purchasing power.

A variation of this law applies to banks and bankers. Pretend for a moment that you're an honest banker; think Jimmy Stewart in *It's a Wonderful Life*. The government is creating lots of new dollars and making them available to you, so you have plenty of capital with which to make loans. But you've already given loans to pretty much every credit-worthy customer you can find. Because you're reluctant to lend to people who probably can't pay back a loan, your impulse is to slow down, scale back lending and wait until the economy starts generating more creditworthy borrowers.

But that means giving up the fees generated by new loans which less scrupulous competitors are more than willing to write. Those competing banks become more profitable than yours, and your board of directors begins to question your competence. They make it clear that if your results don't improve they will 1) replace you with a more aggressive (though they use the term "innovative") executive from a more profitable bank or 2) sell your bank to one of its fast-growing competitors.

Your choices: start lending to anyone who walks in the door or find another career. Whatever you decide, the banking world comes to be populated with the kinds of people who pioneered sub-prime mortgages and liar loans – and who currently operate in Wall Street investment banks and view customers as prey to be exploited.

Meanwhile, in today's fiat money system, the government, Fed and major banks get to use that newly-created currency before its rising supply lowers its value, giving a huge advantage to the government-sanctioned banking monopoly (for more on how this process works, see Section III). And banks – facing the pressures mentioned earlier – have been using this money in increasingly aggressive ways, creating products like asset-backed bonds, junk bonds, and over-the-counter derivatives that generate fees in the moment but vastly increase systemic leverage and fragility. In effect, the largest banks have become hedge funds, rolling the dice with their depositors' money.

With some of the profits thus generated, they then buy more favorable treatment from Washington. To take just three of many possible examples:

Repeal of Glass-Steagall

In the aftermath of the Great Depression, the Glass-Steagall Act of 1935 divided the banking industry into commercial banks, which were banned from risky investments in return for the government guaranteeing their depositors' money, and investment banks that were free to make big bets on pretty much anything while putting their partners' and investors' money at risk. This division kept the banking system from behaving too crazily for several decades. But the restrictions bothered increasingly-powerful bankers who envisioned "financial supermarkets" offering everything to everyone. Over time they were able to carve out legal loopholes that enabled them to conduct investment banking, money management and speculative trading through separate subsidiaries. And in 1999 they were finally powerful enough to overturn what was left of Glass-Steagall. With the stroke of a pen, the final distinctions between commercial bank, investment bank, and hedge fund largely disappeared.

De-regulation of Over-the-Counter Derivatives

Recall from Chapter 5 that over-the-counter derivatives are contracts between two consenting financial institutions – known as counterparties – that bet on changes in interest rates, currency exchange rates and the probability of bond defaults, among other things. As they became ever-more-profitable, the banks were able to convince Congress to exempt them from oversight by the Commodity Futures Trading Commission, the regulatory body responsible for other kinds of derivatives. The market then exploded to half-a-quadrillion dollars of notional value. (In an interesting example of what happens in unregulated financial markets, banks were able to value their derivatives however they liked, meaning that it was possible for both parties of a given derivative to report it as profitable.) The multi-trillion dollar bailouts of the 2008 financial crisis were a direct result of these contracts blowing up when counterparties failed.

The Right to Own Warehouses and Refineries

In 2010 banks convinced regulators to allow them to own and operate a wide range of heavy-industrial assets, and Goldman Sachs quickly bought Metropolitan International Trade Services, a string of Detroit-area aluminum warehouses. It then, according to numerous lawsuits outstanding in late 2013, set about shuffling the metal from warehouse to warehouse, creating the illusion that it was shipping when in fact it was holding metal off the market to raise prices – from which its traders then allegedly profited in the futures market.

The term for this buying of official favor is "regulatory capture," and lately it has become a major profit center for powerful industries. A few million dollars directed to the right political campaigns can yield billions of dollars in advantages over competitors. The predations of the banking, agriculture, drug and defense industries are a book-length (and fascinating) subject. But here we'll focus solely on the banks by pointing out the difference between the handling of the Savings & Loan crisis of the early 1990s and the housing bubble collapse of 2008.

In the former, which was much smaller in scope and less damaging than the latter, over 1,100 S&L executives were prosecuted and 800 jailed. In the more recent crisis, despite vastly more serious and blatant crimes being committed, not a single Wall Street executive had gone to prison by the end of 2013, fully five years after the crimes took place. On the infrequent occasions when banks behave so blatantly that even their pet regulators can't look the other way, the result is a fine amounting to a few days' or weeks' profit, with the bankers who committed the crimes remaining anonymous and unmolested.

Illustrating how completely the regulatory apparatus created to supervise markets has been co-opted by the big banks, consider that in late 2013, Securities and Exchange Commission (SEC) head Mary Jo White was a former litigator with Wall Street law firm Debevoise & Plimpton – where she defended banks from charges of corruption. The CFTC was run by Gary Gensler, a former partner at Goldman Sachs, where he served as Co-Head of Finance. And Treasury Secretary Jack Lew was a former Citigroup banker whose contract had a clause that paid him a $940,000 bonus if he left the bank for a high-level government or regulatory position.

Just for fun, here's an incomplete but representative list of headlines detailing the kinds of shenanigans the banks have been up to lately:

Bond Deal Draws Fine for UBS
JPMorgan Settles Electricity Manipulation Case for $410 million
Deutsche Bank Net Profit Halves on Charge For Potential Legal Costs
US Sues Bank of America Over Mortgage Securities
Senate Opens Probe of Banks' Commodities Businesses
US Regulators Find Evidence of Banks Fixing Derivatives Rates
Goldman Sachs Sued for Allegedly Inflating Aluminum Prices

SAVERS BECOME BORROWERS

Besides corrupting bankers, systematic inflation discourages thrift and savings and encourages borrowing and profligacy. To illustrate the process, imagine two neighbors, Bob and Martha. Bob saves a big part of every paycheck (which in the non-inflationary past was considered wise behavior) and puts the proceeds into a traditional bank savings account on the assumption that it will be safe and available when needed, while earning a reasonable return, let's say 3 percent, each year.

Now assume that the government, in order to finance its deficits and create lots of speculative opportunities for large banks, chooses to depreciate the dollar by 8 percent a year (while reporting inflation of only 2 percent). The purchasing power of the dollars in Bob-the-saver's bank account actually falls in real terms by 6 percent a year, so that at the end of a lifetime of saving, his nest egg has far less purchasing power than he expected.

Bob's neighbor Martha, meanwhile, sees that interest rates are low and that everything seems to cost a lot more every year, so she doesn't bother to save, instead taking out the biggest possible mortgage on her house at a government-subsidized rate of 4 percent. With real inflation running at 8 percent, her mortgage becomes less onerous every year, until its monthly payments have been reduced to a pittance in real terms. She spends a life deeply in debt, but ends up richer than Bob because the government's policy of currency inflation significantly lessened the burden of her debts.

Seeing similar things happening all around them, Bob and Martha's friends and neighbors make the rational decision to emulate Martha, producing a society in which everyone borrows and no one saves. Which is exactly what the US has become. As Figure 6.5 illustrates, the national savings rate fell from an average of 12 percent in the 1970s to less than 3 percent in 2007, and was only slightly higher than that in 2013. The grasshoppers, who in the parable end up begging for food when winter comes, now vastly outnumber the ants.

Another explanation for this sudden behavior change is that as a currency loses value, real (i.e., inflation-adjusted) incomes don't keep up. Paychecks rise, but not enough to maintain the average family's lifestyle, and the only way to stay even is to borrow a bit each year to make up the difference. Because federal policy since 1971 has for the most part been designed to encourage exactly this kind of behavior, Americans found it difficult *not* to embrace debt as a way of life.

Figure 6.5: US Personal Savings Rate, 1971–2013

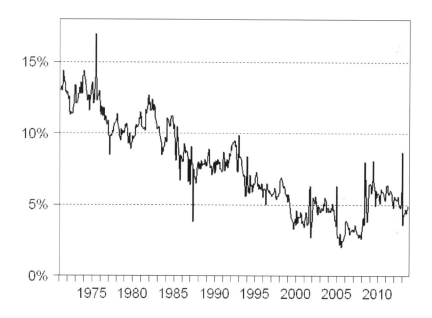

TRUSTED BRANDS BECOME UNTRUSTWORTHY
Now let's say you're running a cereal company or fast food restaurant chain. Your costs are rising at the real inflation rate of about 8 percent. But everyone thinks inflation is 2

percent, so you can't raise prices in line with costs without alienating your customers. Neither can you eat the cost increases without seeing your already razor-thin profit margins evaporate. So what do you do? Perhaps you give customers a little less for their money, but secretly. You put less cereal in each box, or you mix a bit of soy filler or "pink slime" into your formerly all-beef patties, and hope no one notices.

In 2012 ABC News sent reporters out to analyze what was in the newest packages of a wide range of brand name products. They found that many looked the same and cost more-or-less the same as previous versions, but contained slightly fewer tissues or nuts or whatever. A few examples:

Kashi cereal: taller box but less cereal
Box of Scott Tissues: 12 fewer tissues
Bag of Ghirardelli chocolate chips: 48 fewer chips
Can of Planters Deluxe Mixed Nuts: 52 fewer nuts
Can of Maxwell House Coffee: 30 fewer cups
Pillsbury Cake mix: Three ounces less, 3 fewer cupcakes
Roll of Brawny paper towels: four and a half feet fewer towels

This study was small and random and covered only consumer products. But its findings imply that the conflict between cost increases and limited pricing power is leading to the use of cheaper ingredients and deceptive packaging across the economy. Trusted brands, in short, are becoming untrustworthy. And customers who see that they're getting less for their money find their trust in institutions eroding just a bit more with each experience.

CONTRAST WITH A SOUND MONEY ENVIRONMENT

When a currency holds its value, government has less incentive to lie about its performance. It can honestly state that its money is sound and that its citizens' savings are becoming a little more valuable each year. Savers are rewarded for their thrift while borrowers are punished for their profligacy (the ant's prudent strategy is favored over the grasshopper's lack of concern about the future). Banks, no longer the distributors of a torrent of newly-printed currency, are far less powerful, have less incentive to make unwise loans for immediate fee income, and control fewer resources with which to buy government favor. Industrial companies, which make real things rather than shuffling paper, become relatively more powerful. Manufacturing, or more generally production of all sorts, becomes the core of the economy, with finance a support function rather than the source of most power and wealth.

Companies in a sound money system, meanwhile, see their input costs fall or remain stable, so instead of degrading their products and lying about it, they are incented to give customers more for their money – and to brag about it. The result: higher-quality ingredients, larger packages, better products – and advertising that tells consumers that they're getting more for their money. Trust in business grows rather than erodes.

This was the way of the world for two centuries under the Classical Gold Standard (which is explained a couple of chapters hence), when national currencies actually became a little more valuable each year. Today's world, alas, is very different.

CHAPTER 7

PERPETUAL WAR
AND THE EMERGING POLICE STATE

"There was of course no way of knowing whether you were being watched at any given moment. How often, or on what system, the Thought Police plugged in on any individual wire was guesswork. It was even conceivable that they watched everybody all the time. But at any rate they could plug in your wire whenever they wanted to. You have to live - did live, from habit that became instinct - in the assumption that every sound you made was overheard, and, except in darkness, every movement scrutinized."

– George Orwell, 1984

In what seems like the blink of an eye, the US government has taken the espionage and coercion techniques traditionally employed in foreign affairs, updated them with 21st-century technology, and turned them on its own citizens. Washington can now spy on virtually anyone anywhere without a warrant, detain citizens and foreign nationals indefinitely without due process, torture its prisoners both at home and abroad, and kill virtually anyone with drone strikes if they are suspected of being up to no good – all of which were until recently thought to be unconstitutional.

At first glance it may seem a stretch to tie this emerging high-tech police state to the financial corruption discussed in previous chapters. But it's actually very easy: Thanks to America's ownership of the world's reserve currency, it is able to spend more on "defense" than anyone else – by a mile. The resulting sense of omnipotence has led the US to intervene around the world, invading whomever it perceives as threatening and using its financial and military power to intimidate nearly everyone else. The enemies thus created are legion, and some of them have begun to take the fight to US soil.

Figure 7.1: Comparison of 2012 Military Budgets

	Spending (US$ billions)	% of GDP	World share (%)
World Total	1,753	2.5	100.0
United States	682	4.4	39.0
China	166	2.0	9.5
Russia	91	4.4	5.2
UK	61	2.5	3.5
Japan	59	1.0	3.4
France	59	2.3	3.4

The realization that this "blowback" has reached dangerous proportions has coincided with the emergence of technologies that allow the authorities to monitor and analyze literally every electronic signal crossing the domestic grid. Add in the fact that soaring debt has increased the risk of catastrophic collapse – with all the domestic civil unrest and geopolitical turmoil that that implies – and the result is both motive and opportunity for the US to become more intrusive, secretive and coercive.

But just how intrusive, secretive and coercive may still come as a shock. What follows is a very brief chronicle of the US government's descent into authoritarianism.

Surveillance: Big Brother Is Watching

After a post-Watergate Senate investigation documented abuses of government spying, Congress in 1978 passed the Foreign Intelligence Surveillance Act, or FISA, to impose limits and order on the intelligence community. The law created a secret court that issued warrants for electronic surveillance or physical searches, albeit with a lower standard than for domestic law enforcement. Instead of probable cause, the authorities just had to prove that they sought foreign intelligence.

Then came 9/11 and the subsequent passage of the Patriot Act, which gave the newly-created Department of Homeland Security the ability to monitor the business documents, tax records, and library check-out lists of "suspected terrorists." The Act allowed for the prosecution of librarians and other record keepers if they revealed that such information had been subpoenaed and enabled police to listen in on jailhouse conversations between attorneys and clients and, if they choose, deny lawyers to Americans accused of crimes. The FISA court, originally charged with limiting such activities to clear, specific cases of terrorist activity, became a rubber stamp that approved nearly every request that came its way.

In the early 2000s, the National Security Agency began installing equipment in private telecommunications networks that allowed it to monitor emails, web surfing, and voice calls. It created data centers capable of storing this torrent of information and supercomputers capable of mining it and breaking even high-level encryption. In 2006 the FISA court gave blanket approval to the NSA's broad-based spying, and in 2007 Congress ratified the program via the Protect America Act.

Also in 2007, a secret program called Prism gave the NSA and FBI access to user data from Microsoft, Apple, Google and several other major telecommunications companies. Congress then granted immunity to telecom companies for their participation in warrantless wiretapping. It was subsequently revealed that Facebook shares member information with the authorities.

Another program called XKeyscore makes available everything a target has ever done on the Internet — browsing history, searches, content of emails, online chats – to even low-level NSA analysts. All without a court-issued warrant or even a superior's signature. As NSA whistleblower Edward Snowden told a reporter in early 2013, "I, sitting at my desk could wiretap anyone, from you or your accountant, to a federal judge or even the president, if I had a personal email."

Snowden also revealed that the NSA had hacked into computers to snare messages before they were encrypted and (going beyond spying to become a saboteur) introduced weaknesses into the encryption standards followed by hardware and software developers around the world. The result: less security for not just terrorists' emails but also bank transactions, medical records and communications among coworkers and friends.

In 2013 it was revealed that the data being gathered for the war on terror was being used not just against suspected terrorists but against suspected drug offenders within the US. Because even the current government recognizes that this is unconstitutional, the data is being "laundered" via the falsification of evidence. The following passage from a *Salon* article describes the process:

"A secret branch of the DEA called the Special Operations Division – so secret that nearly everything about it is classified, including the size of its budget and the location of its office – has been using the immense pools of data collected by the NSA, CIA, FBI and other intelligence agencies to go after American citizens for ordinary drug crimes. Law enforcement agencies, meanwhile, have been coached to conceal the existence of the program and the source of the information by creating what's called a 'parallel construction,' a fake or misleading trail of evidence. So no one in the court system – not the defendant or the defense attorney, not even the prosecutor or the judge – can ever trace the case back to its true origins."

The amount of money being devoted to surveillance, meanwhile, is immense. In 2013 the Washington Post reported that the so-called "black budget," most of which flows to the above programs, was $52.6 billion – or only slightly less than Japan and the UK spend on their entire militaries.

Torture, "Rendition" and Assassination: Big Brother Gets Physical

The original Patriot Act allowed the government to detain foreign nationals indefinitely, without access to an attorney or the chance to confront witnesses. The 2012 National Defense Authorization Act extended indefinite detention to American citizens and appeared to give the president the ability simply to kill, without judicial review, citizens he believed to be involved in terrorism. A public backlash caused the administration to promise not to do so without clear justification, but the law remains on the books for future administrations that have not made any promises about how it will be used.

The Central Intelligence Agency, meanwhile, began kidnapping suspected terrorists in foreign countries and shipping them (a practice known as "rendition") to secret prisons around the world, where they were tortured and sometimes murdered. According to a team of British researchers tracking the program, the CIA, with the help of 54 foreign governments, has organized thousands of flights carrying terrorism suspects to other countries. In several documented cases, the wrong person was kidnapped, held and tortured for several months before being released without comment.

And then there's the "kill list" of terrorist suspects marked for execution – many by unmanned drones circling in on a target from several thousand feet. President Obama is intimately involved in populating and managing the list, while signing off on a soaring number of drone strikes – many of which kill civilians along with the intended targets. The extent of this collateral damage is unknown because the US counts all military-age males in a strike zone as combatants, though press accounts of funerals and wedding parties being bombed are becoming common.

Through it all, debate over the treatment of prisoners has raged. According to the Constitution's Eighth Amendment the federal government cannot impose "cruel and unusual" punishments, which by logic and general agreement include torture. But while the US was declaring that no torture was going on, prisoners held in Iraq and elsewhere were reportedly subjected to amputations, beatings, burnings and lashings, and in several cases were beaten to death. When such stories reached the Pentagon, officials reportedly declined to intervene if no uniformed US soldiers were involved, implying that free rein was being given to hired mercenaries. Closer to home, the US was employing torture directly via "enhanced interrogation techniques" like waterboarding, sleep deprivation and sexual humiliation at its Guantanamo Bay prison, with acquiescence, if not direction, from higher ups.

A growing number of whistleblowers, appalled by what they're seeing, have begun to leak classified information detailing just how far the US has strayed from its ideals. To take a few of the hundreds of disturbing recent revelations:

- Egyptians allegedly given "human rights" training by the FBI were actually trained to torture.

- In 2013 the US had tapped the phones of the leaders of Germany, Brazil and France, among others, and in a single month monitored over 60 million phone conversations in Spain.

- The Justice Department stole two months of telephone records of Associated Press reporters and editors in what the news cooperative called a "massive and unprecedented intrusion" into news organizations' freedom to operate.

Local Police Become an Occupying Army

Municipal police forces are being reshaped by the same confluence of rising threat level and new technology, in the process transforming the cop on the beat into a something resembling a soldier in an occupying army. Arrests traditionally made by a handful of uniformed officers knocking on a door are now increasingly executed by SWAT teams of a dozen or more officers using special-forces tactics. Stories abound of such commando raids in which doors are kicked in and occupants beaten or shot – some of which turn out to be cases of mistaken identity.

Increasing amounts of property are being seized under civil forfeiture laws, which allow police to seize assets of suspected law-breakers before a trial has found them guilty.

According to one study, the number of paramilitary drug raids in the US totaled a few hundred per year in the 1970s, a few thousand per year in the 1980s – and perhaps 80,000 currently. Using asset-forfeiture funds, police forces around the country are augmenting their revolvers and batons with stun grenades, heavily armored cars, tanks (believe it or not), and other paramilitary equipment. Meanwhile, the US Department of Defense has distributed billions of dollars' worth of surplus Iraq and Afghanistan military gear to local police forces.

This, alas, is just the beginning. Currently under development by Homeland Security is BOSS, short for Biometric Optical Surveillance System, which can scan entire crowds and use facial recognition software to pick out individual targets up to 100 meters away. And the Transportation Safety Administration (TSA) has begun conducting random bag searches and interrogations at train and bus stations. The division responsible for these searches is named Visible Intermodal Prevention and Response (VIPR), pronounced "viper."

Turn-Key Totalitarian State

Add it all up, and the US certainly appears to have shredded its Bill of Rights. Freedom of assembly and speech, along with prohibitions on unreasonable search and cruel and unusual punishment that Americans used to take for granted are fast disappearing.

To be fair, when viewed in the context of today's "asymmetrical" battlefield in which formal armies are replaced by terrorist cells with potentially devastating weapons, some parts of Big Brother's new tool kit may seem justified. If terrorists are shipping a suitcase-nuke to a US city, we all want the police to find it before it detonates, and if that means reading a few emails or even torturing the plans out of perpetrators, then maybe in that moment of stark choice the end – saving millions of lives – justifies the means. And for the most part, FBI agents are not yet the KGB, and local police officers are not an occupying army.

But the infrastructure of which they are a part is evolving into a "turn-key totalitarian state" just waiting to be switched on by some future desperate, deranged, or simply corrupt leader. And if history teaches anything, it is that such people are always in the pipeline and tend to appear in greater-than-usual numbers when financial collapse begets political crisis.

CHAPTER 8

MANIPULATED MARKETS

"There are no markets anymore, just interventions."

– Chris Powell, Gold Anti-Trust Action Committee

Once upon a time, a handful of countries sometimes described as "capitalist" claimed to operate on the principal that consenting adults should be free to buy, sell, build and consume what they wanted, with little interference or guidance from the authorities. The idea, derived from Adam Smith's 1776 classic *The Wealth of Nations*, was that all of these self-interested actions would in the aggregate form an "invisible hand" capable of guiding society towards the greatest good for the greatest number of people. Coincidentally, the political framework for such a society was envisioned the same year on the other side of the Atlantic, when Thomas Jefferson penned in the American Declaration of Independence that in addition to life and liberty, there was a third inalienable right for every individual – the pursuit of happiness. The resulting "market-based" societies were messy but brilliant, producing more progress in two centuries than in the previous 50.

But those days are long gone. After four decades of unrestrained borrowing, the developed world is in a constant state of near-collapse and governments everywhere feel compelled (or perhaps liberated) to tinker with markets, sometimes overtly and sometimes secretly, but of late with an increasingly heavy hand. The system that is evolving does not yet have a modern name but certainly looks like the central planning that failed so miserably for the Soviet Union and social democratic Europe in decades past. What follows is a brief overview of the manipulations that now dominate the global economy. Most are covered in greater depth in later chapters, so here we'll just introduce them without excessive background. If a term or event is not clear, read on for an explanation.

Artificially-Low Interest Rates

Interest rates are, in effect, the price of money and as such they're a crucial signal to virtually everyone in every market. When rates are high, that's an incentive to save, because the resulting yield is attractive. Low rates, meanwhile, are a signal that money is cheap and borrowing is potentially more profitable than saving.

Prior to World War II interest rates were set mostly by supply and demand. When there were lots of productive uses for a limited supply of money, demand for it went up and interest rates rose, and vice versa. Market participants had a fair idea of what the economy was asking for and government generally let them respond to these signals. (The term "laissez faire," French for "let [them] do," is aptly used to describe this version of capitalism.)

When the Fed began playing a bigger role in the economy in the 1950s and 60s, it chose as its main policy tool the Fed Funds Rate, the rate at which it lent short-term money to banks. Long-term interest rates (i.e., the bond market) remained free to fluctuate according to the supply and demand for loans. But following the crisis of 2008 the Fed and other central banks expanded their focus from short-term rates to all rates, including long-term. Today, the Fed intervenes aggressively "across the yield curve," pushing short rates down to zero and buying enough bonds to push long-term rates down to historically-low levels.

These interventions have preempted the market's price-signaling mechanism, encouraging borrowing and speculation and discouraging saving, as we explained in Chapter 6. We expand on what this means for society in Chapter 10: Variable Rate World. But for now suffice it to say that the entire yield curve – from short to long-term interest rates – is now dominated and manipulated by the government.

Dishonest Interest Rates and Currency Exchange Rates
While governments have been actively depressing interest rates, the world's major banks have been manipulating the London Interbank Offered Rate (Libor) for their own ends. Libor is the reference rate for trillions of dollars of loans world-wide. And in a scandal that is still escalating as this is written in late 2013, it has been revealed that the banks responsible for setting this rate have been arbitrarily moving it around and then trading on the advance knowledge of the movement, enhancing their profits and yearend bonuses. Other banks lied about the rates at which they were borrowing to make them appear less fragile during the 2008 financial crisis, misleading market participants as well as government regulators. Meanwhile, many of the loans based on sham Libor rates disadvantaged the entity on one side of the transaction, costing, in the aggregate, hundreds of billions of dollars.

And in 2013 US, Swiss and British regulators opened investigations of more than a dozen major banks alleged to have manipulated currency exchange rates and traded on inside information by "front-running" (trading for the bank's own account before executing customer orders).

Artificially-High Stock Prices
Until very recently share prices, by general consensus, were set purely by market forces (though they were influenced

somewhat by the Fed's control of short term-interest rates and government tax and spending laws). Whether the market went up or down was not generally seen as a pressing policy matter for the federal government or central bank. Then in 1988 – presumably in response to the previous year's flash-crash that had sliced about 30 percent from US stock prices in a single month – the Reagan Administration created the Working Group on Financial Markets to either prevent or manage such events in the future.

This shadowy organization came to be known as the "Plunge Protection Team (PPT)," and is now thought by many to funnel government money into the market to boost share prices when it perceives the need. The origin of this idea goes back to 1989 when former Federal Reserve Board member Robert Heller told *The Wall Street Journal* that, "Instead of flooding the entire economy with liquidity, and thereby increasing the danger of inflation, the Fed could support the stock market directly by buying market averages in the futures market, thereby stabilizing the market as a whole." In August 2005, Canadian fund manager Sprott Asset Management released a report arguing that the PPT was indeed manipulating stock prices.

But the PPT is just one of the ways that the government now intervenes in the stock market. Interest rates, as mentioned above, are manipulated in part to make stocks more attractive relative to bank accounts and cash. And the repeated bailouts of banks and major industrial companies when their failure threatened the economy – and therefore share prices – are widely perceived as a government "backstop" for equities. The goal isn't higher share prices per se but to engender optimism among investors who are then more willing to borrow and spend because their portfolios are rising. This so-called "wealth effect" is now a central lever of government policy.

Cheap Mortgages, Inflated Home Prices

For most of the 20th century, homes were bought with either cash or 30-year, fixed-rate mortgages. And because long-term interest rates were not set by the Fed, the price of money with which to buy a house was determined mostly by the market. But after the 2008 financial crisis, when the Fed began forcing down long-term rates, cheap mortgages and rising home prices became government policy objectives. The Fed now buys mortgage backed bonds in addition to government bonds, which both lowers mortgage rates and funnels money into the mortgage market, generally making home loans easier to obtain and inducing individuals to buy the biggest possible house with most aggressive possible financing. Here again, rising home prices are just a means to a positive wealth effect.

Figure 8.1: 30-Year Mortgage Interest Rates, 2007–2013

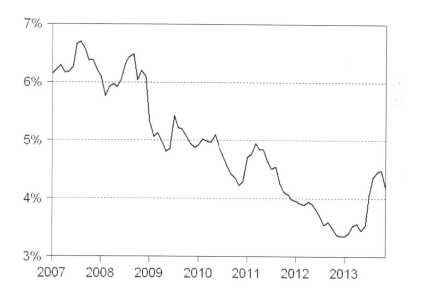

Suppressed Gold Price

We cover gold in much greater detail in Part IV, but for now suffice it to say that because the metal is a competing form of money, when it rises in dollar terms it makes the dollar and the dollar's managers look bad. So for nearly two decades the US, along with several other governments and their central banks, has been systematically intervening in the gold market to push down its exchange rate to the dollar. They do this by covertly dumping central bank gold onto the market and instructing large commercial banks to sell huge numbers of gold futures contracts into thinly traded markets. Together, these secret machinations have held gold's exchange rate far below where a free market would have taken it. Gold's ability to signal market participants that inflation is rising and/or national currencies are being mismanaged is being short-circuited. As a result, market participants who might otherwise be converting those currencies into hard assets are not doing so. The Gold Anti-Trust Action Committee, a not-for-profit organization aimed at restoring a free market in gold, has thoroughly documented this manipulation, and makes its archives freely available at www.gata.org.

All of the Above

The Exchange Stabilization Fund (ESF) was established in 1934 to enable carte blanche market intervention by the federal government, outside of Congressional oversight. As Dr. Anna J. Schwartz, at the time a Distinguished Fellow of the American Economic Association explained in a 1998 speech, "The ESF was conceived to operate in secrecy under the exclusive control of the Secretary of the Treasury, with the approval of the President, [quoting here from the 1934 legislation] 'whose decisions shall be final and not subject to review by any other officer of the United States'."

The ESF now functions as a "slush fund" available to the Treasury Department for wide-ranging, frequently-secret market interventions. It provides "stabilization" loans to foreign governments. It influences currency exchange rates – including that of gold. It has been used to offer insurance to money market funds and to bail out Mexico. Most recently it was drained to provide the government some breathing room during the late 2013 debt ceiling impasse. As for the stock market, well, why not? Perhaps the ESF is the real – or at least another – Plunge Protection Team.

Distorted Signals and Lost Trust

What happens to a society when market signals are distorted by the government? In a word, "malinvestment." Factories are built that produce the wrong things, houses are bought that cost more than their owners can afford, bank CDs are cashed in to buy stocks just before a market correction, gold and other hard assets are converted to paper currency when they should be accumulated and held for the long haul. The market, in short, stops directing capital to its most productive uses, wealth creation grinds to a halt, and chaos eventually ensues.

Along the way, people begin to notice that the markets they thought were more-or-less honest are being secretly manipulated for the benefit of others, and trust begins to erode. The next chapter explains what happens then.

Chapter 9

Shrinking Trust Horizon and the Crack-up Boom

"Whenever destroyers appear among men, they start by destroying money, for money is men's protection and the base of a moral existence. Destroyers seize gold and leave to its owners a counterfeit pile of paper. This kills all objective standards and delivers men into the arbitrary power of an arbitrary setter of values."

– Ayn Rand, Atlas Shrugged

As the scope and nature of the corruption detailed in the previous three chapters become common knowledge, Americans are beginning to conclude that:

- The economy is in worse shape than the government says it is.

- Consumers are getting less value for their money than previously and instead of rising, their standard of living is actually eroding.

- Markets once thought to be fair are being secretly manipulated by the government to the detriment of the average citizen.

- The police and military are spying on and threatening them in seemingly-unconstitutional ways.

- Banks and other corporations are using their dominance of the financial system to commit increasingly blatant and far-reaching fraud.

Pollsters have been noting this shift in sentiment for some time. Congress' approval rating, always low, plunged to single-digits in 2013; 50 percent of respondents in one recent poll viewed the president as "not trustworthy"; 77 percent in another poll no longer trust TV news. The list goes on, but the point is clear: The perception is growing that society's institutions no longer work for the folks they were originally designed to serve.

When people realize they're being misled by their leaders, one typical response is to re-focus closer to home, on friends, local producers of necessities, local government, and family – in other words, the people and organizations that can be seen and judged face-to-face. This "shrinking trust horizon,"[1] shows up in a number of trends:

- Owning gold and silver – or "crypto-currencies" like Bitcoin[2] – instead of dollars.
- Buying locally produced food instead of national brands.
- Banking with community banks instead of money center banks.
- Home schooling children rather than sending them to public school.
- Tuning out national politics.
- Voting for – or at least admiring – libertarian candidates like Ron Paul.
- Buying guns and ammunition.
- Stocking up on survival rations.
- Investing in offshore assets.

---

[1] The term "shrinking trust horizon" has been popularized by Nicole Foss of the Automatic Earth website.

[2] See Chapter 18

At first glance, these trends might seem to be random and unrelated because they emanate from different points on the political/social spectrum. Home schoolers and local food buyers are frequently motivated by different ideologies, for instance, while offshore investors and gun enthusiasts frequently lead very different lives. But all of the above behaviors share one motivation that cuts across political affiliation and social class: a growing distrust of the systems and institutions that run the country and the world.

And therein lies the rub. Fiat currency in the end is based on trust. Trust in government, trust in banks, trust in currency issuers. As that trust erodes, so does the currency's purchasing power.

THE CRACK-UP BOOM

The early stages of a shrinking trust horizon are accommodated quite nicely by the market. Local banks staff up to handle a surge in deposits, local farmers expand to meet the new demand, companies are formed to supply home schoolers with materials or to facilitate offshore trusts and LLCs, etc. But as the trend progresses, it comes to be understood that the central, underlying system that is being corrupted is the currency, that most of today's political and financial malfeasance depends on easy money, and *that inflation is an ongoing policy of this pervasive new regime.* When this realization becomes sufficiently wide-spread, the trends towards alternate means of saving money (gold and silver), employing capital (putting it into real assets like farmland) and transacting in everyday commerce (with Bitcoin and other non-national currencies) reach a tipping point.

In the Austrian School of economics (which is, we believe, the only branch of that profession that actually explains how modern financial systems work) this tipping point and what follows is known as a "crack-up boom." Austrian economist Ludwig von Mises explained it as follows:

"This first stage of the inflationary process may last for many years. While it lasts, the prices of many goods and services are not yet adjusted to the altered money relation. There are still people in the country who have not yet become aware of the fact that they are confronted with a price revolution which will finally result in a considerable rise of all prices, although the extent of this rise will not be the same in the various commodities and services. These people still believe that prices one day will drop. Waiting for this day, they restrict their purchases and concomitantly increase their cash holdings. As long as such ideas are still held by public opinion, it is not yet too late for the government to abandon its inflationary policy.

But then, finally, the masses wake up. They become suddenly aware of the fact that inflation is a deliberate policy and will go on endlessly. A breakdown occurs. The crack-up boom appears. Everybody is anxious to swap his money against 'real' goods, no matter whether he needs them or not, no matter how much money he has to pay for them. Within a very short time, within a few weeks or even days, the things which were used as money are no longer used as media of exchange. They become scrap paper. Nobody wants to give away anything against them.

It was this that happened with the Continental currency in America in 1781, with the French mandats territoriaux in 1796, and with the German mark in 1923. It will happen again whenever the same conditions appear. If a thing has to be used as a medium of exchange, public opinion must not believe that the quantity of this thing will increase beyond all bounds. Inflation is a policy that cannot last."

So how close is the point where "finally, the masses wake up?" No one knows. In late 2013 stocks and houses were approaching previous-bubble levels, propelled higher by the Fed's aggressive currency creation. Banks, after three years of almost preternatural caution, were loosening lending standards and beginning to turn their mountain of liquidity into business and home loans. There were many signs, in short, that yet another manic phase was beginning in the financial markets.

And what would another asset bubble do to today's even-more-leveraged financial system? Doug Noland, manager of the Prudent Bear mutual fund, addressed this in an early 2013 issue of his weekly *Credit Bubble Bulletin*:

"I don't mean to imply that today's environment is comparable to 1999. The U.S. economy was sounder in 1999 – and the global economy was a whole lot more stable. Global imbalances in 1999 were insignificant compared to the present. The U.S. economic and Credit systems had yet to be degraded by a doubling of mortgage debt and a massive misallocation of resources. The federal government hadn't doubled its debt load in four years. Europe had not yet terribly impaired itself with a decade of runaway non-productive debt growth. China and the "developing" economies had not yet succumbed to historic Credit booms, overinvestment and economic maladjustment. Central banks hadn't yet resorted to really dangerous measures."

The implication: Today's world, levered to the hilt in response to the policy mistakes and financial crises of the past few decades, is even more complex and fragile than the economies that (barely) survived the bursting of the tech stock and housing bubbles. So the next bubble and its aftermath might be a whole different animal, and a crack-up boom is a very plausible way to explain it.

Too Little Faith, Not Too Much Currency

As we've described it so far, a crack-up boom may sound like simply a fancy name for accelerating inflation. But the two, while related, represent very different stages in a fiat currency's life cycle. Inflation – a rising supply of currency that leads to asset bubbles and/or generally higher prices – can persist for years or even decades without triggering a definitive crisis. 1990 - 2013 was such a time, when consumer prices rose at a (reported) 3 or so percent a year and asset bubbles expanded and popped approximately once per decade.

A crack-up boom, in contrast, is the end game, the point where inflation comes to be seen as permanent and a critical mass of people act on that assumption, potentially causing a hyperinflation/currency collapse within a very short time. This crisis is not necessarily due to a sudden increase in the supply of currency but can also occur from a sudden loss of faith that results in *plunging demand* for currency. In other words, a crack-up boom is a psychological/emotional event that builds slowly and erupts suddenly. When it does, economic activity falls, leading to more currency printing in an attempt to arrest the decline, and this new supply results in an even greater drop in demand for the currency, in a downward spiral that ends with the currency's total failure.

Imperfect But Useful Indicators

Are there financial indicators that can signal the advent of a crack-up boom? A few. Gold's exchange rate is an obvious one. When it spikes, that's a sign that global capital is losing faith in fiat currency – which explains why governments intervene in the precious metal markets so aggressively.

Also potentially useful is the velocity of money. Recall from Chapter 3 that this is a measure of how many times a given dollar in circulation turns over. When banks are lending aggressively and the recipients of loans are spending what they're borrowing, the velocity of money is high, and each newly-created piece of currency has an outsized effect on the overall economy. And vice versa: Since 2009 the velocity of money has fallen to record low levels as banks, traumatized by their near-death experience, have been reluctant to lend and borrowers, burdened by the debts they took on in the housing/consumer bubble, have been in no mood to borrow. This reticence on the part of both borrowers and lenders explains why the massive increase in bank reserves had little initial impact on economic growth.

If the velocity of money rises gradually from here, the result would probably be modest expansion accompanied by an equally modest rise in general price levels. But if velocity spikes, then something much more extreme is developing.

Then there's inflation itself. When price increases cease to be confined to a few asset classes like equities, houses and college tuition and become more broad-based, people begin to notice. And if those general price increases seem to be accelerating, people really notice. Table 9.1 shows the soaring number of Reichsmarks needed to buy one US dollar, which indicates the trend in consumer inflation in Weimar Germany preceding and during its hyperinflation.

Figure 9.1: Reichsmarks Needed to Buy US$1

	Reichsmarks/US$1
January 1922	201
February 1922	227
March 1922	338
July 1922	670
August 1922	1,975
October 1922	4,500
December 1922	8,470
January 1923	48,390
June 1923	193,500
August 1923	11,400,000
October 1923	170,500,000,000

Note that the increases were (relatively) modest at first, then significant, and then – in the space of few months – parabolic. Virtually overnight, the German Reichsmark simply ceased to function. That's what a crack-up boom looks like, and it occurred in a country with a generally well-educated populace that previously had enjoyed one of the best standards of living in the world. And the US is creating a very hospitable environment for something similar.

Chapter 10

Variable-Rate World Death Spiral

"One of the great mistakes is to judge policies and programs by their intentions rather than their results."

— Milton Friedman

In Chapter 6's look at the ways in which fiat currency corrupts a society, we left out the fact that today's combination of a depreciating currency and artificially-low interest rates leads many to not just borrow heavily, but to borrow at variable rather than fixed rates. This form of corruption takes a bit of explaining, but is so important that that it deserves a chapter of its own.

The story in a nutshell: If government policy is to push interest rates a little lower each year in order to make a rising debt burden easier to manage, then it makes sense for individuals, businesses and governments themselves to either borrow for very short periods and roll maturing debt over at ever-lower interest rates, or to choose debt with variable rates like an adjustable rate mortgage (ARM) or a business loan tied to a benchmark like Libor or the prime rate. And it encourages leveraged players to speculate on lower rates in the future, creating a mountain of highly-volatile bond portfolios and derivatives.

The resulting "variable-rate world" seems stable and prosperous while ever-cheaper loans free up cash for other uses. But interest rates can't fall forever because forcing rates down to abnormal levels requires the creation of excessive amounts of new currency, which produces generalized inflation, a falling currency exchange rate, or booms and busts of increasing magnitude – or all of the above – eventually destabilizing the financial system. So at some point rates will reverse course and begin rising to historically-normal levels. The virtuous cycle of lower interest rates leading to lower interest expense will shift into reverse, with higher interest rates raising debt service costs to intolerable levels and potentially crashing the whole system.

In mid-2013 the US got a glimpse of its future when rates began to rise on fears that the Fed would soon scale back (or "taper") its QE bond-buying program. Both bonds and equities went into tailspins, threatening to undo in a few months the (paper) gains of the past few years' debt monetization. The speed and violence of the reaction caused the Fed to backtrack, and as this is written in late 2013 tapering has yet to occur.

If the dollar is to survive as a functioning currency, then at some point interest rates will have to rise to normal levels. But the global financial system is both unprepared and *unable to prepare* for that day. The following sectors, in ascending order of systemic impact, are where rising interest rates will cause trouble:

Long-Term Bonds
Retail investors poured about $1 trillion into bond funds between 2009 and 2012, in part because bond prices (which go up when interest rates go down) had been rising for three decades, and in part because investors were anxious and bonds are viewed as relatively low-risk assets.

For a while it worked. Bond prices soared as long-term rates kept falling, which helped both individuals and pension funds rebuild capital lost during 2008's debacle. But when interest rates spiked in mid-2013, US bond mutual funds saw $60 billion depart, while bond prices fell hard. Figure 10.1 shows the price of US 20-year Treasury bonds, which dropped by about 12 percent between April and August – a stunning move for this traditionally staid asset class.

Figure 10.1: Treasury Bond Prices (TLT), 1 April–31 October 2013

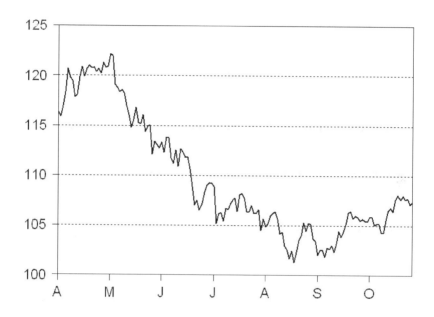

Exactly how much this jump in interest rates cost the economy is unknown because most bondholders don't report their day-to-day results. But commercial banks own huge portfolios of long-term bonds and report their results to the Fed, which compiles a report called "Net unrealized gains (losses) on available-for-sale securities." Figure 10.2 shows the unrealized gains falling from $43 billion in December 2012 to essentially zero by July, with losses beginning to appear in August as interest rates continued to climb. And this was just the commercial banks. Assume similar results for pension funds, bond mutual funds, hedge funds and private individual accounts, and the carnage was probably north of $1 trillion, or about 8 percent of the entire economy – in three months, on a move that left interest rates still far below historical norms.

Figure 10.2: Bank Bond Portfolio Gains/Losses, 2012–2013

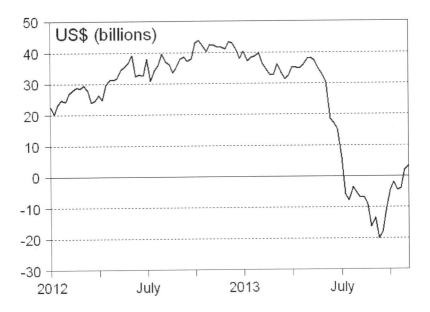

Government Budgets

Banks and pension funds losing trillions of dollars on their bond portfolios is serious. But true systemic risk enters the picture with sovereign debt. One of the many ways the US, Japanese and European governments hide the effects of their mounting liabilities is by doing most of their borrowing for short periods of time – a few months to one year – where interest rates are now close to zero and money is effectively free. In 1990, for example, the US paid $265 billion in interest on $3.2 trillion of debt. In the ensuing 23 years, its debt rose more than five-fold to $16.7 trillion, while its annual interest expense rose only 57 percent, to $416 billion. This apparent miracle was made possible by the lower interest rates engineered by the Federal Reserve, which dropped the average rate on federal debt from 8.3 percent to 2.4 percent.

Figure 10.3: US Federal Debt and Interest Expense, 1990–2013

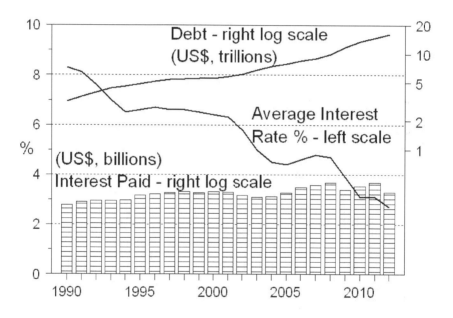

This party ends when long-term rates start rising, at which time governments will have three choices: (1) roll even more of their maturing debt into very short-term paper, which would keep interest costs down but necessitate the refinancing of greater amounts each year; (2) keep the average maturity of their debt constant and see their interest costs rise dramatically; or (3) have their central banks buy even more debt, which might prolong the deception for a while but at the risk of a tidal wave of newly-created currency wreaking various kinds of havoc.

Japan is the poster child for the variable-rate-world dilemma. Recall from Chapter 4 that its government debt is higher as a percent of GDP than that of any other major country. It was able to borrow this much because its citizens were aggressive savers willing to park their nest eggs in government bonds. This huge pool of domestic capital soaked up most of the debt issued by Japan's government, at very favorable rates. Between 2000 and 2013 its debt more than doubled, but its interest costs actually fell because it was borrowing and refinancing at declining rates.

Figure 10.4: Japan Trade Balance, 2007–September 2013

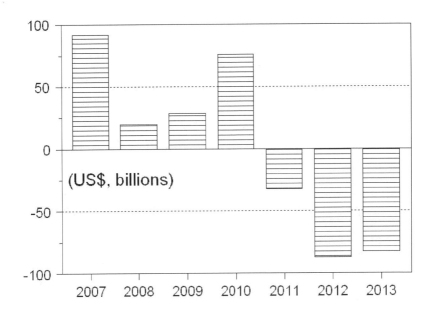

But this uniquely-enabling situation is over, for several reasons. First, Japan is the world's most rapidly-aging nation. To cite just one of many extraordinary data points, in 2012 its citizens bought more diapers for adults than for children. Retirees tend to spend rather than save, which means less domestic demand for government bonds. One indicator of this inflection point is the fact that Japan's perennial trade surplus – which brought in hundreds of billions of dollars each year to finance its budget deficits – became a trade deficit in 2011, which is before the Fukushima Daiichi nuclear disaster forced the country to import more energy than previously, further worsening its trade deficit. But demographics are also having an impact, and as Japan's population of retirees – who consume more than they produce – continues to swell, its trade deficit will only grow wider.

In the future, Japan will have to look abroad for funds and will have to pay interest rates more in line with the US and Europe, which are considerably higher than what it currently pays. The ratchet will start turning in the other direction, raising total interest expense with each new borrowing and refinancing.

The resulting fiscal crisis would be catastrophic for Japan, but also disruptive for the rest of the world. Japan owns over $1 trillion of US Treasuries along with a sizeable chunk of euro-denominated debt. Should it have to sell – or even stop accumulating – such bonds, the US and Europe would have to pay more to borrow elsewhere, further straining *their* budgets. In effect, Japan would export its debt crisis to the rest of the developed world.

But even leaving Japan out of the equation, the US and Europe are headed for the same fate. With $17 trillion of Treasury paper outstanding, a 1 percent rise in its average borrowing rate increases the US deficit by $170 billion. Let rates rise from the year-end 2013 average of 2 percent to a historically-normal 6 percent and the cost of servicing the national debt would swell by nearly $700 billion annually. This extra interest would have to be borrowed, thus increasing the following year's deficit and requiring that much more borrowing – and probably leading investors to demand an even higher interest rate, further raising the government's interest cost. And so on, until the federal budget enters a death spiral that ends with the US being priced out of the debt market and forced to live within its means – or to print so much new currency that the dollar collapses.

Interest Rate Derivatives
Now for the big one: Recall from Chapter 5 that financial derivatives – unregulated bets between banks and institutional investors on various financial events – have risen from a face value of less than $1 trillion in the mid-1990s to $693 trillion by year-end 2013 without a corresponding increase in reported liabilities. That's because banks and hedge funds (i.e., the "counterparties") net out their long and short positions and only report the remainder, which is miniscule compared to the total value of contracts outstanding.

Amazingly, over 80 percent of this market is now made up of interest rate swaps (see Figure 5.1), which are essentially bets on the direction of interest rates. If interest rates keep rising, the players betting on stable or falling rates will lose big. If these counterparties then default on their obligations, the holders of the other side of the bet suddenly find themselves with a losing ticket – which they had neglected to report as a potential liability. They are impaired by this loss, are unable to make good on their losing bets, and stiff *their* counterparties, and so on, until the entire financial system freezes up. This is not mere theory; it actually happened with credit default swaps in 2008, when the failure of insurance company AIG and investment bank Lehman Brothers would have devastated Wall Street and much of the rest of the global financial system if the federal government had not bailed them out. As legendary investor Warren Buffett famously observed, derivatives truly are "weapons of financial mass destruction."

All At Once

The interesting (if that's not too neutral a word) thing about rising interest rates in a variable-rate world is that all the events mentioned here will happen simultaneously. Bank and pension fund bond portfolios will report massive losses; governments will see their interest costs spike, making borrowing more expensive and risking a flight from their clearly-mismanaged currencies; and interest rate swaps will become highly unstable, possibly threatening the house of cards that is the global banking community.

The world's governments thus find themselves in an ever-shrinking box. And all it will take to trigger the crisis is a return to historically-normal levels of interest rates. As recently as 2000, 30-year Treasury bonds yielded over 6 percent and 30-year mortgages cost 7.5 percent. Let rates return to those levels and the global financial system implodes. But continue to force down interest rates by creating trillions of new dollars, euros, and yen, and the near-certain result is even bigger asset bubbles and rising inflation, culminating in a crack-up boom that will sweep the world's fiat currencies into the dustbin of history. And there is no third choice. As every addict eventually discovers, there is pain today or even greater pain tomorrow, and that's it.

CHAPTER 11

THEY'RE COMING FOR YOUR SAVINGS: CAPITAL CONTROLS, WEALTH TAXES AND BANK BAIL-INS

"If there is a risk in a bank, our first question should be 'Okay, what are you in the bank going to do about that? What can you do to recapitalize yourself?' If the bank can't do it, then we'll talk to the shareholders and the bondholders, we'll ask them to contribute in recapitalizing the bank, and if necessary the uninsured deposit holders."

– Jeroen Dijsselbloem, Dutch Finance Minister

For most Italians, June 7, 2012 began like any other day – which is to say uncertain and stressful, given their country's starring role in the eurozone crisis. But for customers of Bank Network Investments SpA (BNI), things took an even darker turn when they discovered that the troubled bank had frozen their accounts, leaving many unable to pay rent or buy groceries.

Individual banks sometimes run into trouble, of course, so BNI was easy to dismiss as an isolated event – until two weeks later, when the eurozone announced that it was considering system-wide capital controls, including bank withdrawal limitations, to prevent the crisis from spreading. Suddenly, the life-changing difficulties of BNI's Italian customers were a possible "new normal" for much of the continent.

And Europe is not alone. The whole world has entered an era in which the rules governing financial accounts and capital movement are routinely changed with the stroke of a pen. To take just a few recent examples:

- Iceland responded to its 2008 financial meltdown by requiring that firms seeking to invest abroad get permission from the central bank, and that individual Icelanders get government authorization to buy foreign currency or travel overseas.

- Greece pulled funds directly from bank and brokerage accounts of suspected tax evaders, without prior notice or judicial due process.

- Argentina banned the purchase of US dollars for personal savings and required banks to make loans in pesos at rates considerably below the true inflation rate.

- The US Federal Reserve proposed that money market funds be allowed to limit withdrawals of customer cash in times of market stress.

- The International Monetary Fund proposed a 10 percent tax on eurozone household savings, noting that, "The appeal is that such a tax, if it is implemented before avoidance is possible, and there is a belief that it will never be repeated, does not distort behavior (and may be seen by some as fair)."

- And beginning with Cyprus (see below), a growing list of countries are planning to directly confiscate their citizens' financial accounts in a banking crisis.

Bank Bail-Ins: What's Yours Is…Ours

The developed world responded to the 2008 banking crisis by creating immense amounts of new currency and giving it to insolvent banks. No strings, not even restrictions on year-end bonuses to bank executives and traders. Responding with the tone-deaf sense of privilege that has since become so familiar, Wall Street proceeded to pay out record bonuses – with taxpayer money. This in-your-face arrogance, combined with the fact that the trillions of dollars of bail-out funds produced little growth on Main Street but extreme strain on government finances, have made bail-outs a political non-starter going forward. So the developed world needs a new way to stop a banking crisis from going systemic.

Enter the "bail-in," in which the depositors and creditors of a failed bank are required to pay for the institution's rescue. Cyprus, a eurozone country, was the first to go this route in 2013, when its leading banks failed and the rest of the eurozone insisted that in return for financial assistance, it confiscate 47.5 percent of domestic bank accounts over €100,000.

Poland – not a eurozone member – then followed with its own variation on the bail-in theme, responding to a budgetary shortfall by confiscating the assets of the country's private pension funds (many of them owned by brand-name multinationals like Allianz, AXA, and Generali), without offering any compensation.

Also in 2013, it was revealed that Spain had, in effect, looted its largest public pension fund, the Social Security Reserve Fund, by ordering it to use its cash to buy Spanish government bonds. By year-end, 90 percent of the €65 billion fund had been invested in Spanish sovereign paper, leaving the fund's beneficiaries dependent on future governments' ability to manage their finances.

Since Cyprus, the bail-in model has been adopted by the rest of the eurozone, Switzerland, New Zealand and even Canada, while the Bank for International Settlements has published a blueprint showing other countries how to use creditors' and depositors' money to recapitalize failed banks. (That bail-ins ignore legal niceties like creditor hierarchy and the sanctity of contracts by inflicting losses on bondholders before shareholders have been fully wiped out is yet another reason for a shrinking trust horizon.)

Just the Beginning

Will more countries introduce capital controls or asset confiscations in the next few years? Almost certainly. The predicament in which most central banks find themselves has only two exits: continued monetization of ever-greater amounts of debt at the cost of ever-greater hot money flows and asset bubbles – which will destabilize developing countries and lead them to impose capital controls, bail-ins and other forms of asset confiscations. Or the scale-back of debt monetization at the cost of rising interest rates, which will destabilize the variable-rate world – again leading to various kinds of asset confiscation as money-hungry governments, reluctant to cut spending in a crisis, look for new sources of wealth to tap.

So recent capital controls and bank bail-ins are, alas, just the beginning, and what follows will make them look tame by comparison. In the US, bank checking and savings accounts, while containing a lot of money, are peanuts compared to tax-advantaged accounts like IRAs, 401(K)s, and private pensions. These plans contain trillions of dollars of stocks, bonds and money market funds, much of which is not currently taxed. For a government desperate for resources in a system spinning out of control, such accounts will be too tempting to pass up.

Interestingly, the recently enacted Affordable Health Care Act (aka Obamacare) provides the constitutional rationale for their seizure. By claiming – and then gaining Supreme Court acquiescence to the assertion – that the government has the power to force Americans to buy health insurance, the Act has eliminated the Constitutional argument preventing the federal government, for instance, from demanding the conversion of stocks, bonds, and mutual funds in brokerage accounts into Treasury bonds. In effect, this would force investors to finance ongoing government deficits.

Thus armed with both motivation and legal justification, desperate governments will, at some point in the not too distant future, begin taking productive assets from citizens' accounts and replacing them with government bonds paying the same number of dollars (or euros or yen) each year – just in time for a sudden, massive currency devaluation. This asset-grab will resemble Franklin Roosevelt's 1933 confiscation of citizens' gold and subsequent 70 percent devaluation of the dollar against gold (more about this in a couple of pages). With one big difference: In 1933 the government didn't know where all the gold was and gold owned by Americans outside the United States was not confiscated, so it was possible for citizens to ignore FDR's demand and keep their gold. This time, the government knows exactly where every financial account is located and what it contains, making it virtually impossible to sidestep any confiscation.

To sum up, in an era of capital controls, asset confiscations, a shrinking trust horizon and increasingly desperate governments, the money in your financial accounts – that is, your bank CDs, brokerage accounts, money market funds and maybe even insurance policies – may not be yours after all.

Historical Digression -- Notable Asset Seizures of the Past.

Desperate governments have, throughout history, done what they had to do to survive, which often includes simply stealing their subjects' wealth. The pretexts vary, but the ultimate act is generally the same: people with weapons (physical or legal) show up at homes, banks, or businesses and take what they want, leaving the victim with little or no recourse. Here are a few of history's more notable examples:

- *Ancient Rome had a rule called "proscription" that allowed the government to execute and then confiscate the assets of anyone found guilty of "crimes against the state." After the death of Julius Caesar in 44 BC, three men, Mark Anthony, Lepidus, and Ceasar's adopted son Octavian, formed a group they called the Second Triumvirate and divided the Empire between them. But two rivals, Brutus and Cassius, formed an army with which they planned to take the Empire for themselves. The Triumvirate needed money to fund an army of its own, and decided the best way to raise it was by kicking the proscription process into overdrive. They drew up a list of several hundred wealthy Romans, accused them of crimes, executed them and took their property. It worked. The Triumvirate won the war and Octavian went on to become Augustus, who transformed what had been a republican state into a dictatorship and became the first Roman emperor.*

- *In the mid-1530s, England under Henry VIII was short of funds, and his agents began seizing monasteries and claiming their property and income for the Crown. As historian G. J. Meyer tells it in The Tudors: The Complete Story of England's Most Notorious Dynasty:*

"By April fat trunks were being hauled into London filled with gold and silver plate, jewelry, and other treasures accumulated by the monasteries over the centuries. With them came money from the sale of church bells, lead stripped from the roofs of monastic buildings, and livestock, furnishings, and equipment. Some of the confiscated land was sold – enough to bring in £30,000 – and what was not sold generated tens of thousands of pounds in annual rents. The longer the confiscations continued, the smaller the possibility of their ever being reversed or even stopped from going further. The money was spent almost as quickly as it flooded in – so quickly that any attempt to restore the monasteries to what they had been before the suppression would have meant financial ruin for the Crown. Nor would those involved in the work of the suppression ... ever be willing to part with what they were skimming off for themselves."

- *Soon after the French Revolution in 1789, the new government confiscated lands and other property of the Catholic Church and used the current and future proceeds to back a new form of paper currency called assignats. Recall from Chapter 1 that once begun, this money-printing binge spun out of control, resulting in hyperinflation and the rise of a dictator.*

- *During the US Civil War, Congress passed laws confiscating property used for "insurrectionary purposes" and of citizens generally engaged in rebellion.*

- *In 1933, with America mired in the Great Depression, President Franklin Roosevelt banned the private ownership of gold and ordered US citizens to turn in their gold. Those who did were paid in paper dollars at the then-current rate of $20.67 per ounce. Once the process was complete, the dollar was devalued to $35 per ounce of gold, effectively confiscating 70 percent of the purchasing power of citizens who surrendered their gold. Much has been written about how FDR's real aim was not simply to accumulate gold but to remove gold as an obstacle to the power and growth of government. As you might expect, we agree wholeheartedly with this analysis.*

- *In 1942, after entering World War II, the US arrested and moved Japanese citizens to concentration camps, with severe limits on what they could take with them, causing forced selling at a great financial loss. Their remaining property was seized and sold. The detainees were released in 1945, given $25 and a train ticket home – and were never fully reimbursed for their lost wealth.*

CHAPTER 12

CURRENCY WAR: THE WORLD TARGETS KING DOLLAR

"[Americans] are living beyond their means and shifting a part of the weight of their problems to the world economy. They are living like parasites off the global economy and their monopoly of the dollar. If [in America] there is a systemic malfunction, this will affect everyone. Countries like Russia and China hold a significant part of their reserves in American securities. There should be other reserve currencies."

– Vladimir Putin, Russian President

When a country borrows too much and begins to suffer for its sins, it frequently concludes that the only viable way out is to devalue its currency in order to generate rising exports and faster growth. To illustrate how this works, pretend that you're in charge of Japan and would like to pump up the domestic economy, ideally by selling more cars to the US. You cut taxes, increase government spending, and create more yen, which taken together lower your currency's value versus the dollar, thus making Toyotas and Hondas cheaper when their yen price is converted to dollars. Americans buy more Japanese cars, their makers book higher profits and hire more workers, and the Japanese government receives more tax revenue. And you, the architect of the strategy, are hailed as a genius and re-elected in a landslide.

But the view from the US is less rosy. For every Toyota that its citizens buy, one fewer Ford or Chevy is produced, which leads US automakers to lay off workers and book lower profits. The American economy suffers, and its leaders get the blame.

So what do they do? They emulate their successful Japanese counterparts by running higher deficits, lowering taxes and pressuring the Fed to lower interest rates in order to make the dollar less valuable on foreign exchange markets. This also works. A cheaper dollar lowers the effective price of American exports, which leads to more sales and faster growth, and incumbent politicians see their poll numbers rally.

And so it goes, as Europe, China and the developing world respond in turn by lowering the value of *their* currencies. This series of "competitive devaluations" contributes to and exacerbates the mess caused by the previous decade's over-borrowing.

According to hedge fund manager James Rickards, whose book *Currency Wars* is required reading for anyone who wants to understand this process, there have been two previous currency wars in modern times. The first was during the 1930s when the US and the major European countries, suffering from the debasement of currency created to pay for World War I and the collapse of the 1920s debt bubble, either went off the gold standard or sharply devalued versus gold. The second was during the 1970s when the US ended convertibility of dollars into gold, setting off a decade of monetary chaos in which inflation hit double-digit levels and gold soared from $35 to $850.

Rickards believes that today's world is deeply into Currency War III. We concur, and view this one as far more dangerous than its predecessors, for three reasons. First, recall from chapter 4 that the amount of debt the developed world has accumulated dwarfs anything that has come before. Second, everyone is still borrowing. Debt, even when measured in real terms by adjusting for inflation, continues to rise in the US, Europe, and Japan – and though no one really knows what's going on in China, it seems to be on a similar path. Third, the mountain of derivatives that has accumulated is, as we may have mentioned once or twice already, a highly destabilizing wild-card. So to avoid a 1930s-style debt-driven collapse, successive rounds of currency devaluation are all but guaranteed.

The most recent – and in many ways most remarkable – shot was fired by Japan, where the Bank of Japan is explicitly trying to engineer inflation and in late 2013 was buying up Japanese bonds at a rate that would double the size of its 2011 balance sheet within another year.

No Neutrals

Sitting this war out is not an option. If a country chooses not to devalue, its currency soars versus the others and its exports are priced out of world markets. This is politically unacceptable, leaving it with no choice but to join in.

Switzerland, for instance, was able to remain neutral in the past century's shooting wars. But a currency war (especially a *fiat* currency war) is an entirely different challenge for a global banking center. When capital in search of a safe haven began pouring into Swiss franc accounts in 2010, the franc soared to record highs, which sent the country's exporters into a tailspin. In response, the Swiss did the previously-unthinkable, pegging the franc's value at 1.20 to the euro and vowing to create unlimited amounts of currency to keep it there. The franc plunged 8 percent versus other major currencies on the day of the announcement, which is another way of saying the Swiss devalued the franc by that amount. And with its currency now pegged to the euro, it is committed to eurozone levels of inflation going forward. In effect it has joined the currency war on the side of the euro.

Meanwhile, even the better-run developing countries find themselves at the mercy of the major trading powers. As dollar, yen and euro interest rates have plunged in recent years, hedge funds have been able to borrow virtually-unlimited quantities of major-country currency for next to nothing. Meanwhile, developing countries like Brazil, Thailand, and Russia offer bonds yielding far more than US Treasuries. So speculators – on a vast scale – have found it profitable to borrow dollars or yen, use them to buy, say, Brazilian bonds, and reap a wide, lucrative spread, which is frequently made even wider when capital inflows strengthen the developing country currency.

This "carry trade" is great for the developed world in general and hedge funds in particular, but not so much for developing countries, where alternating in-and-out torrents of hot money can destabilize smaller, more fragile economies, leading the latter to resort to the kinds of centralized planning that frequently do more harm than good. Brazil, for instance, reacted to soaring real estate prices and consumer indebtedness in 2011 by raising interest rates and imposing capital controls, which sent its currency, the real, soaring, which in turn priced its exports out of world markets and slowed its economy. By 2012 Brazil was forced to change course, easing aggressively to lower the real's value. Yet long-term Brazilian bonds still yielded nearly 10 percent in early 2013, making them as attractive as ever for the carry trade.

Then in mid-2013 the Fed announced its intention to "taper" its debt monetization, US interest rates soared, and hot money poured out of emerging markets and back into dollar-denominated debt. Several developing countries nearly imploded, with the Indian rupee and Brazilian real hitting multi-year lows, forcing their governments into yet another round of extreme and possibly counterproductive capital controls and monetary interventions. Throughout this saga their leaders vocally complained about being victims of a currency war, though no one really listened.

The Victims Retaliate

The combination of the dollar's reserve currency status and America's willingness to blatantly abuse the resulting advantages is a huge problem for much of the rest of the world. Consider the situation from the Russian or Chinese point of view: You not only face torrents of hot money pouring in and out, severely distorting your economy. But your desire to be a great power, at least in your own neighborhood, is continually stymied by the omnipotent US military – which is paid for with newly-created reserve currency. The dollar's dominance, in other words, is a key to America's ability to bully other countries not just economically, but militarily.

During the Cold War, US dominance was tolerated because its allies and trading partners valued the protection afforded by the US nuclear umbrella. But with the collapse of the Soviet Union, external threats have diminished while US arrogance has, from their point of view, only increased.

So the developing world's rising powers are now attempting to change the balance of power. In recent years, China has agreed to currency swaps (in which two countries exchange currencies to be used in bi-lateral trade) with France, Britain, Japan, Australia, Russia, and Iran. Iran cut similar deals with India and Russia, while Japan and India have begun trading in their own currencies. In late 2013 China and the Association of Southeast Asian Nations (ASEAN) were discussing the creation of a central bank that would settle in Chinese yuan. Russia, Iran, Angola, Sudan and Venezuela have begun accepting Chinese yuan for oil, and in 2013 more than one million barrels per day were traded in that currency. All of these transactions take place without the need for dollars, reducing demand for it and diminishing America's reserve currency advantage.

China is obviously the key player here, with good reason. Its economy is the world's second largest but its currency accounted for less than one percent of foreign exchange transactions in 2012. Logically, this percentage should be a lot higher. And unlike most other currency war combatants, China is pursuing this goal with what looks like a well-thought-out, coherent plan.

Recently, for instance, it announced its intention to make the yuan fully convertible and to transact half its foreign trade in its own currency within five years. And it has begun shifting its massive foreign exchange reserves (accumulated by running huge trade surpluses with the US) out of dollars. In 2006, 74 percent of China's reserves were parked in Treasury bonds. By yearend 2013 that figure was 54 percent.

With its excess dollars, China has been buying up real assets like mines and oil fields around the world. And it has been accumulating gold. Its gold mining sector has become the largest in the world, and its entire output stays within the country. Meanwhile, China has been buying gold on the open market on a vast scale. By some estimates it imported nearly 600 tons through Hong Kong in 2012 and over 1,000 tons in 2013. At this pace of accumulation, it will soon (if it doesn't already) have gold reserves exceeding 4,000 tons, sufficient to rank its reserves among the world's largest. China is gaining the ability, in short, to back its currency with gold, an act that would give the yuan instant global credibility as a store of value and seriously challenge the purely fiat (and therefore inferior) dollar as a medium of exchange.

Figure 12.1: China's Gold Imports From Hong Kong 2012 - 2013

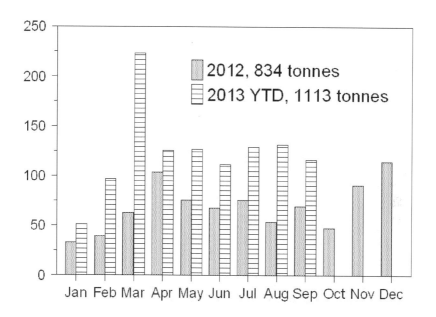

Two hints that a reserve-currency yuan is being contemplated came during 2013. First, Yao Yudong of the Chinese central bank's monetary policy committee called for a new Bretton Woods system. Under this post-World War II fixed-exchange-rate regime, one currency – the dollar – was convertible to gold, while other currencies were pegged to the dollar. A new Bretton Woods-style monetary system, designed when China has the world's only gold-backed currency, would presumably have the yuan at its center and the dollar, euro and yen as mere satellite currencies.

A few months later, China's official press agency, Xinhua, published an article stating that "US fiscal failure warrants a de-Americanized world" while calling for a new reserve currency "to be created to replace the dominant US dollar, so that the international community could permanently stay away from the spillover of the intensifying domestic political turmoil in the United States."

The impact on the dollar of such an event would be catastrophic. In 2013, 60 percent of global central bank reserves were in the form of dollar-denominated paper. So the transition to a world in which the dollar was just one major currency among many would require the sale of trillions of dollars by the world's central banks, and the purchase of commensurate amounts of yuan and gold. Such a massive sale of dollars would, other things being equal, lower the currency's exchange rate and raise US interest rates. No longer in possession of the world's reserve currency, the US would lose the ability to borrow enormous amounts of money, forcing it to live realistically and no doubt painfully with much higher borrowing costs, much lower government spending or a combination thereof.

Since the difference between US tax revenue and its present spending and future commitments, when calculated honestly, is already about $6 trillion a year, or roughly one-third of US GDP, the sudden need to bridge that gap without borrowed money and the unquestioned acceptance of future promises would leave only two options: Greek-style austerity involving a roll-back of the global military empire and the entitlements state, with massive layoffs of government workers and the likely bankruptcy of numerous cities with unmanageable pension funds. Or – the classic currency war scenario – aggressive devaluation in an attempt to maintain economic growth by sacrificing the dollar's value – for as long as they can get away with it. Either way, the post-currency-war world is a very different, much darker place for anyone dependent on the dollar.

CHAPTER 13

PEAK COMPLEXITY AND CATASTROPHIC FAILURE

"Life is really simple, but we insist on making it complicated."

– Confucius

A couple of Christmas vacations ago John and his family tempted fate by booking a multi-stage overseas plane trip...and ended up with cancelled flights, missed connections, and blank-faced airline employees who sincerely didn't care if John and family spent a night or a week on the terminal floor.

While he wallowed in self-pity over this loss of control and the apparent sadism of the airlines, his wife noted that they aren't unique. Big Food, Big Pharma, and Big Banks, among others, are all just as unfriendly to both their customers and society at large. This insight distracted him from his rage, and he spent some time thinking about how strange it is that in a time when Apple and Google are creating Star Trek-level technologies that streamline and simplify their users' lives and Amazon is making shopping almost supernaturally easy, there also exist huge industries that seem to go out of their way to make things complicated and hard. And let's not even start on modern government.

Why do they behave this way when it makes so many people so angry? A pharmaceutical company CEO, for instance, probably can't leave the house without someone accusing him of doubling the price of their heart medication while spending millions marketing erectile dysfunction pills to TV football viewers. An industrial food company executive can't attend a cocktail party without being cornered by someone who reads labels and is appalled by the high fructose corn syrup and preservative-laden "food" his company sells. Goldman Sachs execs must cringe every time they pass a newsstand where the latest *Rolling Stone* is calling their company a "vampire squid." And airline employees, of course, must be abused non-stop by people like John who have had their vacations turned into exercises in enforced patience and asymmetrical negotiation.

But why should this kind of corporate dysfunction, fascinating though it is, appear in a book about the impending collapse of the global monetary system? Because these organizations are suffering from "peak complexity," a concept crucial to understanding the recent evolution – and coming difficulties – of the broader economy.

Let's begin with the "peak" part of the term, which was originally coined by petroleum engineer M. King Hubbert in 1956. He observed that the output of oil wells tended to follow a predictable bell-shaped curve, rising strongly, plateauing, and then beginning a decline that steepened with time. He predicted that the same curve would apply to the output of national as well as global oil reserves, and turned out to be generally right (though new drilling technologies may have delayed the inflection point by a decade or two). In subsequent years the "peak" appellation has been applied to numerous other markets, including food, water, and prosperity itself. In each case it refers to the point at which the growth in the supply of something plateaus and begins an inexorable, accelerating decline. It seems that entropy, after death and taxes, is the third certainty of this world.

Now for "complexity" which is, ahem, a more complicated topic. To understand it, a little systems theory is helpful: Systems come in several forms, beginning with "simple" versions where the constituent parts are similar or identical and behavior doesn't vary much with scale. A bucket of sand behaves pretty much like a handful, for instance. A "complicated" system like a watch or internal combustion engine may have components with different shapes and functions, making the resulting device very different from its parts. But those parts don't change – i.e., grow bigger or smaller, or exhibit different behaviors or properties – based on their interaction. A watch is a watch, and always behaves that way.

But a "complex" system like a weather front, living organism, or pre-avalanche snow-covered mountainside contains numerous parts that do change in response to their communication and interaction. This process can create feedback loops begetting "emergent properties" that differ radically from the system's constituent parts or its previous state. Think of a tropical depression becoming a Cat-5 hurricane overnight and you have a sense of the power and potential instability of a complex system.

Such systems have some other notable features:

- As they grow larger the energy required to maintain their stability rises exponentially. Double the size of a complex system and its energy requirements might increase ten-fold.

- They are prone to catastrophic collapse, and this propensity also rises exponentially as the system becomes bigger and more complex.

- With a highly-complex and therefore fragile system, small inputs can have exaggerated effects. When a mountainside has a sufficient amount of snow, for instance, a single snowflake can start an avalanche. But the snowflake itself wasn't special in any way; the system was simply ready to go. As Harvard historian Niall Ferguson explained it in a 2010 *Foreign Affairs* article, "Such systems can appear to operate quite stably for some time; they seem to be in equilibrium but are, in fact, constantly adapting. But there comes a moment when complex systems 'go critical.' A very small trigger can set off a 'phase transition' from a benign equilibrium to a crisis...In such systems a relatively minor shock can cause a disproportionate -- and sometimes fatal -- disruption."

- The details of a complex system's collapse are inherently unpredictable. Set a fire in a dry forest, for example, and the scale of the resulting conflagration can vary from a few square yards to hundreds of miles.

Death by Complexity

Systems theory is a useful framework for understanding the dysfunctional industries that opened this chapter. Each is huge, concentrated, and after decades of centralization and empire building now has to generate sales on pretty much any terms, no matter how questionable, in order to avoid death by complexity. Both the customer and society take a back seat to the desperate institutional need to survive, and quality deteriorates until the production/delivery system breaks down.

This brings us to the point of the exercise, which is that financial markets are complex systems, and today's global financial system is orders of magnitude more complex – and therefore less stable and more prone to catastrophic failure – than ever before.

Was this exponential increase in complexity avoidable? Absolutely. In 1998, when the collapse of hyper-leveraged hedge fund Long Term Capital Management nearly brought down the Western financial system, the US and other major financial centers could have responded by preventing commercial banks from running proprietary trading desks and doing mergers and acquisitions that increased their size, so that risk remained broadly dispersed. Instead, in 1999 the US went the other way, repealing the Glass-Steagall Act, which had separated commercial banks that took insured deposits from investment banks that took big risks with owners' and clients' money. In 2000 the US liberalized the regulation of swap agreements, which made possible a vast expansion of derivatives. In 2006 broker/dealers were allowed to double their leverage. The result: banks of every stripe became hedge funds, i.e., effectively-unregulated investment companies that could expand in any direction with virtually unlimited amounts of borrowed money. The system became vastly more leveraged, which is to say bigger and more complex.

Another chance came after the near-death experience of 2008, when multi-trillion dollar bail-outs could have been used as leverage to re-impose limits on bank risk-taking. But that was not to be. Wall Street banks by this time were so thoroughly in charge of the government that they got their bail-out essentially for free. Since then they've used their "too big to fail" status – and the implied government backstop should things go wrong – to obtain cheaper financing than smaller banks, and have vastly expanded their role in mortgages and other consumer markets, while their derivatives books have continued to grow.

After each bubble – junk bonds (1990), dot-com stocks (2000), housing (2008) – the amount of debt (i.e., "energy") required to maintain the system has risen. Recall from Chapter 4 that in the US, a dollar of new debt produced nearly that much new GDP in the 1960s, but by 2013 the return on new debt was virtually zero. From here on, the US and the rest of the developed world can borrow as much as they want and the only result will be more debt. Wealth won't increase, while complexity continues to soar.

But stopping would mean the instant dissolution of the system, with horrendous near-term consequences for asset values and incumbent political parties. So sitting politicians will instinctively delay the inevitable with more debt, which causes the system to become even more complex, requiring even bigger infusions of new money, and so on. This is peak complexity, and it is virtually always followed by a radical simplification of the system, either voluntarily (though this is rare) or catastrophically via some sort of phase change as in 1920s Weimar Germany or 1930s America.

To understand how the current system might spin out of control and where the unraveling might begin, look at where the complexity – aka systemic risk – is of late being concentrated most quickly. Post-2008, the two areas that stand out are government debt – which has been substituted for private debt as governments have borrowed unprecedented amounts to bail out the banking and housing sectors – and the derivatives books of the major banks, which remain gargantuan and lately have begun to cluster in interest rate swaps. Recall from Chapter 9 that fully three-quarters of over-the-counter derivatives are now bets on the direction of interest rates.

The survival of today's financial system thus depends on the ability of governments to continue to borrow, which depends on the value of fiat currencies. Let the dollar, euro, or yen begin to lose value (another way of saying let inflation spike), or let the global bond markets demand higher interest rates to compensate for rising systemic risks, and the game is over.

But the straw that breaks the market's back might also be something less obvious. With a system at peak complexity there is simply no way to predict which snowflake will set off the avalanche – and really no reason to care. The important thing to understand is that the after the global financial system's most recent jump in complexity, the potential for a catastrophic crash has never been greater. When the crash comes it will dwarf what almost happened in 2008 – and what actually did happen in the 1930s.

CHAPTER 14

BLACK SWANS: LESS LIKELY BUT STILL VERY SCARY

"The punch you don't see is the one that gets you."

– Old boxing saying

Each of the scenarios presented so far in this section is terrifying in its own way. But at least they're visible. We can see them coming and deduce, more or less, the kinds of havoc they're likely to wreak. This gives well-informed individuals a chance to protect themselves and maybe prosper during the resulting changes.

More dangerous, for both society at large and a typical person's nest egg, is the "black swan" that few see coming – the next Pearl Harbor or flash crash, the financial/political asteroid that hits without giving its victims a chance to prepare. Here are four especially interesting and/or disturbing possibilities:

A DEBT JUBILEE RESETS THE SYSTEM

The central theme of this book is that fiat currencies and the crushing debts they beget are at the root of the world's troubles. Virtually everywhere, governments and their citizens are borrowing more than ever before, and in many places are already far beyond any hope of orderly repayment. As Australian economist Steven Keen puts it, "We're at the debt event horizon, the point of no return where interest payments begin to swamp society's ability to generate free cash to cover those payments."

However, says Keen, things aren't completely hopeless for the current system. He sees one policy option that might reset the clock and buy time for a motivated people to avoid a descent into monetary chaos: an updated version of the biblical "debt jubilee," a wide-spread forgiveness of debt, to be engineered by governments.

The problem with the classical jubilee concept is that every debt is someone else's asset, so forgiving a mortgage in Boise or Dusseldorf inflicts a loss on Citigroup or Deutsche Bank, which is a political non-starter. Keen, in response, proposes a "quantitative easing for the masses," that would give money directly to borrowers with the proviso that they use the money to pay off debts. Individuals would see their balance sheets improve while banks would swap loans for cash, ending up in more-or-less the same place.

Keen's hypothetical jubilee comes packaged with some fairly serious policy changes. "You don't want to reset the system and just start blowing bubbles again. So you'll need a combination of tighter lending standards and tighter monetary policy going forward," he says. "Banks should be intermediaries rather than creating money as they do now," implying an end to fractional reserve banking (an idea we endorse in Chapter 15). "And asset prices will have to fall because they've been inflated by excess borrowing for the past couple of decades. A debt jubilee will just accelerate a process that has to happen in any event. Pension funds will benefit from the cash infusions but be hurt by the decline in asset prices."

If the details of a future debt jubilee are impossible to predict, so is its impact on financial markets. Traders and investors have responded to previous "extend and pretend" policies with enthusiasm, so it is very possible that the Fed buying up and then writing off trillions of dollars of debt would be seen as giving the markets a few more years of debt-centric normalcy. If so, it might delay the crisis we're predicting. On the other hand, market participants could recognize that the cash injected into the system via QE will remain after the bonds are forgiven, meaning that the government is henceforth financing itself directly by printing money, which is wildly inflationary and destabilizing. In that case a jubilee, especially a one-sided version that eschews painful but needed reforms, might hasten the demise of the current monetary system.

Another variation on the debt jubilee theme is simply having central banks write off the bonds they're now accumulating through quantitative easing. Since the bonds were bought with newly-created fiat currency, they could, in theory, be extinguished just as easily.

In 2011, Texas Congressman Ron Paul actually introduced a bill (HR 2768) that would cancel the $1.6 trillion of Treasury debt then held by the Federal Reserve and simultaneously lower the debt limit by that amount. "Where did they get the money to buy our debt?" asked Paul at the time. "Well, they created it out of thin air. It's a fictitious debt. It's a dishonest debt and I would say that we're not obligated [to pay it off]."

A debt jubilee, especially one that involves governments and banks giving up their printing presses, remains highly unlikely. But the Ron Paul version – minus the lowering of the debt limit – might appeal to desperate governments (especially in Japan, where government debt makes up the bulk of that society's obligations). Such a gain-without-pain approach would, as Keen warned, allow the powers that be to "reset the system and just start blowing bubbles again." That's not a happy prospect, but it might be exactly the strategy the monetary authorities are looking for when things start spinning out of control.

In any event, the jubilee idea seems to have captured the imagination of the financial public. In November 2012, Société Générale economist Michala Marcussen noted that the most frequent question being asked by clients is "Can central banks just cancel their government debt holdings?"

A CYBER-ATTACK CRIPPLES THE ECONOMY

By making it possible to share information with a mouse click, the Internet has revolutionized everything from shopping to dating to war. Unfortunately, it has one little drawback: Because it was originally designed to allow researchers to communicate conveniently, ease of use was purchased with the sacrifice of privacy. It's hard to protect data when multiple people can access it from different locations using different passwords. And the developed world, with stunning naiveté, has put the whole show – military and scientific research, power grid, banking and stock trading, everything – on the backbone of this inherently-insecure system.

As a result, crucial systems are vulnerable to attack from multiple sources. Passwords can be stolen (new software makes even the most convoluted password easy pickings). Malware can infect systems and take them over. Laptops and tablets (and now smart phones) can be stolen and used to penetrate their former-owners' networks. And once inside a network, a hacker has the same capabilities as any authorized user. "If you can penetrate a publicly-accessible network to steal information, you can also corrupt the information on the network, or wipe it, or shut the network down – or even physically fry the equipment," writes Joel Brenner, former head of US counterintelligence and author of *America the Vulnerable: Inside the New Threat Matrix of Digital Espionage, Crime, and Warfare.*

Hacking, meanwhile, has moved from the domain of smart/sociopath teens (though they're still out there causing mischief) to well-financed criminal organizations with much more ambitious goals. Even more ominous, every major military now has well-funded units tasked with penetrating and exploiting adversaries' crucial systems. Because today's networks are easier to penetrate than defend, the predators are succeeding on a scale that would send multitudes back to using cash and snail mail if it was widely understood.

In recent years, according to Brenner, "An electric generator was blown up using nothing but a keyboard and a mouse. A water system was polluted using a laptop. In Iran, nuclear plant centrifuges have been physically destroyed with software. In 2012 a computer virus wiped all the information off 30,000 computers at Saudi Arabian Oil Co. If Saudi Aramco can wake up and find 30,000 of its computers wiped, the same thing can happen to your company or your bank."

Why aren't these vulnerabilities being addressed? "In most companies, nobody really owns cybersecurity," says Brenner. "The lawyers think it's an IT problem. IT doesn't control the usage rules and probably doesn't have a sufficient budget. Line management wants to push the problem down to the lawyers and IT." And most people – including the supposedly-tech-savvy – simply don't understand the systems that they depend on, says Brenner. "About five years ago, a Washington, DC area financial advisor installed music sharing software on his office computer. He didn't know – and most people still don't know – that when you install it, you open everything on your system to being 'shared.' The next thing he knew, his clients' personal data was out the window. That was five years ago, but it's still happening."

This asymmetry between offense and defense implies that sooner or later, a major act of cyberterror, cybercrime, or cyberwar will occur. It could be part of a conflict over resources or territory (if the dispute between China and Japan over offshore oil rights, for instance, were to escalate). Or an incursion by some foreign mafia that takes down one or more financial institutions, which in turn causes a broader crisis of confidence. It could be a corruption of the clearing mechanism of a national banking system or a prolonged blackout of a major power grid. Whatever it is, it will happen suddenly, with little advance warning and therefore no chance to make portfolios less vulnerable – as if "less vulnerable" has any meaning when the banking system or power grid is in the hands of shadowy enemies.

THE POLITICAL BUBBLE BURSTS

Just based on the numbers, the global financial system should have collapsed long ago. That it hasn't has less to do with economics than politics. The people in charge have arranged things so that they can keep borrowing, spending and printing into the indefinite future – as long as they can agree on "compromises" that give each faction most of what it wants. That's how US military spending can soar (thus keeping the right happy) while entitlement programs can simultaneously spread to every corner of American life (keeping the left happy). As long as the resulting deficits can be financed and the bond, currency and precious metals markets tamed with repeated government interventions and newly-printed currency, then the game can continue.

But if this log-rolling political consensus breaks down, all bets are off. And there are signs that this is indeed beginning to happen. An entire book could be written about the political turmoil that was roiling the world of 2013, but since we have just a few pages, we'll present the juiciest European example and then focus on the US, which is emblematic of what's happening everywhere.

In October 2013 Marine Le Pen's eurosceptic National Front party won a local French election and for the first time ever took the lead in a national poll. As she famously told London's *Daily Telegraph*before the election, the European Union "is just a great bluff. On one side there is the immense power of sovereign peoples, and on the other side are a few technocrats."

Generally portrayed by the two major (center-right, center-left) parties as racist or neo-fascist, the National Front's public goals of limiting immigration, especially from Africa and the Middle East, and withdrawing from the eurozone and going back to the French franc were beginning to resonate with voters exhausted by the feeling that recent immigrants aren't assimilating and the PIIGS countries aren't managing their own affairs. An actual French withdrawal from the euro would collapse the monetary system, causing continent-wide chaos. And the French experience is being replicated in numerous other eurozone countries, where anti-euro parties once on the fringe are drawing serious support. Greece in particular has actual neo-Nazis and communists contesting major elections.

In the US, the late-2013 battle over the debt ceiling has exposed similar, equally colorful fault lines. Within the Republican party, the mainstream (log-rolling, back-scratching) career politicians wanted, as the October default deadline approached, to cut a deal to keep the government up and borrowing. But a small band of Tea Party-affiliated conservatives and libertarians were having none of it, and forced a dramatic game of chicken in which neither side, for a while, was willing to blink until a day before the Treasury was due to default on its bond interest payments.

This was more than simple political brinksmanship. There seemed to be, gasp, actual principles beyond career longevity involved, and it presages both more turmoil between Republicans and Democrats and very possibly the birth of an influential third party, currently within the Republican tent but soon to be outside of it. It will be semi-coherently anti-debt and pro-small government – and it might, like France's National Front, attract enough support to gum up the borrow-and-print consensus, perhaps forcing real choices.

Why does this matter? Because the markets by late 2013 had come to believe that political turmoil is always followed by a deal that feeds more currency into the hands of banks and consumers, thus supporting asset prices. Looked at this way, the American political system is a bubble of unrealistic expectations, just as certainly as were dot-coms in 1999 and home prices in 2006.

The complacency engendered by this political bubble is exactly why the ending of political consensus matters. With bonds, stocks, houses and pretty much everything else "priced for perfection" in the expectation that newly-created money will always save the day, any interruption in that flow – or perception that it might be interrupted in the future – would cause a broad-based re-pricing (i.e., a bear market) that could easily spin out of control – especially with a government grid-locked by incompatible ideas about how to proceed.

This asset re-pricing would be global, and would include Treasury bonds and the dollar itself, which would lose its reserve currency luster if the US was seen as no longer willing or able to automatically finance its deficits. In that circumstance, the Long Wave would return with a vengeance, taking the US and much of the world from the realm of the unreal (paper currency) into the surreal (hyperinflation, complex system catastrophic failure, and authoritarian government). And it would happen suddenly, when a spending bill fails, or an anti-Fed party has a surprisingly good election, or a debt ceiling extension just can't be sold to Congress, bringing an immediate end to the easy-money gravy train.

THE BREAKAWAY CULTURE...BREAKS AWAY

Another of this book's premises is that the folks running the global financial system are making the same mistakes as many of their predecessors throughout history. They're borrowing too much money, attempting to inflate away the resulting debts, and in the process *inadvertently* destroying their currencies and perverting the market mechanisms essential for a capitalist society to function. In other words, we're describing an unchanging aspect of human nature expressing itself through recurring historical cycles.

But what if this time the people running the global economy aren't inept and historically clueless? What if they know exactly what they're doing and are quite far along in a plan to funnel the wealth of the world's middle and working classes into the accounts of the super-rich and technically savvy, in the process creating a separate culture that is to middle-America what middle-America is to a village of 15th century peasants?

Our friend Catherine Austin Fitts of the *Solari Network* makes a coherent case for this worldview, in which a "breakaway civilization" is already nearly done with its truly grand theft. The recent banking crises and subsequent monetary experiments are, she says, tools to that end, and the next stage is a global "debt-for-equity" swap that sends tech stocks through the roof while starving old-style industries and government entitlement programs (what she calls "legacy systems"). In Fitts' own words, taken from an October 2013 interview with the *Daily Bell* website:

The plan's origin: "Starting in the 1990s a decision was made to move significant amounts of capital out of existing systems in the developed world, and literally trillions of dollars of financial fraud was engineered to do that."

The role of the Fed: "I think what the Fed has been doing with quantitative easing is running a shredding operation where they buy up the fraudulent mortgage securities paper and shred it. If you look at the Treasury, they've run a very tight regulatory process where that money doesn't seep out on Main Street. It's quite phenomenal the way they've managed to control it... So far the Fed's policies have done what they're intended to do. We've moved a tremendous amount of money out of the economy, and the legacy systems can't get the money back. So the financial coup d'état has been successful and now the cover-up is pretty much over."

What happens next? QE will not only continue, says Fitts, but will be ramped up. Central banks will buy up all the bonds issued by their governments and much of what is outstanding in the private sector. Much of the resulting torrent of cash flowing into the banking system will find its way into equities, extending the bull market of 2013 into truly uncharted territory. "We're literally coming into what I consider to be a planetary debt-for-equity swap," she says.

The breakaway civilization will feast on the flow of new money while globalization and automation will combine to pressure working class wages. State and local governments will be starved for revenue and will be forced to cut public sector pensions and salaries. The result, she says, will be "A 'slow burn' world in which for most people income is flat or falling and expenses are steadily rising. For the next couple of years, the Administration and the Fed are going to be managing the decline of legacy system expectations, just gutting their way through retirees' disappointment."

UNCHARTED TERRITORY

The challenging thing about the four black swan scenarios described here is that both their timing and their impact are very hard to predict. A debt jubilee might take many forms and have many effects depending on the way it is implemented. A cyber-event could be large or small and involve industrial, financial or military systems – and will by definition come without warning. The bursting of the political bubble will likely happen in Congress rather than the markets and again might come without warning. And the breakaway culture's equity melt-up might, by creating the mother of all equity bubbles – and considerable discontent within the 99-percent – lead to market and geopolitical distortions that no one, including the plan's architects, can accurately foresee. In short, this is the realm of unintended consequences, where forecasts become guesswork and uncertainty is the only guarantee.

PART III:
THINGS YOU SHOULD
UNDERSTAND

CHAPTER 15

FRACTIONAL-RESERVE BANKING: FROM GOLDSMITHS TO HEDGE FUNDS TO…CHAOS

"Issuing promises to pay on demand in excess of the amount of goods on hand is simply fraud, and should be so considered by the legal system… This is legalized counterfeiting; this is the creation of money without the necessity for production, to compete for resources against those who have produced. In short, I believe that fractional-reserve banking is disastrous both for the morality and for the fundamental bases and institutions of the market economy."

– Murray N. Rothbard,
The Case for a 100 Percent Gold Dollar

Banking didn't start out as a reckless, parasitical plaything of a moneyed and politically-connected aristocracy. In the beginning, in fact, bankers weren't even bankers. They were jewelers and goldsmiths who had to maintain their inventory with vaults, guards etc., and offered storage services to others with valuables to protect. So the original banks were essentially very safe warehouses.

Eventually some goldsmiths noticed that the paper receipts they gave to their customers to evidence the valuables left in storage began to circulate as currency alongside their country's coins. A shopkeeper accepting these receipts in payment knew that he could go to the goldsmith to redeem them for gold and silver, and also recognized that a paper receipt was more convenient to use as currency than were pieces of metal. Gradually these receipts became a widely-accepted form of payment, circulating among buyers and sellers and saved like other forms of wealth.

The goldsmiths then noticed something else about their new paper-money invention: Only a tiny fraction of their clients asked for the return of their valuables in any given period, which led to a bright – but legally and morally-dubious – idea. Why not start issuing receipts in excess of the gold and silver on hand? The goldsmiths could spend this currency themselves or lend it to others – thus inventing the business/consumer loan. Henceforth the total gold and silver in the vault (the goldsmith's reserves) would equal only a fraction of the receipts circulating as currency.

"Fractional reserve banking" was thus born of deception if not outright fraud, because for the receipts to retain their value the goldsmiths had to pretend that those paper claims to gold and silver were backed by an equal amount of metal and were therefore of equivalent value. They were not, of course, because a tangible asset is more valuable than a promise to pay a tangible asset, particularly when the latter outnumbers the former.

The goldsmiths, having evolved into more-or-less recognizable bankers, then realized that more deposits equaled more profits. So they began paying people for deposits of gold and silver rather than charging for their storage, thus inventing the interest-bearing account.

The resulting system had some inherent dangers, most obviously that it tempted bankers to lend out ever-greater multiples of deposits, increasing the odds that they would be unable to meet withdrawal requests and collapse. This happened frequently early-on, eventually leading governments to regulate the amount that a given bank could lend against its capital.

For a sense of how this works, imagine a bank with $100 in capital that is required to hold a reserve equal to 20 percent of its loans outstanding – which based on experience is usually more than enough to satisfy a typical day's withdrawal requests. In our example, the bank can lend 4/5ths of its depositors' money, or $80, while 1/5th, or $20, remains in reserve. Now here's where it gets interesting: When our hypothetical bank makes a loan, the recipient deposits the proceeds in another bank, which can lend out 4/5ths of that deposit. The recipients of *those* loans make deposits in other banks, and so on, until a huge multiple of the original deposit base has been turned into circulating currency.

The result is an "elastic" money supply. When borrowers are optimistic and want to increase their borrowing, banks in a fractional reserve system can in the aggregate offer them immense amounts of new credit. So the money supply, instead of being determined by the amount of gold, silver or other bank capital in the system, can expand dramatically to accommodate an energetic society's demands.

But it can also contract dramatically. If an economy that has greatly increased its money supply through bank lending suddenly takes a downturn or is unnerved by an unexpected crisis, borrowers will pay off their loans or default on them and banks won't replace them, while depositors seek the return of their cash. These actions cause the money supply to collapse, potentially all the way back to the level of base money in the system. The result of this fluctuation in the supply of circulating currency is a recurring series of booms and busts that wipe out businesses, individuals, and banks and frequently send the general economy into recession or depression.

Fractional reserve banking was, in fact, a major cause of the Great Depression. To condense a long, complex story into a single paragraph, the extra currency that was printed by the belligerents during World War I (which ended in 1918) was recycled through the fractional reserve banking system and massively amplified via the process we've just described. This tsunami of new credit caused the Roaring Twenties bubble in asset prices – especially global equities – that popped in 1929, destroying the pseudo-wealth created in the previous decade. The collateral supposedly guaranteeing bank loans evaporated and sentiment turned negative, sending the fractional reserve credit machinery into reverse and collapsing both the banking system and the real economy.

The US government responded to the imprudence and outright corruption of the 1920s by passing the Glass-Steagall Act of 1933, which separated commercial banks, which were to focus solely on the needs of commerce, from higher-risk activities that would henceforth be permitted only within investment banks. To further reassure the public, the government provided insurance for commercial bank deposits, and hired regulators to monitor bank solvency.

Constrained by new regulations and the gut-churning memories of the Depression, banks played a mostly constructive role in the years following World War II, helping to make the 1950s a relatively stable decade. Also contributing to this brief period of sensible banking was the fact that most investment banks were partnerships in which the owners had their personal capital on the line and so had an incentive to act prudently.

But rising government spending on the Vietnam War and Great Society social programs produced a credit boom in the 1960s, resulting in the US decision to break the dollar's formal link to gold in 1971. The adoption of a pure fiat currency – as we've mentioned once or twice in previous chapters – changed everything. Bank reserves, previously at least theoretically exchangeable for gold, became pieces of colored paper that the Federal Reserve could – and did – create with increasing abandon.

Easy money made the banks more profitable and powerful, and the restrictions on leverage and risk-taking began to fade. In the 1980s, most Wall Street investment banks "went public," selling shares to outside investors. The infusion of new capital both enriched the original owners and changed their incentive structure. By the 1990s, both commercial and investment banks were playing mainly with investors' money and were thus encouraged to take ever-bigger risks, safe in the knowledge that immediate profits would translate into huge year-end bonuses and a higher stock price, while the resulting problems might not manifest for years – by which time the architects of those strategies would be retired.

Attracted by the profitable new financial instruments being designed by investment banks' "financial engineers," the commercial banks successfully lobbied for the repeal of Glass-Steagall in 1999 and (recall the list from Chapter 6) numerous other regulatory favors. But banking didn't return just to the excesses and bad practices of the 1920s; this time it was much worse. Deregulation has combined with a rapidly-inflating fiat currency to take fractional reserve banking to its logical extreme. Formerly staid commercial banks have become hedge funds, jumping feet first into risky assets and even riskier derivatives while taking de facto control of the legislative and regulatory machinery. The result is the world described in this book's first two sections, where soaring debt is producing ever-more-dramatic booms and busts and increasingly authoritarian governments. And where the worst is yet to come.

CHAPTER 16

CENTRAL BANKS TAKE OVER THE WORLD

"The only viable solution for monetary stability is to get government out of the money business permanently. The way to bring this about is through currency competition: allowing parallel currencies to circulate without any one currency receiving any special recognition or favor from the government."

– Ron Paul

Early in the development of fractional reserve banking, the system's inherent instability became apparent to the goldsmiths cum bankers, who after all were personally threatened by bank runs. They convinced governments to create a new kind of bank, called a central bank, to act as a lender of last resort to prevent bank runs from spreading. The Bank of England, for example, was founded in 1694 when London bankers enticed the British monarchy, then near bankruptcy because of endless wars with France and rebellious Scots, to finance its military adventures with borrowed money. But from a banker's point of view the central bank's real job was to prevent individual lenders' bad decisions from threatening the rest of the financial community.

The central bank concept soon spread to the rest of Europe, and by the end of the 19th century every major country except the United States had some form of central bank. And the US was not far behind. Though the 19th century was a period of exceptionally high, non-inflationary growth for America, it was also a time of periodic bank panics which both bankers and governments found disquieting. So after a contentious debate and considerable behind-the-scenes maneuvering[3], the Federal Reserve was created in 1913.

By today's standards these original central banks were limited in both power and objective; their main goal was to moderate the inherent instability of fractional reserve banking. But like commercial banks, over the years they've evolved into something different and much more dangerous. The main themes of their evolution:

Replacement of Gold with Paper

During the Classical Gold Standard, which ran from 1700 to 1914, banknotes circulating as currency were, in effect, warehouse receipts for a nation's precious metal reserves. Put another way, the dollar, pound, and franc were simply names for different weights of gold or silver. The central bank's other job (besides intervening to keep bank failures from spreading) was to issue the paper that circulated as a "money substitute" and to stand ready to exchange metal for paper at the discretion of currency holders.

Countries, meanwhile, were required to ship gold from their reserves to their trading partners to make up for trade deficits. These flows moderated differences in national economic growth rates by moving gold from fast-growing countries to slow-growing, thus lowering the money supply of the former while increasing it for the latter. This constant circulation of central bank reserves didn't prevent booms and busts but did limit their damage. Consumer prices actually fell a bit each year, mainly as a result of technological developments that enhanced production,

---

[3] See in particular The Creature from Jekyll Island by G. Edward Griffin.

meaning that money was becoming more and more valuable – it was gaining rather than losing purchasing power. Thus encouraged, savers saved and investors invested, making the 19th century a kind of "golden age" of steady, non-inflationary progress that lifted millions world-wide from poverty and into the middle class.

But governments chafed at the restrictions on spending imposed by a limited money supply, and with the outbreak of World War I in 1914 began to leave the gold standard and adopt unbacked fiat currencies which they could create as needed. In order to preserve their new power, governments expanded the role of central banks to include setting interest rates and deciding how much currency to create, without reference to any external limit. This discretion gave central bankers immense power and importance. By the 1970s their decisions regarding interest rates became front-page news and more recently their experiments like QE and ZIRP have entered the lexicon as widely-recognized terms. Leading central bankers gained celebrity status commensurate with their power, appearing on magazine covers and television talk shows. Today the heads of the European and US central banks are generally considered to be the second most powerful public figures in their respective systems, and the central banks they run are the major actors on the modern economic stage.

Loss of Independence

Once upon a time there was a quaint notion that central banks should be independent of government to avoid the never-ending pressure to finance elections or otherwise placate important constituencies. By giving central bank managers fixed tenures and insulating the appointment process from politics, it was hoped that monetary policy would be conducted with the value of the currency rather than partisan politics in mind. In modern times, the best example of a truly independent central bank was the German Bundesbank, which was designed by the victorious powers after World War II to be immune to political pressure in order to prevent Germany from using the money-printing ability of a central bank to rearm and start another world war. The perhaps-unintended result was several decades of near-perfect monetary policy to make the German mark one of the world's strongest currencies, while restoring Germany to its prior industrial glory in a single generation.

The US Fed, meanwhile, is not actually a branch of the government, but instead is a private consortium of major banks, with 12 regional branches, each run by a governor appointed by the president. A "Board of Governors" sets monetary policy and overseas bank regulation. The governors serve staggered, fixed terms that in theory confer independence and encourage rational monetary policy.

But over time the walls separating central banks from their governments have eroded. The Bundesbank was superseded by the European Central Bank when most of the Continent adopted the euro in 1999. And the US Fed and the central banks of Canada and Japan, among others, have become de facto if not de jure branches of their governments. In 1977, for instance, the Fed was given a "dual mandate" that made full employment one of its stated goals, virtually guaranteeing excessively-easy money from that point forward. And in 2013 the incoming Japanese president simply demanded that the Bank of Japan target and achieve a 2 percent inflation rate – and the BoJ acquiesced.

This combination of commercial banks now incented to take extreme risks and central banks under the control of politicians has produced exactly the kind of world one would expect, in which finance dominates production and seemingly-insane amounts of leverage are not just countenanced by the authorities but encouraged.

CENTRALLY-PLANNED WORLD

The term for a system where government controls prices and manipulates markets to achieve its goals is "central planning." The Soviet Union and other collectivist experiments, along with European social democracies and Third World dictatorships have all tried variations on this theme. And all, without exception, have either failed miserably or are about to.

Yet despite the soaring debt, erosion of fiat currency purchasing power, recurring bubbles and busts and extraordinary widening of the gap between rich and poor, the Federal Reserve and its peers – the architects of most of the above trends – continue to command respect. In the US, Fed chairmen and governors are interviewed by serious journalists and quoted on important subjects, as if they actually have unique insight into the workings of a modern economy and the ability to predict its future. And they're given the power to manage the economy by manipulating interest rates, the money supply, the bond market and (surreptitiously) the stock market and gold. Luckily for critics of central planning and the cause of truth generally, the monetary authorities' high profile has left a paper trail that dispels any lingering illusions about their understanding of money or, it seems, anything else related to economic activity. Here are a few telling statements (pulled from literally dozens of possible examples) from the two most recent Fed chairmen or the Federal Open Market Committee (FOMC) during their tenures.

ALAN GREENSPAN, Fed chairman from 1987 to 2006

On the Dot-Com Bubble, from the May 16, 2000 minutes of the FOMC, chaired by Mr. Greenspan:

"Looking ahead, further rapid growth was expected in spending for business equipment and software.... Even after today's tightening action the members believed the risks would remain tilted toward rising inflation."

Less than one year later, the NASDAQ index, where most tech stocks traded, had fallen by 50 percent and the economy had entered a deep recession.

On Derivatives and Financial Stability:

2003. "What we have found over the years in the marketplace is that derivatives have been an extraordinarily useful vehicle to transfer risk from those who shouldn't be taking it to those who are willing to and are capable of doing so. We think it would be a mistake [to expand regulation of derivatives]."

2004. "Not only have individual financial institutions become less vulnerable to shocks from underlying risk factors, but also the financial system as a whole has become more resilient."

In 2008 the derivatives market blew up, nearly destroying the global financial system and requiring a multi-trillion dollar bailout to avoid "marshal law."

On the Housing Bubble:

2004. "Indeed, recent research within the Federal Reserve suggests that many homeowners might have saved tens of thousands of dollars had they held adjustable-rate mortgages rather than fixed-rate mortgages during the past decade…American consumers might benefit if lenders provided greater mortgage product alternatives to the traditional fixed-rate mortgage."

2004. "Overall, the household sector seems to be in good shape."

2004. "While local economies may experience significant price imbalances, a national severe price distortion seems most unlikely in the United States, given its size and diversity."

2005. "A decline in the national housing price level would need to be substantial to trigger a significant rise in foreclosures, because the vast majority of homeowners have built up substantial equity in their homes despite large mortgage-market financed withdrawals of home equity in recent years."

In 2006 home prices peaked and subsequently fell by a nationwide average of 34 percent, leading to record numbers of foreclosures and the financial ruin of countless American families.

BEN BERNANKE, Fed chairman from 2006 to 2013

On the Housing Bubble:
2005. "Housing prices are up quite a bit but it's important to note that fundamentals are also strong. We've got a growing economy, very low mortgage rates, demographics supporting housing growth and a restricted supply in some places…We've never had a decline in house prices on a nationwide basis so it is more likely that house price increases will slow, but not drive the economy too far from its full-employment path…You can see some types of speculation in local areas. I'm confident that bank

regulators will pay close attention the kinds of loans being made and make sure underwriting is done right. I do think that this is mostly a localized problem and not something that will affect the national economy."

2006. "The effects of the housing correction on real economic activity are likely to continue into next year but the rate of decline in new home construction should slow as the inventory of new homes is gradually worked down."

February 2007. "If the housing sector begins to stabilize there's a reasonable possibility that we'll see some strengthening of the economy later in the year...there's not much indication at this point that subprime issues have spread into the broader mortgage market which still seems to be healthy."

July 2007. "The global economy continues to be strong. Supported by solid growth abroad, US exports should expand further in coming quarters. So overall the US economy appears likely to expand at a moderate pace in 2007 with growth rising in 2008 to a pace close to the economy's underlying trend."

By 2008 US the subprime mortgage market had imploded and taken the rest of the housing sector with it. Most major banks were insolvent, and the global economy was falling into the deepest recession since the 1930s.

We present the above quotes not to ridicule these Fed chairmen, but to dispel the notion that today's central bankers are any better at understanding, managing and directing a modern economy than was the Soviet Politburo. Any market populated by emotional, self-interested human beings is far too complex for a handful of bureaucrats to predict and manage. And a modern, technologically-advanced, global economy linked via instantaneous communications networks is vastly more complex than anything that has come before.

An abundance of literature (from Ludwig von Mises, Friedrich Hayek and Adam Smith, among others) exists to explain why central planning is doomed to failure. Their conclusion – with which we agree whole-heartedly – is that government's main role in a modern economy should be to create a stable, predictable stage on which the market's "invisible hand" can operate. This doesn't preclude reasonable regulations, especially in the realm of banking, but it does require that the rules be clear, widely-understood and equitably enforced.

THE ROOT OF MANY EVILS

To sum up, the modern central bank/fractional reserve banking system has three notable flaws:

(1) It depends on perception. Unlike a warehouse full of gold that is worth the purchasing power of those ounces, a fractional reserve bank is worth only, well, a fraction of the claims against it because it lends out rather than stores most of its deposits. If too many depositors want their money back at the same time, they'll be disappointed, and the bank will fail because it cannot turn its loans into dollars quickly enough to meet depositor demands. The same is true of the entire banking system. If enough people begin to mistrust their banks, then "runs" spread from one to another until all the banks (none of which are actually sound in this kind of system) fail.

(2) It inevitably destroys its currency. Today's system can create virtually unlimited amounts of credit. But credit is not wealth. If the supply of money rises faster than the

demand for it – or if the supply of goods and services grows faster than the amount of savings – the result is a "debased currency" that is worth progressively less in relation to the real wealth of the economy. If the process continues, rising prices and a loss of trust cause the currency to stop functioning as a store of value. We'll expand on the concept of inflation in the next chapter.

(3) It distorts markets and misallocates resources. In order to perpetuate the myth that paper currency is as good as gold and silver coin, bankers prevailed on governments to initially require that both money and money-substitutes circulate at equivalent value – when in reality the paper currency should only be accepted at a discount because of the risks it entails. More recently they've dispensed with sound money altogether, leaving only the bank-created paper in circulation, which is perpetuated by "legal tender" laws and other capital controls. The result is a system based on force rather than choice, in an attempt to maintain the illusion of fiat currency safety and soundness.

These interventions and deceptions distort the feedback mechanisms essential to free markets. Recall from Chapter 8 that prices and interest rates are signals that tell economic actors what to do, and when they are systematically falsified, capital is encouraged to flow to unwise uses (i.e., it is misallocated), which exacerbates downturns generally and wastes limited resources. The inevitable result: booms and busts of increasing amplitude, soaring leverage and – eventually – a system-wide meltdown.

So in a very real sense, it is fractional reserve banking and not money itself that is the root of so many of today's evils. Whenever fractional reserves are permitted, the banking system – including the one that exists today throughout the world – comes to resemble a classic Ponzi[4] scheme which can only function as long as most people don't try to get at their money.

A WORLD WITHOUT FRACTIONAL RESERVES

Now, is this critique of the current monetary system just impotent ideological whining over something that, like the weather, can't be changed? Or could fractional reserve banking and the resulting need for economic central planning actually be replaced by something better? Specifically, how could a banking system without fractional reserve lending accommodate depositors' demand that their money be there when they want it *and* borrowers' desire for 30-year mortgages that would tie up those deposits for decades? And could this market operate without the need for government oversight and management?

That's a lot of questions, to which the general answer is *yes*, a better financial system is possible, and here's how it would work:

First, today's commercial banks would split into two types. "Banks of commerce" would take deposits and keep them safe for a fee, like the goldsmiths of pre-banking days. These banks would offer checking accounts where payments are made by transferring depositor currency in return for goods and services without putting depositors' money at risk. "Banks of credit" would pay interest on deposits and lend out depositor money, but would have to match the duration of deposits with the duration of loans,

---

[4] A Ponzi scheme is a fraudulent operation in which returns on investment are paid from money received from investors, rather than profits generated from the employment of those funds, and thus rely upon an ever-increasing flow of new money to sustain the scheme.

while fully informing depositors of the risks so they can decide whether the interest they earn is worth the risks they are taking. Deposits that can be withdrawn anytime (a checking account for instance) could only be used to fund a loan which the bank can "call" on demand, while longer-term deposits (say a 5-year CD) would be matched to longer-lived loans like a business term loan or 5-year mortgage.

Really long-term loans like 30-year mortgages would be funded with deposits for which the bank would have to pay up in order to convince a depositor to part with his or her money for such a long time. The resulting mortgage would carry a high enough rate to provide the bank with a small profit, which would make 30-year mortgages both expensive and hard to get. But the case can be made that they *should* be hard to get. Buying a house – or anything else that requires tying up capital for extremely long periods – should require a hefty down payment, other liquid assets as collateral and a solid income stream. This coverage would give the bank the ability to foreclose and realize more than the value of the loan, which would protect its ability to repay its depositors, thus offering the needed safety to convince depositors to tie up their money for long periods.

A society in which banks operated this way would be a lot less prone to excessive debt accumulation and inflation, while failures would be far less frequent and government deposit insurance would be much less necessary. It would, in short, be a saner world in which individuals managed their own finances, saved with confidence and borrowed only for highly-productive uses, while two sharply differentiated types of banks facilitated wealth protection and real wealth creation rather than paper trading and speculation.

Today's investment banks and hedge funds, meanwhile, would be set free to speculate with their investors' money, making fortunes when they succeed and collapsing when they fail, with no public stake in either outcome. They would be seen as high risk/high reward propositions, and their customers and investors would participate with eyes wide open. No entity would be "too big to fail" because the banking system would be insulated from the vicissitudes of more volatile investment markets.

Central banks in such a 100-percent reserve and duration-matched world would either be completely unnecessary or serve a sharply-defined, very limited function of issuing paper currency 100-percent backed by gold/silver reserves and exchanging one for the other upon request. No need to be a lender of last resort because the banking system is sound and stable. No need to intervene in currency markets to fool citizens into treating valueless paper as a savings vehicle (because paper in this system is a warehouse receipt for real assets and derives value from the tangible asset backing it). No need to centrally control economic activity. Booms and busts will be fewer and less devastating, reducing – and in time probably eliminating – the need for government programs in response. Debt levels would be miniscule by today's standards, and therefore easily serviced from profitable activities.

This hypothetical world is, in short, more modest and far more sustainable. All in all, it's an attractive, completely feasible vision.

CHAPTER 17

WHAT IS INFLATION?

"The first panacea for a mismanaged nation is inflation of the currency; the second is war. Both bring a temporary prosperity; both bring a permanent ruin. But both are the refuge of political and economic opportunists."

– Ernest Hemingway

Over the past 30 years, officially-reported US inflation has been well-behaved – which seems strange in light of the orgy of borrowing and currency creation that has occurred during that time. Historically, this kind of monetary binge has resulted in dramatically higher prices and numerous other economic maladies. Why not this time?

Part of the answer lies in the alterations made by the US government in the way it calculates changes in price levels that lower the reported rate of increase. Recall from Chapter 6 that if it was still calculated by the pre-1980 method, the Consumer Price Index (CPI) would have risen at near-double-digit rates over the past few years rather than the 2-to-3 percent that was reported. And as we explain and/or assert in several other chapters, the monetary authorities are aggressively depressing the exchange rate of gold, which has traditionally been a barometer of monetary excess that inevitably leads to inflation.

The other part of the answer has to do with the definition of inflation. Most people – and certainly most governments and economists – define inflation as a general rise in prices. But this is wrong. Inflation is an increase in the money supply, and a higher general price level is just one possible result. In fact, excessive money creation most frequently shows up as asset bubbles, where the new money, instead of flowing equally to all the products that are for sale at a given time, flows disproportionately into the 'hottest' asset classes. In the 1990s, for instance, the consumer price index rose only modestly, in part because the government had begun changing the way it calculated price changes, but more crucially because huge amounts of money flowed into financial assets. The result was the dot-com bubble. Changing financial asset prices are not factored into the CPI, so this bubble was not seen as raising the cost of living – though it certainly raised the cost of investing.

The same thing happened in the 2000s, when excess currency flowed into housing and equities. In each case, mainstream economists and government officials pointed to modest consumer price inflation as a sign that things were fine. And in each case they were simply looking in the wrong place and completely missing the destabilizing effects of an inflating money supply.

As this is written in late 2013, the pattern is once again repeating, with economists, legislators and Fed officials using low consumer price inflation as a rationale for even easier money, while ignoring epic bubbles in sovereign bonds, equities and real estate around the world. These bubbles are the true signs of inflation, and since they're growing progressively larger, it is accurate to say that inflation is high and accelerating.

Inflationary Expectations
Another term that gets tossed around rather carelessly in discussions of inflation is "expectations," which manages to fit two misconceptions into a single word. The monetary

authorities contend that inflation (which, remember, they mistakenly define as an increase in the general price level) is a result not of the Fed's excessive money printing but of what market participants expect prices to do in the future. In other words, if people expect inflation, there will be inflation, regardless what the central bank might be doing to the money supply. Like so much of modern economic theory and practice, this idea is both wrong and self-serving, in that it deflects attention from the true cause of the problem.

Consider, for a moment, an economy where the money supply is the same from one year to the next. If consumers somehow come to believe that prices are going to soar and act on it by buying, say, cars and houses in anticipation of their being more expensive next year, the prices of those goods will indeed rise. But because the money being spent on cars and houses would, in normal times, have been spent on other things, the demand for those other things falls and their prices decline, offsetting the increase in prices of cars and houses and leaving average prices in the economy unchanged. In other words, the change in the money supply (zero) dictates the change in overall prices.

Since the central bank controls the money supply, why should it have to worry about expectations? Because debt is building up so quickly that without a commensurate increase in the supply of money to pay the interest, the economy will implode. Venerable newsletter writer Richard Russell years ago coined a phrase that still accurately describes the box into which the Federal Reserve and US government have placed the economy: "Inflate or die."

So, unable for policy or political reasons to limit the supply of money, the Fed and the federal government fall back on deception. They attempt to manage expectations through distorted government statistics and "jawboning" – an old-fashioned term for "spinning." The Fed and administration officials make deceptive statements about how "well-behaved" or "anchored" inflation is and how solid the year-ahead economy is looking, all in an attempt to control people and perpetuate the current system.

This need to manage not just the reality of the monetary system but the public's perception of it is one of the traits that distinguishes a fiat currency system from one based on sound money. During the millennia when money was gold (and was therefore "sound") there was no need – in fact no way to – manage expectations about future price levels. Inflationary expectations seldom changed because the price of most things in terms of gold seldom changed. But in a fiat currency system, where money is not redeemable into a tangible asset and circulates solely because the government says one kind of paper is valuable and other kinds aren't, perception isn't just another tool of monetary policy – it is the policy's prime directive. Because once perception-management fails, the next option is direct coercion in the form of capital controls and asset confiscations.

Inflation Is a Stealth Tax
And last but certainly not least, inflation – especially when it is hidden by distorted economic statistics – is a very slick way for a government to siphon resources from its citizens without the discomfort of raising their taxes or cutting benefits. Here's how it works: When the money supply is increased, basic supply and demand dictates that each previously-extant piece of currency is worth a little less. Since the Fed is creating the new currency out of thin air and giving it to the government to spend and the big banks to lend, they get all the benefit from the new money before

the increased supply affects its value, while savers and other holders of currency see their purchasing power decrease commensurately.

A related policy that achieves the same end is to force interest rates down below natural levels. Known as "financial repression" or zero interest rate policy (ZIRP), this shifts income from savers and retirees to debtors – including the government. Taken together, inflation and artificially low interest rates produce a relentless transfer of resources from private to public sector, an underreported aspect of monetary intervention that, once it is well-understood, will make the management of expectations much, much harder.

What About Hyperinflation?

Inflation is so deeply embedded in the fabric of today's fiat currency systems that it goes virtually unnoticed on a day-to-day basis. But inflation's rare and much more destructive cousin hyperinflation is a whole different animal, making life miserable for its victims and frequently destroying the host financial system.

Hyperinflation is always caused by the government turning its debt into currency, generally via a central bank. But it can manifest in two different ways, depending on how important commercial banks are in the economy (i.e., the relative roles of cash-currency versus deposit-currency). In Weimar Germany, hardly anyone had a bank account and almost all commercial transactions involved cash. The government even paid employees with cash-filled envelopes. So when its central bank turned government debt into (far too many) paper notes, the result was a cash currency hyperinflation, with all the attendant images of paper-filled wheelbarrows. The recent hyperinflation in

Zimbabwe was of the same type because few Zimbabweans had bank accounts.

Argentina's recurring hyperinflations were of the other type. No one in Buenos Aires was walking around with wheelbarrows of banknotes because cash-currency was not an important part of commerce. Transactions there were completed with deposit-currency using checks, wire/electronic transfers and plastic cards. So that country had deposit-currency hyperinflations where zeros were regularly added to bank accounts as the currency lost purchasing power.

Frequently, hyperinflations begin with the illusion of deflation, when prices rising faster than the supply of money seems to create a shortage of money. Paychecks fall behind living expenses and generalized hard times ensue, presenting the government with two choices. As the brilliant monetary theorist Murray Rothbard described the situation:

"If the government tightens its own belt and stops printing (or otherwise creating) new money, then inflationary expectations will eventually be reversed, and prices will fall once more – thus relieving the money shortage by lowering prices. But if government follows its own inherent inclination to counterfeit and appeases the clamor by printing more money so as to allow the public's cash balances to 'catch up' to prices, then the country is off to the races. Money and prices will follow each other upward in an ever-accelerating spiral, until finally prices 'run away'…[i.e., hyperinflate]"

James coined the term "Havenstein moment" for this decision point, after Rudolf Havenstein, the head of Weimar Germany's central bank. When faced with the choice of turning government debt into currency or insisting that the government live within its means, he made the wrong choice, producing history's most famous hyperinflation.

This somewhat theoretical discussion is timely and important because the US, Europe and Japan have all faced their own Havenstein moments, and have all made the fateful hyperinflationary choice. But don't expect wheelbarrows full of paper currency. The monetary systems of these countries are all based on deposit-currency, which means their hyperinflations will be of the Argentine variety, primarily decimating financial accounts (though cash under the mattress won't be safe either).

CHAPTER 18

CRYPTO-CURRENCIES: REVOLUTION OR TRAP?

"Bitcoin is a techno tour de force."
– Bill Gates

In the Internet's early days there was general agreement that one of the first killer apps would be some form of cyber-currency. Since money was already largely non-corporeal, existing as entries in bank accounts and ready to spend with plastic cards, the next logical step would be to move the whole thing online and dispense with paper and coins and their costly and burdensome infrastructure of banks, regulators and printing presses. The emergence of such currencies would, in this optimistic scenario, consign relics like the dollar and the Fed to history's circular file and usher in an era of trust, stability, and growth similar to what occurred under the classical gold standard.

But the digital liberation of money turned out to be easier said than done, as the first wave of cyber-currencies came and went without much of an impact. eCash, for instance, was an encrypted, anonymous payment system that allowed anyone anywhere to send and receive instant payments. But it relied on the existing banking infrastructure, and because "anonymous" meant "money laundering" to the police, it faced extreme pushback from authorities who viewed such currencies as primarily empowering drug dealers – and from banks that saw no point in encouraging the competition. Only one small bank ever accepted eCash, and the currency died a quiet death a few years after its introduction.

A larger impact was made by e-gold, which offered accounts denominated in grams of gold from which owners could make and receive payments. It generated some buzz, peaking at five million users and $2 million of transactions in 2009. But here again, the fact that much of this action was apparently money laundering by parties with good reason to stay anonymous led to legal pressure that eventually led to its failure.

James' company, GoldMoney, was originally designed to operate as a gold-based payment system based on several digital currency patents. It avoided the money laundering stigma by requiring users to register under their own names, and also met with early enthusiasm. But other logistical and legal barriers proved to be insurmountable, and GoldMoney's payment system was deemphasized in favor of offshore gold storage. By the late 2000s, purely digital currencies looked, to most observers, like a near-impossibility in a world where governments and banks had the power to prevent such competition.

ENTER BITCOIN

In 2008, a mysterious person or group using the apparent pseudonym Satoshi Nakamoto unveiled a new digital currency called Bitcoin that appeared to solve some of its predecessors' problems. Without going too deeply into the technical details, the Bitcoin system tracks each piece of currency from buyer to seller, eliminating the possibility of one person spending the same piece of currency multiple times before the counterparties catch on. The network is distributed, with no central clearinghouse or bank holding everyone's money and imposing rules. "Miners" create more Bitcoins by solving complex algorithms to add more

Bitcoins to the system, with the difficulty of the number crunching increasing as the quantity of Bitcoins grows, thus keeping their supply rising at a steady, predetermined rate until it reaches a preordained limit of 21 million a century or so hence.

Bitcoins, which are a long string of alphanumeric characters, can be stored in a variety of places, from a digital "wallet" on a desktop computer to a centralized service in the cloud, or even completely off-grid by being printed on a piece of paper. And because it operates over peer-to-peer networks similar to those used by techies and teens to download music and videos, it bypasses the established banking/regulatory system, making it, at least initially, free of government oversight.

Nakamoto, whoever he (or she, they) was, disappeared in 2010. But by then the Bitcoin community had taken on a life of its own. Hundreds of users began to mine Bitcoins with increasingly sophisticated computers, and the number of merchants and individuals willing to accept, store, and transact in the currency rose steadily.

As the buzz grew louder, the small community of techie/libertarian early adopters was joined by traders sensing a serious momentum play. The dollar price of a Bitcoin rose from 5 cents in early 2010 to 36 cents in November. In February 2011 it briefly achieved parity with the dollar, and when *Forbes Magazine* ran a favorable story that called it a "crypto currency," the price went parabolic, to nearly $9. More breathless press ensued, sending the price to $27 and putting the market value of Bitcoins in circulation at $130 million.

On the Internet's black market – the network of sites only accessible to computers running anonymizing software such as Tor – Bitcoin was rapidly becoming the preferred form of money. This drew the ire of the establishment, with US Senator Charles Schumer demanding the closure of online drug emporium Silk Road and describing Bitcoin as "an online form of money-laundering."

At about the same time, Bitcoin's Achilles heel became apparent, which is that it has to be stored somewhere, and no place is 100 percent secure. Bitcoins stored on a desktop can be wiped out by a crashed hard drive. Backed up on other storage media, they're vulnerable to hackers. Kept in an online storage service – which sounds like a bank but has no deposit insurance or even physical reality – they can disappear without a trace. Traded on an online exchange they can likewise simply disappear, with no recourse to former owners.

As Bitcoin rose in value the number of high-profile crimes and crashes rose apace. A Tokyo-based exchange was hacked and lost numerous client accounts. A Poland-based storage service accidentally overwrote its customer records. A West Indian storage service simply shut down, and its owner disappeared. And viruses aimed at Bitcoin caches proliferated. Newcomers, meanwhile, discovered that working with Bitcoin required skills not yet common among the non-techie 99 percent. The press turned scornful, and a consensus formed that the concept was fatally flawed and without much of a future.

The Comeback
Throughout that boom and bust, Bitcoin retained a core user base that saw its possibilities and worked to overcome its flaws by developing point-of-sale hardware and online merchant services while lessening its dependence on a small number of exchanges.

And then, just when the outside world had stopped paying attention, Bitcoin recovered. From under $20 at the beginning of 2013 it rose to $240, crashed to below $100, and then in one dramatic arc soared to more than $400. (Note that Figure 18.1 is drawn on a log scale to encompass this 10,000-plus-percent move). In November 2013 Bitcoin's market value exceeded $5 billion and the number of merchants willing to accept it began to soar. The market appears to have spoken: Bitcoin is for real.

Figure 18.1: Bitcoin US$ Exchange Rate, Weekly, 2010–2013

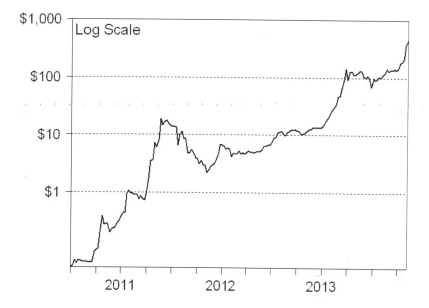

Is Bitcoin the New Napster?

In 1999 a brilliant, erratic iconoclast named Sean Parker aimed an arrow at the heart of the recording industry. Called Napster, it allowed owners of music to swap it with others online, from one hard drive to another – without paying for it. The recording industry sued, and Napster went bankrupt. But the genie was out of the bottle and file sharing services have since proliferated, changing the world of digital media forever.

If the growth rates seen in file sharing reappear in crypto-currencies, the implications would be profound. By allowing anonymous person-to-person (P2P) transfers of *money* with no national origin, Bitcoin's widespread acceptance would move the global financial system beyond the control of the world's central banks, something just as scary to them as the unlimited sharing of music was to the record labels.

By late 2013 the world's governments were wondering whether to try to co-opt Bitcoin or destroy it. The New York Department of Financial Services began questioning businesses that accept Bitcoin about their anti-money laundering safeguards. The US Senate Homeland Security and Government Affairs Committee began an investigation into who should regulate virtual currencies, and how they should do it. And Germany's finance ministry announced that the country would recognize Bitcoin and other digital currencies as "private money" and start taxing their capital gains.

At this writing in late 2013 it is not clear that regulating and/or taxing a crypto-currency is even possible. Attempts to shut down other kinds of file sharing (though not individual file sharing sites) have failed, and the Internet market for drugs, stolen property and even murder contracts is surviving in the face of official disapproval.

So the questions become: Are national currencies about to go the way of the $16 music CD? Is Bitcoin the agent of this change? Or is it a bleeding-edge pioneer like Napster, opening doors that others will walk through?

Or Is It a Trap?

What if, instead of threatening the powers that be, crypto-currencies like Bitcoin and its eventual competitors play into the hands of the emerging police state by giving them even greater control over our financial lives? Catherine Austin Fitts examined the dark side of online money in a recent interview with GoldMoney's Andy Duncan:

"There's nothing the top people driving and managing the financial system would love more than a digital currency. Nicholas Negroponte used to run MIT's Media Lab and said that 'in a digital age, data about money is worth more than money.' If you can ultimately merge digital currencies [into one global currency] the people who control the digital systems and the Internet will have far more centralized power. Their access to real-time data on what we're all doing will be fantastic and amazing. So clearly if your goal is centralized governance of financial systems, you love digital money that is anonymous to the user, where you don't have to put sovereign insurance behind it, but is completely transparent to you."

Another disturbing angle involves the growing cyber-war capabilities of the US and other major nations. In the aggregate they are throwing tens of billions of dollars each year at developing the tools to hack virtually any system. If they gain the capability to override the algorithm that governs the increase in the supply of a given crypto-currency they would have the ability to hijack it for their own ends, either to finance themselves or punish/control those who depend on it.

Their lack of physical reality means that crypto-currencies have a huge hurdle of market perception to cross before they can be considered as "money." That is, they function beautifully as a currency, but as a store of value they are suspect because they lack a corporeal existence.

But don't count them out. Given the speed with which other Internet applications – and the Internet itself – have evolved from techie playthings to user-friendly essential tools of modern life, it would not be at all surprising to see crypto-currencies travel the same path. They have the potential, once their kinks are ironed out, to function as an efficient online currency complement to the time-tested store-of-value attributes of precious metals.

PART IV:
CRISIS EQUALS OPPORTUNITY

CHAPTER 19

THE GREAT MIGRATION
FROM FINANCIAL TO TANGIBLE ASSETS

"When US Treasuries and IBM certificates are museum pieces, gold will still be money."

– Richard Russell, Dow Theory Letters

Wealth comes in many forms, but only two general categories: tangible and financial. Tangible wealth is made up of real, physical things like buildings, farmland, oil wells, commodities, etc., which can be seen and touched, and – crucially – don't have counterparty risk. That is, no one else has to make good on a promise for a tangible asset to have value.

Financial assets like bank deposits, insurance policies, bonds, and annuities do have counterparty risk, which is to say they depend on someone else's promise. A bank deposit, for instance, only has value if the bank is willing and able to return that money when the account holder requests it. Even an insured bank deposit is only as good as the financial capacity of the government or insurance company standing behind the bank. And of course a piece of paper currency is only valuable if the government manages the money supply properly.

Equities, because they represent ownership shares in public companies, can be either near-tangible or financial depending on the underlying company. A share of Exxon Mobil stock is for all practical purposes like a tangible asset because oil wells are real, while a share of Goldman Sachs or JP Morgan Chase would be financial because a bank's wealth is primarily in the form of loans and other financial instruments.

Over long periods of time these two asset categories tend to move in and out of favor, with tangible assets being more prized in hard, uncertain times when preservation of capital is paramount and counterparty risk is suspect, and financial assets being favored when times are good and people have grown to trust major financial institutions and governments to keep promises and generate big returns.

One of the keys to successful money management is to understand which category is ascendant and therefore the more profitable/safe place to be. During a boom, one should own financial assets until they become relatively overvalued (as they did in 1929, 1968, and 2000), then shift into tangible assets and own them until they become overvalued (1947 and 1980). As Figure 19.1 illustrates, when it takes about 20 or more ounces (622 grams) of gold to buy the Dow Jones Industrial Average, financial assets have become overvalued and are topping out, and it's time to shift into real assets. Conversely, when less than two ounces (62 grams) of gold can buy the Dow Jones Industrials, then financial assets are cheap and attractive.

Figure 19.1: Dow Jones Industrial Average Priced in Gold

Another way of visualizing this process is to compare the relative sizes of the finance and manufacturing sectors. During the expansion of the credit bubble that began after World War II, Americans gradually became more and more optimistic about the future and more trusting of banks and governments. Because the good times seemed likely to continue, using other people's money to achieve one's ends came to be seen as increasingly reasonable and wise. Debt expanded and finance (i.e., the debt industry) became an ever-more important part of the economy, while manufacturing in particular and tangible assets in general became relatively less important.

Finance doubled as a percent of GDP between 1947 and 2008 while manufacturing fell by nearly two-thirds. For investors, the standard diversified portfolio of stocks, bonds and dollar cash was a great way to build wealth, with very little long-term downside risk.

That faith was shaken by the crash of 2008, which should have marked the end of the post-WWII cycle of credit expansion and ushered in a mass-migration out of finance and into tangible assets. Instead, the world's fiat currency managers upped the ante, cutting interest rates to zero and flooding the system with newly-created currency in an attempt to re-inflate the financial sector. They handed the biggest banks effectively-unlimited amounts of free money, and the banks, reluctant to lend so soon after their near-death experience, simply deposited their excess reserves with the Fed, earning a small but risk-free return. And the biggest banks, as the recipients of most of the Fed's largesse, reaped most of the rewards. In the first half of 2013, the 1.5 percent of banks with the largest asset bases earned about 80 percent of the industry's profits. The debt monetization experiment had succeeded in lengthening what was already an extreme pendulum swing toward financial assets.

Figure 19.2: US Bank Profits, 1990-2013 (Quarterly)

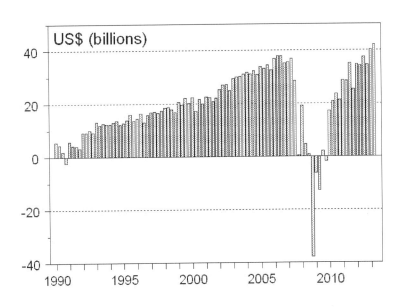

So now the question becomes, will the monetary authorities be able to push the pendulum even further, or was the financial asset recovery of 2009-2013 the last gasp of a dying trend? By now you know that we're firmly in the latter camp. The expansion that began after World War II has produced extraordinary amounts of debt, leverage and complexity, from a financial standpoint achieving "peak" everything. Finance has no further to go, and the great migration out of financial assets and into tangible things is about to begin, on a scale commensurate with the historically unprecedented size of the post-WWII credit bubble.

Investors and savers who position themselves for this trend change will both protect their capital and, potentially, earn outsized returns. The next few chapters will present some strategies to help achieve this outcome, ranging from money-under-the-mattress conservative to bet-the-farm aggressive.

CHAPTER 20

WHAT IS GOLD, AND WHY DOES IT MATTER?

"Gold is an expression of the world's distrust of the way our central bankers conduct their affairs."

– James Grant, Grant's Interest Rate Observer

Most discussions of the world's ongoing monetary mess eventually touch on gold. But all too frequently the result is more heat than light, in part because so many people carry both preconceptions and misconceptions into the debate and in part because many participants have been at it for so long that they no longer feel the need to provide background or state their premises. They just launch into their assertions, pro or con, safe in the knowledge that most of their listeners already understand the context.

This is understandably frustrating for newcomers curious about how and whether a chunk of shiny metal can matter in a modern economy. So this chapter will provide a little background to help readers understand gold's role in the coming monetary "reset" and why, in our judgment, it never stopped functioning as money in this era of fiat currencies.

Brief digression: value versus utility. *On the subject of money, there are two concepts – value and utility – that appear similar (or even identical) but differ in important ways. Because they're crucial to a deeper understanding of the distinctions between sound and unsound forms of* *money and currency, we'll take a moment to define and contrast them.*

The Austrian School of economic thought holds that value is not intrinsic to any asset. Instead, the value of a given thing is subjective and situational. That is, it depends on what people need or want and can afford at that moment. But utility – what the thing can do – is intrinsic and objective. A hammer is always a hammer, and can always pound nails. But whether it is valuable to a given person at a specific moment depends on whether it meets their immediate needs. One person's junk is indeed another person's treasure.

In today's world, several forms of money and currency exist simultaneously, but with differing utilities. Buying a newspaper with a credit card is not as easy as using coins, which is not as easy as using dollar bills, but each are able to do the jobs of money and currency. A gold coin, meanwhile, is of little use for buying a newspaper but does a great job of preserving purchasing power without counterparty risk.

Markets, being subjective and emotional, frequently do a terrible job of equating utility and value. As a consequence, assets prices (or exchange rates in the case of money) frequently differ from fair value. These divergences can occur for a variety of reasons, but are most common – and most extreme – when conventional wisdom takes one of its periodic detours into shared hallucination. During such times, those with a clear understanding of asset values are able to profit from their insights, while those (generally the vast majority) who follow mainstream opinion make disastrous mistakes.

During the dot-com bubble, for instance, it was widely accepted that profits didn't matter and that market share – in the form of "eyeballs" – was the true measure of a company's value. That conventional 'wisdom' was shattered when dot-com stocks crashed. A few years later, majority opinion held that house prices only go up, and we all know how that worked out. History is also full of excessively pessimistic – and equally wrong – thinking at market bottoms.

How does this tendency of markets to misprice assets relate to gold? By late 2013, after a grinding two-year bear market, the conventional wisdom had concluded that gold's time had passed. Illustrating this view, an October 28, 2013 Wall Street Journal article opined that "Gold...yields nothing and can be costly to hold," and quoted a fund manager to the effect that "Gold really doesn't have much to offer." Conventional wisdom appears to be sending another of its clear, if inadvertent, messages, which Chapter 21 will explore in great detail. In the meantime, back to the nature of gold.

WHAT IS GOLD?

Recall from Chapter 1 that sound money has certain properties, including rarity, dependable supply, and portability, and that after much trial and error, gold and silver coins were chosen almost unanimously by every market-based economy as the best tools for the job (more about silver in Chapter 22), and remained central to the global monetary system until 1971. As for what gold is in a physical sense, according to Wikipedia:

"Gold is a chemical element with the symbol Au and atomic number 79. It is a dense, soft, malleable, and ductile metal with a bright yellow color and luster that is considered attractive, which is maintained without tarnishing in air or water. Chemically, gold is a transition metal and a group 11 element. It is one of the least reactive chemical elements, solid under standard conditions. The metal therefore occurs often in free elemental (native) form, as nuggets or grains in rocks, in veins and in alluvial deposits."

These characteristics place gold among the world's most eternal substances. It can rest for centuries at the bottom of the ocean or buried in desert sands or a back yard without tarnishing or eroding. And because it is almost exclusively a monetary metal, it doesn't disappear after use. In contrast to base metals, very little gold is used in industry, and when it is, much of it is recycled and reused because of its high value.

So virtually all the gold that has ever been mined is still here, accumulated in an aboveground stock estimated at 160,000 metric tonnes. That may sound like a lot, but isn't. Twenty-six times as much steel (by weight) is produced *each day*. And all of the gold mined throughout history, if poured into a cube, could fit under the arches of the Eiffel Tower. Gold is indeed rare, one of the essential characteristics of sound money.

Because the supply of gold is constrained by geology and the economics of mining, new production adds only about 1.8 percent a year to the aboveground stock, making its growth inherently stable and explaining why its purchasing power remains relatively constant over long periods of time. This growth rate is approximately the same as those of world population and new wealth creation, which are key determinants of the demand for money. Gold thus achieves what economist Milton Friedman's "k-percent rule" intends for central banks, which is that to control inflation the money supply should increase by the same modest percentage rate every year. No central bank comes close to achieving Friedman's target, so no fiat currency matches gold's consistency in providing stable purchasing power over time.[5] Gold, in short, does the job of money very well.

So despite the fact that gold no longer circulates as currency, it is still valued and held throughout the world as money. Different cultures prefer different forms – in India, for instance, high-karat gold jewelry (best described as "monetary jewelry") makes up a large part of a typical family's wealth. But whether held as coins, bars, or necklaces, gold is seen virtually everywhere as a form of savings that preserves purchasing power over not just years, but generations.

WHO DECIDES WHAT IS MONEY?

During a 2011 congressional banking subcommittee hearing, Texas congressman Ron Paul – long a champion of gold's role in the financial world – asked Federal Reserve Chairman Ben Bernanke if gold is money. "No," replied Bernanke, "It's an asset." Video of this exchange went viral in the gold-bug community, because the difference between money and an asset is, to people who care about such things, both profound and crucial to the future of the global financial system.

The subtext of the Paul/Bernanke exchange was a slightly different but equally important question: Can a government simply decree that what has functioned as money for 5,000 years no longer be money? This question has been debated in various forms and forums since the first government began debasing its currency eons ago. But the modern iteration can be traced back to the Great Depression. Recall that at the time the US was on a gold standard, and a paper dollar was simply a warehouse

---

[5] See: The Aboveground Gold Stock: Its Importance and Its Size
http://www.goldmoney.com/images/media/Files/GMYF/theabovegroundgolds tock.pdf

receipt for 23.222 grains of gold (approximately $1/20^{th}$ of a troy ounce), while a dollar in a bank account was in theory exchangeable for those paper receipts (dollar bills). But because the Federal Reserve issued up to 2½-times more receipts than gold and because banks operated on a fractional reserve system, the total quantity of claims vastly outnumbered the weight of gold held in reserve. After the 1929 stock market crash, the fractional reserve system began working in reverse (see Chapter 15), leaving the US – and much of the global – economy on the verge of imploding.

For countries on the gold standard, currency devaluation was seen as an admission of failure and deemed dishonorable because it allowed a country to pay off its debts in currency that had less purchasing power than at the time the loans were made. Nevertheless, devaluation was grudgingly accepted as last-ditch strategy for badly-run countries to boost economic growth and avoid a depression or more direct form of default. The US, as it turned out, chose to both devalue its currency *and* default on its debts.

Shortly after his inauguration in 1933, President Franklin Roosevelt concluded that US problems were serious enough to warrant devaluation of the dollar, among other aggressive policies. Under Article I, Section 8 of the Constitution, only Congress had the power to "regulate"[6] the relationship between the dollar and gold,

---

[6] The term "regulate" is generally misunderstood today. Congress was given a non-exclusive power to "coin" money, not "print" it. As part of this coining power, it was also given the power to "regulate" the gold/silver ratio in order to ensure that sufficient gold and silver was available for circulation. For a thorough analysis of the original intent of the Framers of the American Constitution, see "Pieces of Eight: The Monetary Powers and Disabilities of the United States Constitution" by Edwin Vieira Jr.

but FDR claimed that authority for the presidency. And instead of simply decreeing that henceforth the dollar was worth less gold than before, FDR first confiscated Americans' privately-held gold and made it illegal to own the metal – and *then* devalued the dollar against gold, effectively taking the difference between the purchasing power of the gold citizens turned in and the dollars they received in return. This was, to put it bluntly, theft. It was also a partial default on US debt, much of which carried "Gold Clause" provisions specifying that it was payable in specific weights of gold.

The implications of FDR's actions, however, went far beyond a garden-variety asset confiscation or currency devaluation. By making gold ownership illegal, FDR was asserting the primacy of government over the market in deciding what constitutes money. In the process, it made the right of private contract – a fundamental pillar of law heretofore considered sacrosanct – subservient to the government's conception of the "national interest."

By lifting the restraint that sound money places on federal spending, FDR fundamentally altered the relationship between Americans and their government. Previously, governments could borrow modestly (by today's standards) but for the most part could spend only the money that they had on hand. Money was gold, and the coins and bars in the national treasury helped define the government's wealth while limiting its ability to promise all things for all constituencies.

In the future FDR created, governments would be free to act as they saw fit, simply creating a desired amount of paper fiat currency and spending it to make the world a better place – as defined by the people in charge. Perhaps FDR's goal was the public good rather than what is now often called an "imperial presidency." But regardless of his intent or motivation, as the brief tour of monetary history in Chapter 1 makes clear, a government with a printing press is a monster in the making.

Nixon Closes the Gold Window

For a few decades after FDR's gold confiscation, the separation between gold and national currencies was only partial. Under the terms of the post-WWII Bretton Woods monetary system, the dollar was convertible into gold by foreign governments and non-Americans, while other currencies were pegged to the dollar. Governments continued to view gold as the basis of their monetary system, keeping bullion in vaults as "reserves" to back currencies that circulated in commerce as substitutes for those reserves. Gold thus remained the foundation of the value of the dollar, German mark, French franc and other major currencies, and could be used for settlement of government-to-government debts. So while individuals no longer used gold for everyday transactions in the US, it retained the functions of money and, crucially, continued to restrain government spending and currency creation because other countries could demand gold in return for excess, unwanted dollars.

The onset of the Vietnam war and creation of Medicare and other "Great Society" programs in the 1960s ("guns and butter" as the simultaneous pursuit of ambitious military and domestic goals came to be known) put mounting pressure on the US budget and led the Federal Reserve to ramp up the supply of new dollars. France, already chafing at the "exorbitant privilege" conferred on the US by its ownership and control of the world's reserve currency, began converting some of its dollars into gold. In March 1968 these redemptions led to the collapse of the "London Gold Pool," the mechanism through which central banks had been maintaining the gold/dollar exchange rate of \$35 per ounce even while the US was pursuing its expansive monetary policies. But France kept up the pressure and was soon joined by a growing number of countries and individuals who recognized the ongoing debasement of the dollar and, more to the point, the failure of the US to maintain a sound dollar for the smooth functioning of the international monetary system.

By 1971 President Richard Nixon was faced with a dilemma. If the US continued to exchange gold for paper, its gold would soon be gone. The traditional response to such a situation would be to devalue the currency by offering less gold per dollar, making dollars more attractive relative to gold, as FDR had done. But Nixon instead "closed the gold window," thereafter refusing to provide gold in return for dollars. As US Treasury Secretary John Connally put it to a group of finance ministers just before Nixon's decision, "The dollar is our currency, but your problem."

And so the US once again defaulted on its gold obligations and, through its dominance of the International Monetary Fund, convinced the rest of the world to follow it into a paper money world. The break between the supply of gold and national currencies was now complete, and the latter became pure fiat currencies, circulating by force of legal tender laws rather than the belief in their monetary value from a direct link to gold. The US government, now highly confident in the primacy of the paper dollar, in January 1975 again allowed citizens to own gold.

Today, gold still resides in government vaults as part of central bank monetary reserves but, except in very limited instances in a few countries, is not exchanged in payment of debts or spent as currency by governments or individuals, even where legal to do so. Those who own gold are mimicking central banks by keeping their gold in safekeeping. After all, currency can be spent or saved, and today gold falls mainly into the latter category.

The Shadow Monetary System

Today, most people agree with Ben Bernanke that gold is an asset, more like oil or soybeans than money. That such a misguided belief can gain widespread acceptance has more to do with the ability of monetary authorities and academic economists to obscure facts and shape public opinion than with any changes in gold's role. The key to understanding why this is so is Gresham's Law (mentioned briefly in Chapter 6 in a different context), which states that bad (i.e., unsound) currency will drive good (i.e., sound) currency out of circulation when the government mandates that they both trade at face value.

Readers of a certain age will recall that in the 1960s and early 1970s US coins containing silver gradually disappeared, as Americans hoarded them for their (increasingly valuable) silver and spent the newer coins made of cheaper metals. The silver coins were still money. They just stopped circulating in commerce as they gradually accumulated in jars and boxes in American homes. In other words they no longer functioned as currency but continued to function as a form of savings.

Today, good currency is not driven out of circulation by fixed exchange rates but by legal tender laws mandating that national fiat currencies be used in commerce. And in a very similar way to when silver was removed from coinage, gold is saved because it remains a store of purchasing power. Each year's mine production is bought with national currencies and saved by (a wise handful of) individuals, private institutions and even some central banks. The fiat currencies (bad money) used to pay for gold continue to circulate while gold, as the soundest money, is mostly hoarded as savings.

There are instances, however, where gold still circulates and is used for transactions. 400-oz bars along with smaller bars and coins are moving around continuously, generally in return for fiat currency rather than goods or services. But in a handful of countries gold is still used for some types of commerce. It is used to purchase real estate in Vietnam, for instance, and often to rent space in Istanbul's bazaars.

Meanwhile, gold, like national currencies, can be borrowed and lent at interest. This is not widely known because the market is dominated by central banks and open only to the large banks that trade bullion and a handful of specialist fabricators of gold jewelry. Their activity is further obscured by the fact that they call borrowing "leasing" and the interest rate a "lease rate." The acts taking place are identical to the lending and borrowing of any national currency, except that borrowing gold requires moving a tangible asset around in addition to posting bookkeeping entries and signing promissory notes. In Chapter 21 we explain how gold lending is used by central banks to artificially depress the metal's price. But for now suffice it to say that gold continues to be lent and borrowed, just like dollars, euro, and yen.

And finally, gold continues to provide a highly useful alternative method for calculating prices, which is after all the most important function of money. National currencies, because they lose value each year, are a distorted lens for trying to assess changes in the true price of things over time. Imagine the complications that would arise in Olympic scoring, for instance, if meters and minutes got a little shorter each day. Records would become meaningless unless they were filtered through a complex (and easily-corrupted) series of adjustments to offset the debasement of the measuring units. That's exactly the difficulty that inflation-prone fiat currencies present to anyone – whether entrepreneur, chief executive, or individual investor – trying to make sense of long-term price and market trends in order to decide what to do with their accumulated capital.

Using gold as the measure of value presents a much clearer picture. Figure 20.1 shows oil priced in both dollars and gold. Note that in dollar terms oil is way up, while in gold terms it is remarkably stable over more than six decades. The correct conclusion is that oil isn't getting more expensive; rather, the dollar is losing purchasing power. Gold cuts through the haze of monetary debasement to give a clear picture of value over time, and performs this crucial function of sound money better than any national currency.

Figure 20.1: Crude Oil Prices, 1950 Base-100 to 2013 (Monthly)

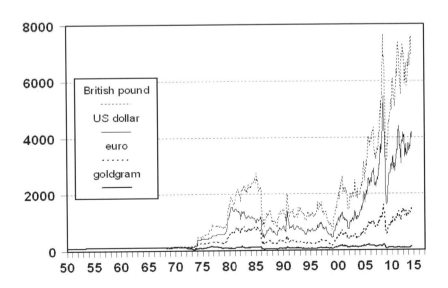

So we come down firmly on the side of Ron Paul, and not Ben Bernanke. Gold is money and will remain so long after today's fiat currencies are justifiably forgotten. But this is far more than a philosophical or ideological point. It is crucial to the financial decisions that savers and investors will have to make to prepare for the coming turmoil.

If gold is money and fiat currencies are not, and if societies always return to sound money when experiments with paper fail and debts become too oppressive, then there will soon be a tidal wave of capital flowing into this relatively small market. When this happens, gold's exchange rate versus the dollar will soar. The next few chapters will explain this inevitable outcome in more detail and show you how to profit from the transition.

CHAPTER 21

WHY GOLD IS ABOUT TO SOAR

"Every great crisis reveals the excessive speculations of many [banking] houses which no one before suspected."

– Walter Bagehot

When gold is viewed as money, the financial establishment's hostility begins to makes sense. Because gold is a formidable competitor of the dollar and other fiat currencies, rising gold implies a troubled dollar, euro and yen – and, by implication, incompetent governments in the US, Europe and Japan. And since fiat currencies have no physical reality and depend for their value on the perceived integrity of the governments that create and manage them, image is everything and looking bad is deadly. A discredited fiat currency can literally fall to zero (as many have), leaving its government with no alternative but coercion to keep the currency circulating (hence the spread of capital controls and wealth confiscations covered in Chapter 11).

So it is emphatically in the interest of the world's monetary authorities to depress gold's exchange rate. And they've been doing this quite aggressively, with the following strategy:

CENTRAL BANK MANIPULATION

The major Western central banks own (or *claim* to own because they don't allow independent inspection of their vaults or adhere to generally accepted accounting principles in their financial statements) 18 percent of the world's gold. And for at least the past two decades they've used that gold to manage the metal's exchange rate by loaning it (inaccurately called "leasing") to large banks known as bullion banks, which sell the gold on the open market. The bullion banks invest the proceeds in bonds or other assets that yield more than the rate at which they've borrowed the gold from the central banks, earning the spread. Meanwhile, the gold they've dumped on the market depresses the metal's exchange rate, making the central bank's fiat currency appear relatively stable by masking its eroding purchasing power. Gold, meanwhile, is made to appear relatively volatile because of short-term fluctuations, while its ability to preserve purchasing power over long periods of time is largely overlooked.

To avoid having to tell the world what they're doing, the central banks employ an accounting trick that no private sector company could get away with: They lump their physical gold and gold loans into one line on their financial reports, despite the fact that unencumbered physical gold stored safely in a vault is a tangible asset, while gold removed from a vault to be loaned is a liability of a bullion bank, i.e., a financial asset with counterparty risk. This accounting deception has enabled central banks to hide the extent to which they've been emptying their gold vaults – and to obscure the fact that the bullion banks are obligated to buy back the gold they've borrowed and then sold in order to return it to the central banks in repayment of the loan. In effect, the bullion banks are "short" gold, a liability that is neither reported to the public nor widely understood by bank shareholders.

The size of this short position could be massive. Analysts working with the Gold Anti-Trust Action Committee (GATA) and other interested parties have pieced together what they believe is an accurate accounting of central bank lending, and have concluded that nearly half of the world's official gold reserves of 29,000 tonnes have been dumped on the market in this way. So the major fiat currencies actually have even less gold backing than previously thought. Less metal in central bank vaults also means less ammunition for future gold lending and price suppression, making it harder to maintain the façade that gold is trading at its fair value.

The Great Gold Takedown

The façade almost cracked in early 2013, as a series of tremors shook the gold market:

- In January, the German Bundesbank (with official gold reserves second only to the US) announced that it wanted about 300 tonnes of the gold it stored in the New York Fed's vault returned to Germany. Since the New York Fed claimed to hold 6,200 tonnes, Germany's order should have been easy to pack and ship within weeks, if not days. Instead, the Fed told the Bundesbank that the transfer would take*seven years.*

- In March, Dutch bank ABN Amro informed customers who had stored gold bullion in its vaults that they could no longer have their gold back on demand, in effect defaulting on the storage agreement.

- In April, stories began to circulate that banks – UBS and Scotiabank were most frequently mentioned – were seeing large withdrawals of gold, as depositors spooked by the ABN Amro news decided that different storage arrangements were in order. A few days later gold analyst

James Sinclair reported that the Swiss central bank had banned the withdrawal of gold from Swiss commercial banks. The question of the day became "Why would banks do these things if they still had their customers' gold?"

- Gold inventories at the Comex (the major US futures exchange) began to fall rapidly, leading to speculation that it might be unable to deliver gold owed to holders of "long" futures contracts, and would default by settling in cash rather than metal. This would have been a catastrophe for both the Comex's prestige and anyone betting that gold would fall, since it would probably have soared in response to the exchange's default.

- Gold held by exchange-traded funds (ETFs – more about them in a moment) worldwide began to decline.

- Chinese gold imports began to soar, implying that the West, where gold was generally perceived to be an investment and out of favor, was shipping large amounts of gold to the East, where buyers saw it as both money and undervalued at prevailing exchange rates.

To avoid a default in which a counterparty failed to deliver physical metal when obligated to do so, the bullion banks and central banks made a pre-emptive strike:

- In early April, several banks that are active participants in the various gold markets started recommending that their clients sell gold, saying the metal was overpriced. Goldman Sachs in particular made a bold and well-publicized recommendation that its clients actually short, or bet against, gold.

- A handful of major banks sold gold futures contracts worth tens of billions of dollars on the Comex futures exchange, frequently at odd times when trading was thin. This pushed the "paper" price of gold through technical support levels, which activated sell programs of momentum-trading hedge funds. The resulting additional selling pressure forced gold down from a high of $1615 per ounce (52/gg) in early April to a low of $1180 (38/gg) by the end of June.

- On April 15 alone, the amount of paper gold traded equaled 82 percent of average annual mine supply and more than 4.3 times the volume of a normal day. And the selling was highly concentrated, with a few huge orders doing most of the damage. This kind of trading is virtual proof of manipulation, since a profit-seeking trader wanting to open or close a position would never move this aggressively, particularly at a time of day when the European and American markets were closed. In such a thin market, the first few trades move the price dramatically, making subsequent trades needed to create or unwind the position far less attractive. If, on the other hand, the goal was to drive gold down, the timing and size of the trades were perfect – and they had the desired effect. Gold declined more than 9 percent in a single trading session.

More such interventions followed, becoming blatant enough to catch the attention of the mainstream press. An October 14, 2013 *Financial Times* article quoted a prominent trader to the effect that, "These moves are becoming more and more prevalent, and to my mind have to either be the work of someone attempting to manipulate the market, or someone who really shouldn't be trusted with the sums of money they are throwing around…There are ways of entering and exiting a market so that minimum disruption is caused, and whoever is entering these orders has no intention of doing that."

- While the paper gold market was being inundated with short futures contracts, the Fed announced that it was ready to begin "tapering" its QE3 $85 billion-a-month asset purchase program, which had been one of the financial system's important sources of liquidity. Less money printing means less free cash to flow into hard assets like gold. It also means higher interest rates – which raise the opportunity cost of owning a tangible asset.

- The final blow was struck by the Indian central bank which decided, supposedly to reduce the country's trade deficit, to impose strict limits on gold imports. The new rules dramatically cut the amount of gold flowing into that normally huge market for gold monetary jewelry.

The attack complete, the bullion banks then covered their short positions at a nice profit. And to restock their vaults with physical gold, they began emptying the SPDR Gold Trust (GLD), a major exchange traded fund that buys and stores gold. The bullion banks that control the flow of metal into the fund are able to convert shares of GLD into physical gold, and did so on a vast scale, pulling more than 400 tonnes from the ETF.

Figure 21.1: SPDR Gold Trust (GLD) Reported Gold Inventory (tonnes)

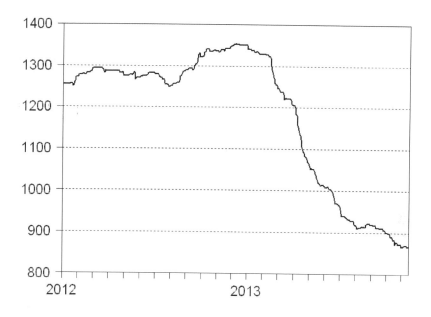

BUT THE GAME IS ABOUT TO END

Based on the ease with which the Fed and the bullion banks were able to crush gold in 2013, it might seem reasonable to conclude that they can do it again whenever they want, and that gold will always be at the mercy of the monetary authorities' desire to keep it cheap, volatile, and irrelevant. But that's not the case. In reality, the great gold takedown of 2013 backfired so disastrously that not only is a repeat less likely, but its opposite, a "short squeeze" or counterparty default that sends the price dramatically higher, has become not just possible but probable in the next few years. Here's why:

Gold Is Migrating from West to East

Recall from Chapter 11 that in order to counter the power that the US derives from having the world's reserve currency, China, Russia and other emerging nations are converting their dollar reserves into hard assets by buying resources of all sorts, but especially gold. The idea is to eventually have enough gold to back their currencies to create rivals to the dollar – or at least to own something that will hold its value while the dollar is being systematically devalued. Either way, they have a lot of dollars and therefore need a lot of gold.

From their point of view, the recent takedown put something they were going to buy in any event on sale. And they responded like enthusiastic consumers, by buying literally all the physical gold that was available at the new lower price. China, India and Russia alone bought more gold than was produced by the world's mines in 2013.

China hadn't previously discussed its reasons for buying so much gold, but an April 2013 article in the Chinese magazine *World News Journal* made its point of view quite clear:

"The US and Europe have always suppressed the rising price of gold. They intend to weaken gold's function as an international reserve currency. They don't want to see other countries turning to gold reserves instead of the US dollar or Euro. Therefore, suppressing the price of gold is very beneficial for the US in maintaining the US dollar's role as the international reserve currency. China's increased gold reserves will thus act as a model and lead other countries towards reserving more gold. Large gold reserves are also beneficial in promoting the internationalization of the [yuan]."

Western Vaults Are Being Emptied
If just three countries bought more gold than was mined in 2013, where did the gold come from to satisfy all the world's other buyers? Some came from GLD, which was looted by the bullion banks. Most of that metal was shipped to Swiss refiners, which turned the ETF's 400oz bars into 1kilo bars (China's preferred size) and shipped them directly to Shanghai or to Hong Kong for importation into China. But this didn't completely bridge the gap between demand and supply, and the only remaining source of significant supply is the Western central banks. Alasdair Macleod, the Head of Research at GoldMoney, broke the news on Max Keiser's popular Keiser Report Internet program, that the Bank of England was a major "dishoarder" in 2013. This shouldn't come as a surprise to gold market analysts: In 2000, when the bullion banks were similarly threatened by their massive short positions, Britain's then Chancellor of the Exchequer (and future Prime Minister) Gordon Brown notoriously bailed them out by selling nearly half of London's gold at bottom-of-the-cycle prices – a transaction dubbed "The Brown Bottom." And Brown's successors are apparently at it again. UK gold shipments to Switzerland exceeded the amount of gold removed from GLD in 2013, implying that the Bank of England shipped some of its own gold reserves – or the gold reserves of other central banks stored with it – to make up the difference.

Meanwhile, on the Comex futures exchange, the amount of gold on hand to satisfy the claims of contract holders who choose to take delivery was, in late 2013, once again shrinking to dangerous levels. Paper claims totaled about 60 ounces of gold for every ounce of physical inventory. In other words, the paper gold market is a fractional reserve system in which claims vastly outnumber tangible assets. Should even a twentieth of contract holders demand gold rather than cash, holders of short contracts – which obligate their owners to supply metal upon demand – would be hard pressed to find the necessary gold.

Backwardation

For much of 2013 the spot exchange rate for gold, i.e., what one pays for immediate delivery, was higher than delivery one month hence. This situation is called "backwardation" and is a sign of extremely strong demand for physical metal. To understand this concept, recall that gold doesn't have debasement risk, and consequently, its interest rates are lower than for any national currency. Because of this difference between gold and dollar interest rates, when calculating the time value of money, the exchange rate for gold increases over time. Don't worry if this isn't immediately clear. The important thing to understand is that gold's spot price should be lower than the price for future delivery.

Backwardation is thus both very rare and historically meaningful. The two previous gold backwardations occurred in 1999 and 2008, and each was followed by a sustained increase in gold's exchange rate. But where those backwardations lasted only a couple of days, 2013's lasted on-and-off for months. The implication? There is not nearly enough available gold to go around at current exchange rates, and central banks are struggling to keep it from rising to market-clearing levels.

WHEN MANIPULATION FAILS, GOLD SOARS

The plunge in gold's exchange rate during 2013 led many to believe that the bull market was over. But the cause of the smack-down – banks and bullion exchanges running out of metal – and the response to it – massive buying in Asia –

imply that this latest round of manipulation was the last gasp of a system that's running out of fuel.

Another perhaps-unintended consequence of taking gold down so dramatically is that the late-2013 exchange rate fell below the average cost of production for the gold mining industry. Chapter 25's look at investing in the miners covers this event in more detail, so for now suffice it to say that the miners responded to gold's correction by shutting down high-cost mines and scaling back new project development, which will lead to less gold being mined going forward. And even at, say, $2,000 per ounce ($64.5/gg), global gold production would probably still shrink over the next couple of decades. This industry is another "peak" producer, which makes sense when you consider that humans have been searching for gold for 4,000 years and have found all the easily-extracted deposits, while many governments are making it harder and more expensive to develop new mines. So future mines will consist of lower grades in harder-to-reach or politically unstable places, and will be less productive and/or more costly to operate.

The result: The supply of new gold from mines will fall for the next few years and will probably never again rise from one year to the next by more than a few percentage points. Mine production is only about 1.8 percent of above ground stocks, so is not the determining factor in gold's exchange rate. But it does matter at the margin. Other things being equal, less mine production means less gold available for increasingly-aggressive buyers, and a growing gap between new supply and the mountain of derivatives and other paper promises that require delivery of physical gold.

Pension Funds Discover Gold

The fact that the East stands ready to buy *all* their gold at late-2013 exchange rates presents developed-world central banks with a dilemma: They can continue their manipulation, in which case they will soon run out of metal. Or they can step back – like they did when the London Gold Pool collapsed in 1968 – and let market forces choose an exchange rate, which will almost certainly be far higher than at present.

To understand how quickly and dramatically the latter scenario might play out, consider the current asset base of the money management industry. Most of the world's approximately $100 trillion of liquid wealth is overseen by mutual funds, hedge funds, insurance companies, sovereign wealth funds and pension funds. And they own virtually no gold.

Shayne McGuire, head of global research at the Teacher Retirement System of Texas, estimates that pension funds, for instance, have allocated about 1/3 of one percent of their $30 trillion of assets to gold. If they were to up their exposure to just one percent (still extremely low) that would represent new demand for about $200 billion worth of gold, or about 4,700 tonnes at the metal's late-2013 exchange rate. That's more than 5-times the weight of gold that now resides in GLD, the biggest gold ETF, and about 125 percent of the late-2013 market capitalization of the entire gold mining sector. If pension funds allocate five percent of their assets to gold – which is still modest when viewed against historical records – the resulting $1.4 *trillion* increase in demand would overwhelm the market, virtually guaranteeing the kinds of defaults and shortages that almost took place in early 2013.

And that's just pension funds. The other institutional investors mentioned above have $70 trillion under management and also own very little gold. A one-percent swing in their allocation would send another $700 billion into this small, thin, already-out-of-balance market, further destabilizing it.

This shift in demand alone would be enough to change the industry's perspective on gold from "ignore" to "get some before the quarterly reporting deadline." Toss in a default by a major metals exchange or an announcement by China that its reserves are actually 4,000 tonnes and it intends to back the yuan with gold and use it instead of the dollar for international trade, and the combination of renewed interest in gold and loss of faith in the dollar would send the gold/dollar exchange rate soaring.

CHAPTER 22

THE CASE FOR $10,000+ GOLD

"Once you eliminate the impossible, whatever remains, no matter how improbable, must be the truth."

– Sherlock Holmes

It's easy to assert that gold is undervalued and heading higher. But *how far* it will rise in dollar terms is both a harder and vastly more important call because knowing when to sell is the true key to successful portfolio management. If you take your profits too soon, you might miss the final blow-off where substantial money can be made. But hold on too long and you risk being "round tripped" out of what would have been a nice gain.

So the big questions are not whether everyone should own some gold (they should), but *what is gold actually worth – and when does it become overvalued?* Each answer's elusiveness is one of the reasons that financial analysts and money managers are so indifferent to gold. It isn't used in major industries where supply/demand trends can be plotted and a price derived from the resulting intersections and divergences. It doesn't generate cash flow that can be projected into the future and discounted back to the present to arrive at a current value. It just sits there, actually costing a bit each year for storage (producing negative cash flow!). As a result, most professional investors are by temperament and training uninterested in owning it.

They are of course missing the crucial point that gold is not an investment. It is money, as we explained in

Chapter 20, and therein lays the key to valuing it. Because gold is stable (both physically as a tangible asset and in terms of supply growth) its value in dollars, euro, or yen depends not on anything going on with gold, but on changes in the demand for those fiat currencies. And that in turn depends on both their supply and the perception of their viability and future value.

James has been tracking the relationship between currencies and gold for decades, and has developed three useful valuation tools:

THE FEAR INDEX

The money in a fiat currency system has two components: the quantity of fiat currency itself, as measured by a broad monetary aggregate like M3, and the main assets backing it, which are gold reserves of the central bank and the marketable assets on bank balance sheets, principally their loans to customers and liquid instruments such as cash and securities held in their trading/investment portfolio. These can be illustrated in a currency's Monetary Balance Sheet.

Figure 22.1: Monetary Balance Sheet of the US dollar, September 30, 2013 (US$ billions)

Assets		Liabilities	
US Gold Reserve	349	Cash Currency	1,207
Bank Loans & Securities	15,043	Deposit Currency	14,185
Total Assets	15,392	Total Bank Liabilities (M3)*	15,392

*M3 calculated by ShadowStats

These numbers are derived as follows:

M3 is the total quantity of dollars in circulation. The Federal Reserve stopped reporting M3 in 2006, but ShadowStats calculates and makes available a credible version.

Cash Currency consists of the paper banknotes and coins that circulate in physical form, a figure which is compiled and reported by the Federal Reserve.

Deposit Currency is the quantity of dollars in bank accounts. They circulate in commerce via checks, wire/electronic transfers and plastic cards. Deposit Currency is derived by subtracting Cash Currency from Total Liabilities.

Total Assets are $15,392 billion because balance sheets must always balance (don't worry about why this is so; it just is).

US Gold Reserve – the balance sheet's tangible asset – is the 261.5 million ounces of gold stored in Ft Knox and other vaults, the market value of which is $349 billion (calculated using gold's exchange rate on September 30th, $1,336 per ounce).

Bank Loans & Securities is derived by subtracting the US Gold Reserve from Total Assets. This is an intangible asset, and therefore has counterparty risk.

Bank liabilities – bank deposits and paper dollar bills in circulation – are fixed. They don't go down if, for instance, interest rates rise, which makes bonds and other fixed rate loans less valuable, or the economy slows, causing a spike in loan defaults. In those circumstances, Bank Loans and Securities on the asset side of the ledger go down, but the liabilities remain unchanged. Because a balance sheet always has to balance, the value of the gold in the system has to rise to make up the difference. In other words, gold's exchange rate rises so that it becomes more valuable relative to the financial assets in the system.

Meanwhile, the value of bank assets also fluctuates based on the emotional state of the populace. When people are happy and optimistic, they tend to trust the local fiat currency and prefer it for its convenience, causing its exchange rate to rise relative to gold. When they're worried, they tend to prefer gold because it is perceived to be a safer asset than any fiat currency. This increased demand causes gold's exchange rate to rise, making it a relatively larger part of the total assets backing the fiat currency.

Which brings us at last to the Fear Index itself, which measures these fluctuations by calculating the ratio of gold valued at its current exchange rate to the amount of fiat currency in the system.

Figure 22.2: Calculation of the Fear Index as of September 30, 2013

$\dfrac{\text{US Gold Reserve * Gold's Exchange Rate}}{\text{M3}}$	= Fear Index
$\dfrac{261.5 \text{ million ounces} * \$1{,}336 \text{ per ounce}}{\$15{,}392 \text{ billion}}$	= 2.27%

Both the level of the Fear Index and its trend are useful pieces of information. A very low Fear Index implies excessive complacency that is probably producing all kinds of malinvestment or other distortions to the economy and will therefore be followed by some form of crisis. It also suggests that gold is undervalued. A very high reading reveals extreme worry about the health of the monetary system, which historically has led to a shaking out of past excesses followed by conservative behavior that repairs and eventually stabilizes the system. The trend of the Fear Index, meanwhile, condenses a lot of cultural cross-currents into illustrative data points with – based on 20th century history – great predictive value.

Figure 22.3 presents the Fear Index plotted monthly since the creation of the Federal Reserve in 1913. Note how the ups and downs correspond to the economic climate:

- Because the dollar was redeemable into gold until 1933, the Fear Index measured the extent to which the fractional reserve banking system had expanded or contracted. Though barely noticeable on the chart compared to the post-1933 period, the boom engineered during World War I ended with a post-war contraction, which was followed by the 1920s boom as banks expanded credit and held less gold in reserve.

- During the Great Depression the Fear Index soared to 29.84 percent, meaning that for every $100 of M3, $29.80 of its value was derived from the gold held in the US Gold Reserve, indicating an extreme desire for financial safety. Once the malinvestment of the 1920s was purged from the system, gradually better times emerged that produced a downtrend in the Fear Index lasting until the fiscal, monetary and geopolitical excesses of the 1970s once again terrified the markets.

- The chaos of the 1970s led to the appointment of aggressive inflation fighter Paul Volker as Fed chairman and the election of fiscal conservative Ronald Reagan to the presidency in 1980. Their policies helped to restore a measure of trust in the dollar and led to a resumption of the Fear Index downtrend that culminated with the tech stock boom of the 1990s. Repeating the experience of the 1920s, malinvestment and other bad decisions had again permeated the economy, but the impact on the banking system was not felt until 2008.

- Since the bursting of the tech stock bubble, fear – and a desire for tangible assets – has been gradually creeping back into the popular psyche, so the Fear Index has been in a well-defined 12-year uptrend.

Figure 22.3: The Fear Index, 1913 – 2013 (Monthly)

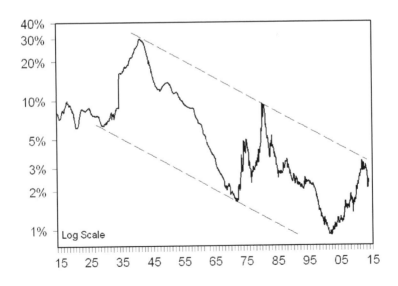

Three things can be inferred from this chart:

1) The historically low reading of 1.06 percent in 1999 meant that for every $100 circulating as currency, only $1.06 of that value was based on gold, and the balance of $98.94 was derived from the intangible assets within the banking system. This extraordinary level of complacency (euphoria, really) was a screaming buy signal for gold, and in the years that followed, gold's exchange rate rose from $255 ($8.198/gg) to a high of $1,920 ($61.729/gg) in 2011. A new dominant trend, this time upward, has been established.

2) The Great Gold Smackdown of 2013 marked a correction but not an end to the uptrend. The fundamentals – a rapidly increasing global money supply, faltering economic activity, soaring government debt, unprecedented financial leverage, questionable bank assets and extreme-but-unsustainable intervention in every major market including gold – point toward a resumption of upward momentum in both fear and gold.

3) The Fear Index is useful to measure gold's true value. The Index's average over the near-century covered in the above chart is 7.09 percent, compared to 2.27 percent in late 2013, which indicates that gold is undervalued. To return to the 'norm' – perhaps not the right word since most of the data measures an era of fiat currency – that this historical average represents and assuming no change in the other components, gold's exchange rate would need to rise to $4,173.

Figure 22.4: Using the Fear Index to Measure Gold's Undervaluation

$\dfrac{\text{Fear Index} * \text{M3}}{\text{US Gold Reserve}}$	= Gold's Exchange Rate
$\dfrac{7.09\% * \$15{,}392 \text{ billion}}{261.5 \text{ million ounces}}$	= \$4,173 per ounce

By assuming that a crisis will push the Fear Index higher in the future, we can also use the above formula to forecast gold's exchange rate. For example, to reach the 9.43 percent attained during the height of the dollar inflation in 1980, gold would need to rise to $5,551. But both history and fundamentals make it likely that the down-channel that has been in place since the 1930s will in time be pierced to the upside as gold returns to the center of the international monetary system and, led probably by the Chinese, takes a more important role in global commerce. So a more reasonable target might be midway between the 9.43 percent achieved in 1980 and the 29.86 percent reading of the Great Depression, or 19.64 percent. Further assume that the US Gold Reserve remains unchanged, and M3 grows by 8 percent per annum over the next three years to $19,389 billion.

Figure 22.5: Using Fear Index to Forecast Gold's Exchange Rate

$\dfrac{\text{Fear Index} * \text{M3}}{\text{US Gold Reserve}}$	= Gold's Exchange Rate
$\dfrac{19.64\% * \$19{,}389 \text{ billion}}{261.5 \text{ million ounces}}$	= $14,563 per ounce

Based on these assumptions, gold would rise to $14,563 per ounce ($468/gg). That may sound farfetched, but it has history on its side: From Sir Isaac Newton's circa-1700 creation of the gold standard until the mid-19th century, Bank of England policy required 40 percent gold reserves to back the British pound. Anything less was deemed too risky for a fractional reserve banking system. Plugging 40 percent into the above formula sends gold soaring to $29,659.

SOUND MONEY BENCHMARK

In 1934 following FDR's gold confiscation and dollar devaluation, it took $35 to exchange for one ounce of gold. Since then the dollar has lost considerable purchasing power. Logic dictates that gold should today be worth the number of dollars it would take to give it the same purchasing power that it held in 1934. In other words, gold should be worth its inflation-adjusted exchange rate.

The problem with this seemingly simple idea is that "inflation" is only one part of the monetary debasement chipping away at the dollar. First, as we explained in Chapter 6, the federal government has repeatedly changed the Consumer Price Index so that it now significantly understates the dollar's true loss of purchasing power. But adjusting for inflation, even when done competently and honestly, doesn't capture currency debasement, i.e., the increase in the supply of currency relative to its gold backing. (The term "debasement" refers to erosion of the dollar's soundness, which is determined by the weight of gold held by the central bank. Like the Roman emperors discussed in Chapter 1 who mixed base metals into coin, today the dollar is being debased by increasing the percent of intangible assets that back it.) Less gold at its current exchange rate is now backing the dollar than it did back in 1934, and this difference – which is measured by the Fear Index – needs to be taken into account to determine the dollar's equivalent value today to $35 in 1934.

The Fear Index captures these two factors – inflation and debasement – and distills them down to a single number. The Sound Money Benchmark (SMB) takes this number and compares it to a starting point. We use 1934, because after that year's devaluation the dollar was once again considered as good as gold, meaning that people were finding dollars more useful than gold, which started flowing back into the Treasury's vaults.

As of September 30, 2013, the Fear Index is 2.27 percent, compared to 14.69 percent in 1934. So the formula for calculating the dollar's equivalent 1934 value is:

Figure 22.6: Dollar Compared to its 1934 Gold Equivalent, September 30, 2013

Current Fear Index / 1934 Fear Index	* 1934 Gold Price	= 1934 Dollar Equivalent
2.27% / 14.69%	* $35 per ounce	= $5.41 per ounce

So in 1934-dollar terms, $35 with 14.69 percent gold backing is equivalent to $5.41 with only 2.27 percent gold in reserve. The changes in the soundness of the 1934-dollar are presented in the following chart, which is prepared to a logarithmic scale. Visually, a tripling from $2 to $6 is the same distance on this chart as a move from $10 to $30.

Figure 22.7: Sound Money Benchmark

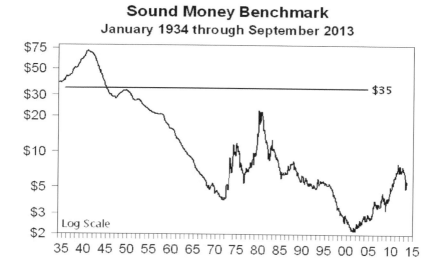

Sound Money Benchmark
January 1934 through September 2013

In the years immediately following the 1934 devaluation, the SMB rose, indicating that the quality of the dollar continued to improve. The deflation of the 1930s and the increasing weight of gold flowing into the Treasury were making the dollar – recognizing that it is just a substitute for gold – a better substitute than it was in 1934. Though never 100% backed by gold, the dollar was getting closer to the 'real thing'.

The SMB rose until the inflation induced by World War II started debasing the dollar, lowering its gold backing. From its all-time high in 1940, the SMB began a protracted decline. Even though the weight of gold in Treasury vaults continued to grow until the end of World War II, M3 increased more rapidly causing the percent of gold in reserve – each ounce of which was fixed at $35 – to drop.

In January 1945, the SMB returned to the $35 level, meaning that the dollar in January 1945 was essentially no different than a dollar in January 1934. But it was of lesser quality than the dollar that prevailed between those dates. And once the $35 barrier was broken, the soundness of the dollar kept falling, until gold started rising in its 1970s bull market. A similar uptrend in the SMB began a decade ago.

While measuring the soundness of the dollar is a useful exercise in its own right, the SMB can also be used in another way. If we assume that the January 1934 level was what was needed to solve the monetary problems of its day – and apparently it did achieve that aim because the previous gold flows out of the Treasury were reversed – we can calculate what exchange rate gold would need to rise to exactly replicate the quality of the 1934-dollar and thereby restore the same level of confidence in today's dollar.

The following formula calculates what gold's exchange rate to the dollar should be for the dollar today to have the same level of soundness – or *quality* if you prefer that term – as it did in 1934:

Figure 22.8: Dollar Benchmarked to its 1934 Gold Equivalent, September 2013

$$\frac{1}{\text{1934 Fear Index}} * \text{Current Gold Price} = \text{1934 Dollar Equivalent}$$

$$\frac{1}{14.69\%} * \$1,320 \text{ per ounce} = \$8,986 \text{ per ounce } (\$289/\text{gg})$$

The calculation here is different from the Fear Index but the conclusion is similar: Not only is the dollar no longer as "good as gold" as it was in 1934, but gold was grossly undervalued – and the dollar grossly overvalued – at their late-2013 exchange rate.

GOLD MONEY INDEX
The first two indicators are US-centric, in that they calculate relationships between the dollar, the US money supply and central bank gold reserves. But these formulas can just as easily be applied to other countries or the entire global financial system. The Gold Money Index does the latter by totaling up the fiat currency reserves of all the world's central banks and dividing that total by their gold reserves.

Figure 22.9: Gold Money Index, December 2012

Central Bank Fiat Currency ($) / Central Bank Gold Reserves (oz)	= Gold's Fair Value
$10,936 billion / 911.1 million ounces	= $12,003 per ounce

The premise is that only goods and services can ultimately pay for goods and services. When fiat currency is used in trade, the transaction is not finished until that currency is itself exchanged for something real. So the reserves building up in the world's major central banks are in effect credit that is being used to defer the payment of goods and services. In other words, China ships refrigerators to the United States which doesn't pay for them with goods and services, but with IOUs – over a trillion dollars worth in the case of China alone – that can in theory someday be turned into real wealth. All this pent-up purchasing power is inherently inflationary, which is to say it lowers the true value of the fiat currencies in which it is denominated.

The Gold Money Index measures this implied currency debasement in terms of gold. Note that the following chart is again prepared to logarithmic scale to more easily illustrate percentage changes in gold's exchange rate.

Figure 22.10: Gold Money Index, 1960 – 2012 (Yearly)

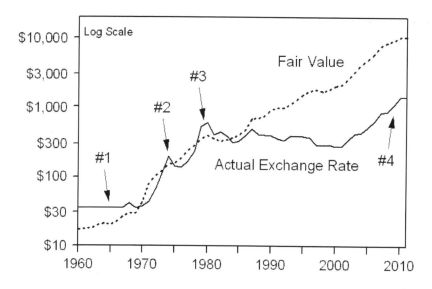

When gold's exchange rate drops significantly below its fair value, the Gold Money Index is saying that gold is undervalued – though it doesn't give precise buy points because undervaluation can continue for long periods and reach extreme levels, which is typical for financial bubbles. More important for this discussion, the Index pinpoints the exact historical moments at which gold was overvalued. At points 1, 2 & 3 on the chart gold was overvalued (i.e., its exchange rate was above its fair value). In 1980, gold's market value was fully twice its fair value (remember, this chart is logarithmic). When that happens again, it will be time to sell (or "spend") gold to buy undervalued productive assets – or just to enjoy life with the greatly-enhanced purchasing power your gold offers.

Since 1960, the amount of dollars, yen and euros held by the major central banks has increased 591-fold, while gold in their vaults has declined by 15.9 percent. Bringing the global monetary system back into balance will require gold to rise to around $12,000/oz ($385/gg). So gold, ending 2012 at point 4 on the chart, was just a little over 10 percent of its target, and its decline so far this year makes it even more wildly undervalued.

Each of the above three methods of valuing gold is useful, but together they are communicating an unmistakable message: Gold is exceptionally undervalued, and therefore offers a wonderful opportunity to both protect and enhance one's wealth as the Money Bubble enters its terminal phase.

CHAPTER 23

THE CASE FOR $100+ SILVER

"We believe silver will be this decade's gold."
– Eric Sprott, Sprott Asset Management

Silver is the other monetary metal. But because it is many other things besides money, its story is both more complex than gold's and potentially even more interesting. So let's start with a bit of history and background.

Silver was first mined in about 3000 BC in Anatolia (modern-day Turkey), where it became jewelry and coins for the early Mediterranean cultures. In the ensuing millennia it was discovered pretty much everywhere else, with the Americas being especially rich in high-grade deposits. Spain's 16th century exploitation of Bolivia, Peru and Mexico produced enough silver to cause one of the few cases of clear-cut inflation in a precious metals-based monetary system. More recently, new mining technologies have combined with major discoveries in Latin America and Africa to bring annual production up to about 800 million ounces. That's about ten times the weight of gold that's mined each year, which reflects silver's greater abundance in the earth's crust.

Rising Industrial Demand

At this point silver's story diverges from gold's. Recall that the vast majority of the aboveground gold stock is fabricated into bars, coins and monetary jewelry that function as a form of savings, with relatively little gold being used in industry or other applications. So gold is primarily money, while silver, despite its long monetary history, is today principally an industrial metal with a growing number of uses. Back in the days of film-based photography, for instance, it was a crucial part of photographic film. But because a lot of silver was recycled from exposed film, the industry wasn't as large a net consumer of silver as it appeared. So the replacement of traditional cameras with digital technology is not the death-blow to the silver market that one might expect. Instead, photographic demand and recycled supply have declined together, while a whole host of other uses have emerged in recent years. Among the most interesting:

Electronics. Silver's combination of conductivity and malleability make it crucial for circuit boards, flat-screen televisions, microwave ovens and radio frequency identification (RFID) tags, among many other things. And new gadgets containing silver are hitting the market on a near-daily basis.

Solar Panels. Most silicon-based solar panels contain silver paste, and with millions of panels being installed around the world, the sector is projected to consume about 100 million ounces per year by 2015. For most of the past decade, however, this market was seen as only a temporary boost for silver demand because "thin film" solar panels made of exotic rare earth elements like cadmium and tellurium were expected to eventually make silicon obsolete. But over the past few years a massive glut of silicon has depressed its price to the point where traditional silicon panels are cheap enough to stave off the thin film challenge. So solar now looks like a growing source of silver demand for at least the rest of the decade. Assuming installations rise at a modest (for that industry) 15 percent a year going forward and the amount of silver per panel doesn't change, by 2020 solar will use more than twice as much silver as in 2013.

Figure 23.1: Global Solar Power Installations (Megawatts)

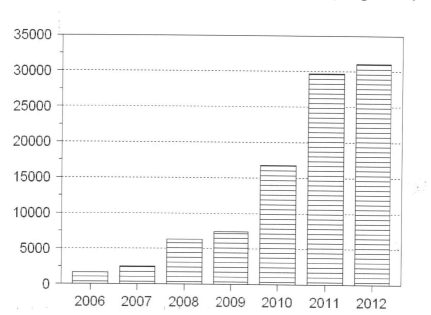

Other Uses. Silver, it turns out, kills germs, which opens up a whole range of interesting niches. Water purifiers infused with silver, for instance, can do the job without recourse to poisons like chlorine. Washing machines with a bit of silver help sterilize clothes, while socks, shirts and underwear with silver threads resist odor. Meanwhile, silver oxide batteries have favorable power-to-weight ratios that make them attractive for uses where weight is a crucial consideration. The list goes on and new uses are constantly being discovered, so silver's prospects in the 21st century industrial world seem bright.

Because in most of the above uses the amount of silver is relatively small, it is seldom recovered when the device is scrapped. So this silver is taken off the market, which is one of the big differences between the two monetary metals. Recall from Chapter 20 that when gold is mined it almost always adds permanently to the aboveground stock because so little of it is used in industrial applications, and where it is used it is generally recycled because of its high value.

Limited Supply

As for how much silver exists aboveground, that's a tougher question. It used to be stockpiled by governments, both as a strategic metal (to guarantee a supply for military and industrial uses) and as part of monetary reserves. But in the 1980s most governments began to sell off their silver, until by early in the 2000s there was virtually nothing left in official inventories.

Because gold is saved while silver is converted to industrial uses and lost, the ratio of available aboveground silver to gold is lower than the ratio of the two metals' mine production. Canadian investment company Sprott Asset Management puts it at about 3:1. In other words, for those who would acquire the metals as money, there is three times as much silver available as gold. But gold's late-2013 exchange rate was 60 times higher than silver's price ($1320 vs. $22), which implies that silver is cheap compared to gold. (Note that we refer to silver's "price" rather than exchange rate because it is an industrial commodity as well as money.)

So think of silver as a gold-substitute, another form of money that can be held as a tangible asset outside of the banking system. A great example of this substitution impulse was the response of Indians to their government's 2013 restrictions on the importation of gold. They simply switched to silver, importing a record 6,000 metric tons, an amount equal to 20 percent of that year's global mine production.

If gold is undervalued and silver is cheap relative to gold, then silver at its late 2013 price appears to be a steal. But here again, the fact that silver is an industrial metal makes its story a bit more complicated. Would, for instance, a jump in the silver price cause demand from solar panel or microchip makers to fall, offsetting the effects of rising coin and bar sales?

Yes and no. With solar panel prices falling, a rising silver price could make the metal an uncomfortably large cost component and lead the industry to minimize the amount of silver in each panel (this happened to an extent during silver's 2011 price spike). But at the moment there is no cheaper substitute in sight, so the industry will use plenty of silver for at least the balance of this decade. In most other kinds of electronics, meanwhile, the amount of silver in each device is miniscule and demand is not price-sensitive. So even at substantially higher prices, industrial demand for silver is likely to keep rising faster than mine output.

Another Manipulated Market

Believe it or not, the manipulation of the silver price in the "paper" futures markets is even more blatant than for gold. Ted Butler, an independent silver analyst who has written extensively to expose silver market manipulation, explained his view in a 2012 interview with Jim Puplava's Financial Sense website. A few excerpts:

"The daily average silver trade on the Comex is approximately 300 million ounces, versus daily mine production of about 2 million ounces. [In the futures market] you have to have one long contract, one short contract to equal one open interest. The long side looks diverse with any number of market participants, whereas the short side is concentrated among what we call the "commercials," mostly New York banks and traders. It is this concentration and large size of the short side that indicates manipulation. The commercials basically have achieved dominance in price. They can put the price on a short-term basis any which way they want.

Why are they doing it? First, to make money in the futures market. Second, because commercial fabricators use silver and [manipulation] enables them to buy it as cheaply as possible."

There is also another reason: A rising silver price would undermine the government's attempt to keep a lid on gold because for silver to rise while gold stagnates would imply that gold is being suppressed.

As for how silver can rise from $6 per ounce in 2006 to $21 per ounce in late 2013 if it's artificially depressed, market intervention can only go so far. When an asset is undervalued, savvy buyers will accumulate it, so the best that manipulators can do is moderate the price increase for as long as possible, much like an army might stage a managed retreat.

In 2008, after being deluged with complaints from silver buyers disturbed by its price action and accusations of numerous analysts and investors, the Commodity Futures Trading Commission (CFTC) opened an investigation of Comex silver trading. Five years later, in September 2013, it dropped the case, claiming that, "Based upon the law and evidence as they exist at this time, there is not a viable basis to bring an enforcement action with respect to any firm or its employees related to our investigation of silver markets." The manipulators are now free to continue their short-term games.

Note, however, how the primary motives of silver and gold manipulators differ. Where gold is depressed purely to prevent it from revealing the weakness of fiat currencies, silver is pushed down mainly to allow the big users of the metal to buy it cheaply. The commercials are, in effect, improving the long-term silver picture by using ever-greater amounts of it, even while they muddy up the short-term market.

Physical Demand Will Swamp Supply

Gold demand now comes mostly from individuals and some central banks, especially in Asia, that are aggressively buying the metal. With silver, the main non-industrial buyers are individuals lured by silver's low price relative to gold. In 2013, Sprott Asset Management reported that its customers were putting the same amount of money into the two metals, indicating that 50 times as many silver ounces were being purchased as gold ounces.

How long can savers continue to buy fifty times as much silver as gold when the ratio of available silver to gold is only 3:1? It's not clear, but this is not the only ratio that is out of balance. Historically – that is, for the 3,000 years prior to the last few decades – gold was generally no more than 16 times as valuable as silver when they were both used as money. As we mentioned earlier, the ratio of silver ounces mined to gold ounces is about 10:1, yet in late 2013 an ounce of gold cost 60 times as much as an ounce of silver.

Meanwhile, the impact of the 2013 gold/silver price correction on the mining industry is far more meaningful for silver than gold. Because virtually all the gold that has ever been mined is still around, annual mine output is only about 1.8 percent of total available gold. So a slowdown in gold production makes relatively little difference to gold's exchange rate. But for silver, since most of what has been produced is gone, current mine output is much higher in relation to available aboveground stocks. And if, as seems likely, silver production declines in coming years as mines that are unprofitable at late 2013 prices are closed and new ones delayed, this will bring the looming supply crunch that much nearer.

We'll go out on a limb to say that when gold makes its epic run from $1,300 to $10,000-plus, silver will not only keep up, it will return to something close to its historical ratio to gold, perhaps 20:1. $1/20^{th}$ of $10,000 is $500, which makes our forecast of a five-fold rise to $100 quite conservative.

CHAPTER 24

BULLION: MONEY, NOT AN INVESTMENT

"Money is gold, nothing else."
– J.P. Morgan

If gold and silver are money, then they are not investments. An investment is something that, if successful, generates cash flow and potentially capital gains, but if less successful can produce a capital loss. Money, in contrast, *is* capital. It is what you receive when you sell an investment. It does not generate cash flow and does not "work" for you the way an investment does. But sound money does preserve existing wealth by maintaining its purchasing power over long periods of time. Physical gold and silver, or "bullion" as they are often called, do this better than any fiat currency.

Think of bullion as cash under the mattress, only better, because today's paper cash loses value steadily, thus eroding your purchasing power, while gold and silver maintain their purchasing power over the long term. Recall from Chapter 1 that an ounce of gold will buy the same amount of life's necessities as it did decades or centuries ago, while a dollar buys maybe 5 percent as much as it did in 1971. Figure 24.1 shows how gold and silver fared versus nine major fiat currencies during the first 12 years of this century.

Figure 24.1: Gold and Silver versus Selected Currencies, 2001 – 2012, Percent Annual Change

Gold

	USD	AUD	CAD	CNY	EUR	INR	JPY	CHF	GBP
2001	2.5	11.3	8.8	2.5	8.1	5.8	17.4	5.0	5.4
2002	24.7	13.5	23.7	24.8	5.9	24.0	13.0	3.9	12.7
2003	19.6	-10.5	-2.2	19.5	-0.5	13.5	7.9	7.0	7.9
2004	5.2	1.4	-2.0	5.2	-2.1	0.0	0.9	-3.0	-2.0
2005	18.2	25.6	14.5	15.2	35.1	22.8	35.7	36.2	31.8
2006	22.8	14.4	22.8	18.8	10.2	20.5	24.0	13.9	7.8
2007	31.4	18.1	11.5	22.9	18.8	17.4	23.4	22.1	29.7
2008	5.8	33.0	31.1	-1.0	11.0	30.5	-14.0	-0.3	43.7
2009	23.9	-3.6	5.9	24.0	20.4	18.4	27.1	20.3	12.1
2010	29.8	15.1	24.2	25.5	40.2	25.3	13.9	17.4	36.3
2011	10.2	8.8	11.9	5.1	12.7	30.4	3.9	10.2	9.2
2012	7.0	5.5	4.8	5.9	5.2	10.7	20.4	4.5	2.2
Avg.	16.8	11.0	12.9	14.0	13.8	18.3	14.5	11.4	16.4

Silver

	USD	AUD	CAD	CNY	EUR	INR	JPY	CHF	GBP
2001	-0.1	8.5	6.1	-0.1	5.3	3.1	14.4	2.3	2.7
2002	4.8	-4.6	4.0	4.9	-11.0	4.3	-5.0	-12.6	-5.3
2003	24.0	-7.3	1.4	23.9	3.2	17.7	11.9	11.0	11.9
2004	14.3	10.2	6.5	14.3	6.4	8.6	9.6	5.4	6.5
2005	29.6	37.7	25.5	26.3	48.1	34.6	48.8	49.3	44.4
2006	45.3	35.3	45.3	40.5	30.4	42.6	46.7	34.8	27.5
2007	15.4	3.7	-2.1	7.9	4.3	3.1	8.3	7.2	13.9
2008	-23.8	-4.3	-5.7	-28.8	-20.1	-6.1	-38.1	-28.2	3.4
2009	49.3	16.1	27.6	49.3	45.0	42.6	53.0	44.9	35.0
2010	83.7	63.0	75.8	77.7	98.5	77.4	61.2	66.2	93.0
2011	-9.8	-11.0	-8.4	-14.0	-7.8	6.7	-15.0	-9.8	-10.7
2012	8.2	6.8	6.0	7.1	6.5	12.0	21.8	5.7	3.4
Avg.	20.1	12.9	15.2	17.4	17.4	20.6	18.1	14.7	18.8

USD = US dollar	CNY = Chinese yuan	JPY = Japanese yen
AUD = Australian dollar	EUR = euro	CHF = Swiss franc
CAD = Canadian dollar	INR = Indian rupee	GBP = British pound

One thing that stands out on the preceding table is the apparent volatility of gold and silver. Using gold in 2008 as an example, how can something rise by 43.7 percent against the British pound *and* fall by 14.0 percent against the Japanese yen in the same year, and still claim to be a stable form of savings? There are two explanations for this seeming paradox.

First, in a dynamic economy the demand for money varies from week to week and year to year. When demand for sound money rises, more capital flows into gold and its exchange rate rises. When demand falls, so does gold when measured in dollars. But these fluctuations even out over time. Recall from Chapter 19 that the price of crude oil when measured in ounces of gold has bounced around in the short run but been remarkably stable over longer periods of time.

The other answer is that the apparent volatility arises from an observer using, so to speak, the wrong end of the telescope. Gold looks volatile when it is measured in fiat currencies – but those currencies are themselves extremely volatile. So variations in the gold/dollar exchange rate are actually fluctuations in the value of the dollar, not of gold. To illustrate the point, pretend for a moment that you're in a boat looking at the shore. You know that the apparent up and down movement of the shore is actually the boat rising and falling on passing waves, and that the shore is stable. It's the same thing with money. Trying to perform economic calculation with a fiat currency is like being in the boat but assuming that the shore is moving up and down. When gold is rising or falling, the price of commodities traded in dollars on international markets rise or fall too, even in the short-term. So if gold falls, say, 0.2 per cent on any given day, crude oil may have also fallen by the same amount, meaning that gold's purchasing power (when measured against crude oil) actually remains unchanged.

The 2008 example mentioned above, when gold fell by 14 percent against the Japanese yen while rising 43.7 percent against the British pound does make gold appear volatile. But if we look at the 12-year average, the results for these two currencies are very similar; gold rose 14.5 percent per annum in yen and 16.4 percent in pounds. Clearly, the volatility in the short-term arises from the fluctuations in exchange rates between the yen and pound, both of which over time are losing purchasing power when compared to gold.

Conventional wisdom views today's national currencies as "floating" relative to one another, meaning that they bob up-and-down depending on factors impacting their supply and demand. But in reality they're all sinking together, relative to the stable purchasing power of gold.

So gold is not something one analyzes like a stock or bond, because standard investment techniques require future cash flows to calculate a present value. Instead, gold is simply where you park the portion of your capital – your money – until you are ready to spend it, invest it or save for the long haul. Figure 24.2 illustrates the role played by money as a store of value in a portfolio, where it forms the bottom layer of capital that is preserved in the safest and most liquid possible form, ready to spend, invest or save. Above that layer, investments are made to take increasing risks in pursuit of higher returns.

Figure 24.2: Portfolio Composition

Measurement	Portfolio Components	Assets by Risk Level	Allocation
Units of Wealth (expressed in terms of purchasing power)	Investments – Risk vs. Reward (wealth producing assets)	other	X%
		real estate	
		bonds	
		stocks	
	Money – Safety & Liquidity (wealth preserving assets)	dollars, euros, yen, etc.	Y%
		gold and/or silver	

Where does dollar cash fit into such a portfolio? In the safety/liquidity layer, but above gold on the risk spectrum. The dollar has counterparty risk, but gold does not. Nor can gold be debased with a printing press. But a certain amount of fiat currency is necessary for day-to-day transactions, both because gold in dollar terms fluctuates in the short run and because fiat currencies are convenient mediums of exchange, highly portable, required for use in many instances, and – for the moment – widely accepted. And because their purchasing power continuously erodes, they're easy to part with compared to gold and silver. How much dollar cash to keep on hand is an individual decision based on spending needs, the interest rates available on bank deposits and money market funds and of course how solid and trustworthy the financial system seems at any given time.

***Brief Digression: Choose Your Bank Wisely.** Dollars are a liability of the Federal Reserve and the commercial banks that issue them. These banks enjoy a government-granted monopoly on the issuance of liabilities that circulate as* *currency, which is why you will never see an IBM banknote or Microsoft coin circulating as currency, and why Disney 'dollars' can only be used in the company's theme parks.*

A liability does not have value in and of itself. So dollars have value only because they are backed by assets that do have value, including the cash, bank loans, and financial securities – mainly government bonds – owned by banks. (See the Monetary Balance Sheet of the US dollar in Chapter 22.)

Legal tender laws mandate that dollars be treated as interchangeable, but not all banks are the same. Some have riskier assets than others, meaning that dollars on deposit in a bank with top quality assets are inherently safer than those on deposit in a weaker bank. This didn't matter when the Federal Deposit Insurance Corporation (FDIC) guaranteed all qualifying accounts without question. But in the current era of bail-ins, where depositors are on the hook for their bank's losses, the differences in bank quality are suddenly crucial. The FDIC has funds sufficient to cover 0.4 percent of insured deposits (that's only 40¢ of every $100). So when banks once again start failing, which one has your money might determine whether you get it back.

The portions of the portfolio allocated to money or investments can vary, depending on one's preferences and perception of the investment opportunities available. Warren Buffett defines investing as "the transfer to others of purchasing power now with the reasoned expectation of receiving more purchasing power...in the future." Logically, money should also be gauged by the same measurement. So to get a true sense of wealth – and whether the portfolio is growing or not – it should be measured in terms of purchasing power, using whatever is the strongest currency for the period being evaluated. For the past twelve years it has been gold, but for two decades prior to that, the strongest currency was the Swiss franc.

But our main purpose here is to make the case for that bottom layer of liquidity to be kept in precious metals as a long-term store of purchasing power. With that in mind, let's consider the technicalities of buying and storing bullion.

Types of Bullion

Physical precious metals come in a variety of sizes and shapes. Central banks and other financial institutions prefer gold bars weighing approximately 400-ounces that meet the purity and shape standards set by the London Bullion Market Association. Individuals, meanwhile, generally own gold bullion in forms including fraction-of-an-ounce coins, 1-ounce coins, and bars up to 1-kilo (31.1 ounces). Silver bullion ranges from one-ounce coins and bars to 10, 100, and 1,000-ounce bars.

Bullion coins and bars are produced by national mints like the U.S. Mint (gold eagles and buffalos, and silver eagles), Royal Canadian Mint (gold and silver maple leafs), and various other national mints (British sovereign, Austrian philharmonics, South African krugerrands). Private mints like Canada's Northwest Territorial Mint and Australia's Perth Mint specialize in non-national silver bars and private-label coins (known as "rounds"). The national mints generally sell to wholesalers who sell to dealers who sell to individuals, which can result in a fairly high mark-up at the retail level. So while there are advantages to owning well-recognized forms of bullion like gold eagles or maple leafs (for example, they often are easier to sell), our advice is to get the most metal for your money and therefore focus on mark-up rather than name recognition.

Also consider that each bar or coin has to be fabricated and shipped. These costs are relatively fixed regardless of the weight of the coin or bar, and are therefore higher per-ounce for smaller coins and bars. So buying the largest possible bar or coin minimizes these costs as a percentage of your outlay. Among the smaller pieces, one-ounce gold coins and bars tend to have the lowest mark-ups (with bars generally being cheaper than coins), so that weight is best for gold. For silver, one-ounce is also a good weight, but larger bars in the 10-ounce and 100-ounce range offer more metal for the money and are also popular.

Meanwhile, do not ignore the added benefit that comes from buying monetary jewelry, namely, that you can wear your savings. At souks in the Middle East and stores in Asia, monetary jewelry – which ranges from 22-karat up to 24-karat, which is 99.9 per cent gold – is sold on the same basis as coins and bars in the West, with a mark-up over the gold content to cover fabrication, shipping and handling costs. Interestingly, whether you are buying a one-ounce coin in New York or one-ounce necklace in Dubai the mark-up is about the same.

Where to Buy It

Local coin shops carry bullion (and in any event are great connections to cultivate) while the best online dealers offer fast delivery and frequently lower prices. In either case, it is crucial to find a *reputable* dealer because the precious metals market is rife with various kinds of dodgy players, from untested and undercapitalized newcomers to predatory established sellers that exploit the public's ignorance with excessive mark-ups, hidden charges, and bad service. So before choosing a dealer, check the firm's online reviews and Better Business Bureau ranking. A good resource for finding a dealer that is both reputable and reasonable is

GoldPrice.org, http://www.goldprice.org, which compares prices across numerous dealers.

How to Buy It

Because the precious metals markets are both naturally volatile and overtly manipulated, converting all of one's cash into bullion in one fell swoop is probably a bad idea – as far too many people discovered during the brutal corrections that occurred in 2008 and 2013. A better approach is dollar cost averaging, in which a buyer orders the same amount of something in each successive time period. For precious metals, this might mean $100 or $5,000 a month (whatever fits your budget) of various sizes of gold and silver coins until the base layer of capital has been created, followed by smaller monthly purchases thereafter. The attraction of a steady, automatic plan is that when prices are low, the same amount of currency buys more metal, and when prices are high it buys less. Over time – at least when the long-term trend is positive, as it is for both gold and silver – the average price ends up being very attractive. And – crucially for psychological reasons – a disciplined strategy eliminates the noise from short-term price swings that can otherwise distract one's attention and disrupt purchase decisions. And last but not least, it gives periodic corrections in the precious metals a positive aspect by making it possible to buy more ounces at lower prices. Recall from Chapter 12 that China and Russia seem to be using a slightly more aggressive form of dollar-cost-averaging by stepping up their buying when prices fall.

How to Store It

Now for the complicated part of the story. Once purchased, precious metals have to reside somewhere, and – we can't stress this enough – *there is no perfect storage solution.* Every option involves risk – some more than others – and requires thought, so it is crucial to choose options with appropriate combinations of risk and complexity that suit your needs and temperament. Since one of the points of accumulating a base layer of precious metals is to be able to sleep peacefully in the knowledge that your assets are diversified, it is advisable to protect your precious metals by dividing them into several caches. Among the possibilities:

Professional Storage. The simplest way to store precious metals is to pay someone else to do it. James' company GoldMoney, for instance, is based in Great Britain and contracts with well-established vault operators in the UK, Switzerland, Canada, Hong Kong and Singapore to store clients' precious metals. The bars are audited, insured and available for delivery upon request. Other storage options include BullionVault in London and Zurich-based GoldSwitzerland.

Not so long ago the list of trusted remote storage options would have included the big Swiss and other European and American banks, but that is emphatically no longer the case. Recall from Chapter 21 that the recent crisis in the gold market began when Dutch bank ABN Amro in effect defaulted on its gold storage promise by refusing to return customers' gold. A similar episode occurred in 2007 when several Morgan Stanley customers alleged the silver they owned was not being stored in a vault, even though they were paying storage fees. The case was eventually settled out of court, but it does provide some insight about the risks of storage and today's unethical global banks which, because their main business is lending, might be tempted to secretly lend out your metal. So when seeking professional storage, use companies that specialize exclusively in that business, and avoid banks.

Safe Deposit Boxes. Most bank branches have vaults full of drawers in which their customers can store valuables. In theory, whatever is stored there stays there, and 99 percent of the time that's how it works. But not always. Banks can fail or be robbed, and given the intrusions the NSA and IRS are making into Americans' private affairs and the growing pressure on developed-world governments to start seizing assets, a safe deposit box poses some risk. So it may be an acceptable choice for some of one's bullion, but emphatically not all of it.

Home Storage. "Metal in hand" is the watchword of a big part of the sound money community, with good reason. If you have it, then it can't just disappear when a coin dealer stops returning customer phone calls or the government decides to seize bank assets. And, truth be told, a big stack of gold and/or silver coins is a very nice, reassuring thing to see, touch, and contemplate.

But here more than anywhere else in the "where to store it" discussion, the devil is in the details. Home storage of precious metals is literally a book-length subject and is a hotly-debated topic online, so when deciding whether and how to store some precious metals at home, plenty of advice is available. And good advice is necessary because the range of factors that must be considered is legion. Besides where to hide a cache of bullion and how to package it to keep it safe from its environment, there's the question whom to tell about it. If too few know, it may never be found. If too many (or the wrong people) know, word might get out and attract unwanted attention.

Meanwhile, each home-storage choice carries its own risks. Hide your bullion in a safe, and that's the first place burglars will look. Bury it in the back yard, and it might be discovered by thieves with metal detectors. Keep it in a dresser drawer, and burglars might get a pleasant surprise when looking for cash or jewelry. Fail to properly insulate it, and bullion can melt or be otherwise damaged in a house fire.

But these risks are all manageable. Over the years, a number of ingenious solutions to the hiding-place question have been developed. Here are four drawn from a highly-instructive article published on the Gold Silver Worlds website in early 2013:

The Freezer. "Regardless of whether you own or rent, the freezer is an indispensable appliance found virtually in all homes, apartments, etc. The accessibility and convenience of this option is excellent, as it does not require any structural modification to your living space. Food items such as turkey, chicken, ice cream containers, etc., can be carefully stuffed with your valuables, effectively fireproofing them in the process. The temperature itself will have preservative effects. Space is a limitation here, but because freezers are rarely robbery targets, they can serve as a discrete secondary storage option."

Artificial Rocks. "Camouflaging your storage site into the local topography is a time-tested solution. Rocks typically do not draw much attention and can fit into a variety of landscapes. Artificial rocks with hollow storage cavities can be purchased online through a simple internet search. Search results will feature a wealth of shapes, sizes, and colors, ranging in capacity to accommodate a few dozen to several hundred ounces. This solution is essentially fireproof and can be extremely labor intensive in the event of theft."

Flower Pots. "The density and weight of larger gardening pots can make them ideal for storing larger quantities of precious metals. Their bases can be altered to feature a spacious non-visible compartment within. Larger pots can weigh several hundred pounds and require skill to successfully penetrate, reducing the probability of theft. The layer of soil acts as a protective fireproof barrier. A larger base can work well for several dozen coin tubes or even bars. Remember to always waterproof your metals before storing."

Unused Pipes. "Pipes are both abundant and distributed throughout most homes. A gas or water pipe which is no longer in use is ideal. Caps can be added to the ends of pipes to hold additional metals. Coins can easily be hidden either within a non-functional pipe or within a pipe cap you may easily purchase. Pipe storage also is a theft deterrent because of the unlikelihood that a time-constrained intruder will have time to scan your entire plumbing or gas pipelines system."

The article's list of possible hiding places continues through table lamp bases, backyard grills, and fake appliances. And the complete range of hiding places is limited only by one's imagination.

But Avoid ETFs!

Among the most popular precious metals investment vehicles are exchange traded funds (ETFs) like GLD and SLV that claim to store gold and silver in vaults and issue shares representing this metal. The idea is that someone wanting exposure to precious metals can dispense with all the previously-discussed thought and work and just buy one of these stocks. But these funds are not what they seem.

For one thing, the rules governing their metal storage facilities aren't tight enough to guarantee that the metal is actually there. It might, like central bank gold, be lent out to other entities that might or might not be able to return it. Meanwhile, their publicly-traded shares are open to manipulation by the bullion banks and others who have an interest in suppressing rather than profiting from higher precious metals. Recall from Chapter 21 that GLD was in effect looted by the bullion banks during the orchestrated gold take-down of mid-2013.

So precious metals ETFs are emphatically not a substitute for owning actual metal because they don't provide ownership. The metal is "unallocated" which means that it belongs to the fund rather than the investor, who is in effect an unsecured creditor totally reliant upon the entity managing the fund. So rather than owning gold or silver, the buyer of a share in one of these ETFs has simply lent the fund manager some money. In a crunch, these ETFs might easily run out of metal, be exposed as frauds, and crash in price – at exactly the moment when precious metals themselves are soaring. So view these funds as having counterparty risk like any other liability of a bank or brokerage house. In other words, with an ETF you own shares, not gold, so they are financial rather than tangible assets and destined to go the way of bank stocks and government bonds in the coming transition.

CHAPTER 25

GOLD AND SILVER MINERS: METAL IN THE GROUND

"In a free country the monetary unit rests upon a fixed foundation of gold or gold and silver, independent of the ruling politicians."

– Howard Buffett, father of Wall Street legend Warren Buffett

The fact that gold is money rather than an investment doesn't mean investors can't "make money" in precious metals. It just means that people wanting to build rather than preserve capital have to look beyond bullion, for instance to the companies that mine it.

Shares in the best gold and silver miners will, we believe, rise far faster than the underlying metals – but will also fall much faster during the metals' periodic corrections. And individual mining companies will do better or worse depending on numerous factors completely unrelated to the precious metals markets, including management decisions, balance sheet issues and political and environmental developments. The resulting variability is what separates an investment, driven by risk-vs.-return criteria, from cash, which should simply protect its owner's purchasing power. As they've demonstrated over the past decade, the miners clearly belong in the investment part of your portfolio.

As this is written in late 2013, the miners are in a uniquely stressful situation. This makes choosing wisely among them even more crucial than usual. So we'll set the stage with a little history:

BUST BOOM BUST

After soaring to record highs in 1980, gold and silver began a long, grinding two-decade-long decline as Paul Volker's Fed restored respect for the dollar in the 1980s and the internet bubble captured the imagination of investors in the 1990s. The pendulum swung away from tangible assets and back to financials, and as the price of their product went down, so, with only rare exceptions, did the miners' profits and share prices. By the late 1990s, neither precious metals nor mining stocks were mentioned in polite financial company.

The pendulum began to swing the other way in 2000 when tech stocks crashed and precious metals began to recover. From a 1999 low of $253 per ounce ($8.13/gg), gold rose fitfully in the early 00s, piercing the psychologically important $500 ($16/gg) level in 2005. And investors, now somewhat excited about precious metals, discovered that a well-run miner offered a double-barreled exposure to its product, since it both mines existing deposits and can find more via exploration or acquisition. Mining shares began to rise.

After a stomach-churning correction during the 2008 financial crisis, the real fun started. The world's governments responded to the bursting of the housing bubble with unprecedented monetary stimulus. Deficits soared, interest rates plunged and the market concluded that unrestrained money creation – implying as it does rising inflation and a weaker currency – was rocket fuel for precious metals. By 2010 investors looked at the sector and saw rising metals prices *and* rising mine production, and they bought in. The miners were among the best performing asset classes, if not the best – for a time.

Easy Money, Bad Decisions

In the heat of this raging bull market, investors' image of the ideal mining company began to change. Where proven, low-cost ore deposits and rock-solid balance sheets once commanded a premium, now low-quality/high-cost-but-potentially-large deposits began to attract investor interest and money. The logic was simple and seemed foolproof: As metal prices moved up, those high-cost ore bodies would yield big profits when they were eventually mined at a much higher metal price. And this financial leverage was viewed as a sign of decisive management.

Thus incented, mining executives embarked on an empire building spree, using investors' money to find or buy big, low-grade deposits in a rush to accumulate the most ounces in the ground. That those ounces might cost more than the current metal price to extract (especially considering the huge capital expenditures required to build the mine) was overlooked because rising precious metal prices would, it was now believed, overcome these and any other obstacles.

This desire for growth at any cost soon began to corrupt the people and processes charged with protecting investors. Engineers hired to assess an ore deposit's size and economics discovered, as had real estate appraisers and bond rating agencies during the housing bubble that their paychecks depended on deals getting done. So reports were generated that made ore deposits look far more attractive and easier to get at than turned out to be the case. Investment banks, ever-willing to feed a hot market, began shoveling new stock offerings into the hands of uninformed investors as fast as the documents could be signed.

Combine overoptimistic projections with huge amounts of naïve money looking for action, and the nearly-inevitable result was an overextended industry ripe for disappointment. Costs began to soar as mines paid top dollar for experienced workers and state-of-the-art earth moving and ore processing equipment, while the price of the oil needed to run those earth movers recovered from post-crash lows. Then the new mines began producing, and all those unrealistic resource quality analyses were exposed, revealing managements', ahem, less-than-perfect foresight. Ore grades (the amount of metal in a given ton of rock) turned out to be far lower than expected, with the cost of producing an ounce of metal soaring above the spot price for many miners.

And even the well-managed miners soon found themselves up against something they couldn't control, when precious metals prices began to fall. This combination of rising costs and falling revenue was hard on the established miners but catastrophic for many "juniors." Small Canadian silver miner Great Panther Silver, to take just one of many, many possible examples, was profitable in 2012 with a cash production cost of about US$9 per ounce. By the first quarter of 2013, its cash cost had soared to $18 and the company was emphatically not profitable. Its solid balance sheet gave it some breathing room, but for dozens of other juniors the sudden evaporation of cash flow was fatal.

Figure 25.1 Average Gold Cash Production Costs of Large Miners (US dollars per ounce)

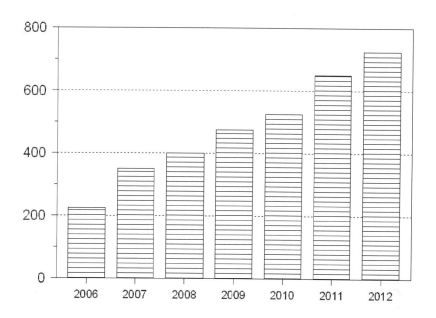

The market value of the average miner plunged, giving back virtually all the gains of the previous bull market. Figure 25.2, which shows the share price of Newmont Mining, a large, diversified gold miner, is representative: A huge few years followed by a precipitous decline, as higher costs ran head-on into a falling gold market.

Figure 25.2: Newmont Mining (NEM) share price, 1990–2013

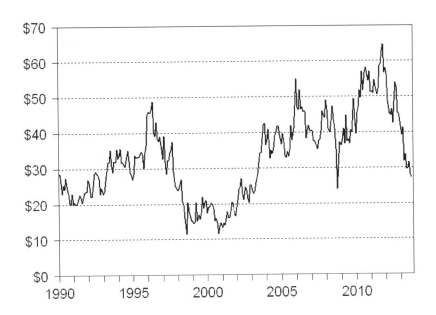

The mutual funds specializing in precious metals miners fared no better. Figure 25.3 shows the Market Vectors Junior Gold Miners ETF (GDXJ), which soared in 2011 and crashed in 2012 as the value of its constituent junior miners shares evaporated.

Figure 25.3: Market Vectors Junior Gold Miners, 2010 – 2013

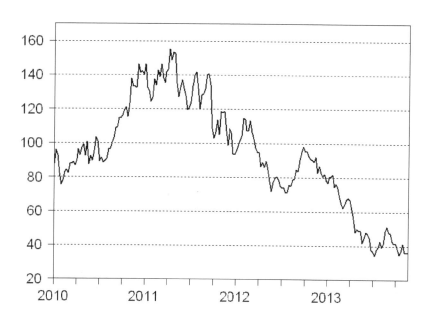

FOCUSED MINDS

The upside of an existential crisis is that it focuses the mind. Mining CEOs responsible for ill-fated acquisitions, uneconomic projects and cost-overruns have been shown the door *en masse*, and their replacements have a very different mandate. As incoming Newmont CEO Gary Goldberg told investors at his 2013 induction ceremony, "My immediate priorities are to drive a more disciplined approach to capital allocation and to set and meet aggressive cost targets." Such sentiments are echoed in virtually every mining company report these days, which in practice means the following:

Delaying or Canceling New Projects

Only low-cost, low-risk projects are being green-lighted. Canadian gold miner Barrick Gold, for instance, recently announced the cancellation or deferral of approximately $4 billion in previously-budgeted capital spending. As it explained in its 2012 annual report, "In today's challenging environment, Barrick has no plans to build any new mines. We have a number of world class ore-bodies around the world which hold sizeable economic potential, but which currently do not meet our investment criteria. In the interim, we will spend the minimum amount of capital required to maintain the economic potential of these assets." Included in the projects put on ice is the huge Pascua Lama project in Chile, which was already over budget and behind schedule, and produced a $5.1 billion write-down in 2013's second quarter.

Reporting Honest Numbers

"Cash cost of production," the standard yardstick by which miners have traditionally been measured, has turned out to be wildly misleading because it doesn't include many other, highly-variable costs of doing business such as administrator salaries, interest on debt, and depreciation of expensive property and equipment. So in 2013 the industry adopted "all-in sustaining costs" as the preferred measure. As Chuck Jeannes, CEO of Canadian miner Goldcorp admitted in his company's 2012 annual report, "The traditional measure of cash costs is not a realistic view. To produce an ounce of gold, we not only incur operating costs, but we spend sustaining capital at the sites, we spend G&A to keep the lights on, and we spend dollars to explore, to sustain our future. If you put all those together, that's an all-in sustaining cash cost. It's a much more transparent and accurate way of judging the real costs of getting an ounce of gold out of the ground."

When calculated in this way, the aggregate breakeven cost for a number of big precious metals miners and most small ones is close to or slightly above late-2013 spot metal prices. That's the number that will be widely reported going forward, giving a much more sober view of the industry.

ONE UGLY YEAR
The precious metals miners are adjusting to their new reality, but the process will be both protracted and painful. In late 2013 and early 2014, the following will be common:

Massive Write-Downs
The past few years' overpriced acquisitions and low-quality ore bodies will have to be shown on future balance sheets at their true, much lower values, and these adjustments will produce lower earnings or outright losses on annual and quarterly reports. So the numbers will be even worse for a while than in the recent past.

Share Dilution
The sudden capital shortage will be felt unevenly across the industry. Miners with low-cost operations and plenty of cash on hand will be able to finance this lean stretch internally. But higher-cost operators in the middle of expansions they were planning to finance have a serious problem. There may not be new capital to be had, and what is available will require either extortionate interest rates or the issuance of so much stock that existing shareholders are "diluted" to the point that their stake in the company is greatly diminished.

Junior Miner Die-Off
At current prices, maybe a quarter of precious metals miners are profitable on an ongoing basis, and many of the unprofitable three-quarters are juniors without the financial cushion to weather a multi-year drought. So write-downs at

the majors will coincide with wide-spread failure among the juniors.

GREAT FOR INVESTORS IN 2014 AND BEYOND

The, um, silver lining for precious metals miners and their would-be investors is that crises of this magnitude tend to cull the weakest players and create survivors that thrive in the next bull market. If mining follows this script it will, at some point, produce another crop of big winners.

The question is when and how this reversal of fortune will occur. Among the determining factors are:

Metals Prices

Obviously, higher selling prices for their products will make the best miners a lot more profitable and give the weak miners some breathing room in which to address their problems. Since we've spent a big part of this book making the case for higher gold and silver prices, all we'll say here is that the mining environment should be a lot more hospitable in 2014 and 2015 than it was in 2013.

Mine Supply

The wide-spread cancellation of new mines means lower future production of gold and silver and, other things being equal, higher prices (though mine supply is a much bigger factor for silver than for gold). In both 2000 and 2008, for example, metal prices dipped to the industry's break-even point, which created a launch pad for subsequent bull markets. With all-in costs more-or-less equal to mid-2013 gold and silver spot prices, the industry is back on the pad.

Takeover Binge

One common sign that a troubled industry has bottomed is a sharp jump in mergers and acquisitions, as the stronger players buy up the weaker at fire-sale prices. Especially in-demand will be deposits located near already-producing mines, offering the potential for economies of scale and other efficiencies by spreading fixed costs over higher production. The precious metals space contains a handful of well-capitalized majors and a hoard of undercapitalized juniors, so the former will buy up (some of) the latter, producing a kind of mirror image of the bad deals of the previous decade, as high-quality deposits bought cheaply make the majors even stronger. Meanwhile, this combination of more buy-outs and more failures will diminish the supply of publicly-traded miners. So when investment money returns to this sector, it will be chasing fewer companies.

Which Miners?

There are three general categories of miners that should be of interest:

- Juniors with high-quality, relatively low-cost deposits and enough cash to finance the next few years' capital budget. They will see their value rise dramatically once the metals begin the next leg of their bull market. Or they'll be snapped up by bigger competitors at nice premiums. But we stress that this applies only to the best juniors. The rest – i.e., those with low-quality properties, extremely high capital costs and/or weak balance sheets will disappear without a trace, taking their investors' capital with them.

- Mid-tiers with relatively-low costs and well-diversified properties; they should rise nearly as much as many juniors, with far less risk.

- Majors able to squeeze costs out of their existing operations and buy up smaller, cash-strapped juniors at favorable prices. This group has the least upside potential because their size precludes the leveraged return available with smaller companies, but they're by far the least risky, so are important parts of a diversified portfolio of mining companies.

CHAPTER 26

THINGS TO AVOID – AND TO BET AGAINST

"Bonds are certificates of guaranteed confiscation."
– Franz Pick

If crisis equals opportunity, then the next few years should produce opportunities that extend far beyond precious metals. Most of these will involve overpriced financial assets returning to their (negligible) intrinsic value, so as this is written in late 2013 the average investor with a diversified portfolio of stocks and bonds is in a very precarious spot. Much of what they own is way up, but as in 2000 and 2007, "way up" might be a prelude to "way down."

Put another way, the tidal wave of newly-created currency that kept the 2008 crisis from becoming another Great Depression has further inflated the Money Bubble, along with subsidiary bubbles in stocks, bonds, and real estate. So the conditions are ripe for the bursting of not just one but several bubbles, all more-or-less simultaneously. The consequences are inherently unpredictable – that's why we devoted an entire section to the different scenarios – but that *something* big and disruptive is coming seems all but certain. In this chapter we'll cover the asset classes most likely to suffer and which should therefore be avoided. And we'll present some strategies for profiting from their pain by betting against them.

SELL YOUR BONDS

In a fiat currency world, where money is just bits stored in or flowing between databases and backed by nothing but promises, waging a currency war is technically quite easy. A central bank clerk just types in a number stating how much government debt his organization is buying and hits send, and voila, the requisite amount of new dollars, yen, or euro are created and added to the banking system. When the supply of new currency exceeds the demand for it, the currency is debased, and its exchange rate tends to decline. A cheaper currency gives domestic companies that rely on exports an advantage in foreign trade, while making the government's debt easier to pay off in real purchasing power terms because of inflation.

But then it gets tricky. How, for instance, does an over-indebted government keep long-term interest rates from rising in response to a depreciating currency? Since higher interest rates would, other things being equal, slow the economy and thus offset the benefits of a cheaper currency, taming the bond market – where long-term interest rates are set – is key.

Quick digression: What is a bond? Readers familiar with bonds and interest rates should skip to the next paragraph. For those who aren't familiar, a bond is a loan made by an investor, usually for a period of twenty years or more, to an entity like a government or corporation that promises to pay a fixed amount of interest each year and then return the principal on the bond's maturity date. Because the annual interest payment, or coupon, is fixed, its purchasing power (and thus the value of the bond) depends on the value of the currency in which the interest is paid. If the currency is stable and holds its purchasing power, the bond generally holds its value. If the currency is depreciating, the income stream received from the bond is worth less each year, which in turn makes the bond worth less. The further in the future the bond's maturity date, the more pronounced the impact of changes in currency purchasing power. So long-term bonds tend to be very sensitive to inflation, and can rise and fall dramatically in different environments. Meanwhile, a bond's yield and its price move in opposite directions. If the price goes up, then the annual interest payments are a smaller percentage of the purchase price, which makes the bond's yield – calculated by dividing the bond's annual interest payment by its price – lower. And vice versa: If a bond's price goes down its yield goes up. As the bond approaches maturity, i.e., the day when the lender is required to pay back the original capital, its price will move toward "par," which is the face value of the bond.

For a major country with a fiat currency, controlling the bond market – at least in the short run – has also turned out to be fairly simple: Create even more currency and use it to buy bonds, a technique known as quantitative easing (QE) or debt monetization. The extra demand from the central bank pushes up the price of bonds, which lowers their yield. Lower interest rates convince individuals and businesses to borrow and spend, increasing everyone's taxable income. The result: All the short-term benefits of currency devaluation without the attendant interest rate issues.

The first half of this book explained this strategy and why it is doomed to fail. So here we'll just assert that in the not-too-distant future the developed world's currency war will reach its natural limit. Governments will lose control of the happy-but-illusory world they created because markets – that is, people using free will to choose what they do with their money – always, eventually, see through such deception. Interest rates will rise as the whole world gives up on dollar, yen, and euro-denominated bonds, and the game will end with a bang, as all bubbles eventually do. Long-term bonds – which financial writer James Grant now calls "return-free risk" – will crash.

Note that we're focusing on long-term bonds and notes, defined as loans with maturities of ten years or longer. Short-term debt instruments, or "bills," that come due within a few years or less are not as sensitive to inflation and interest rates. As financial assets they might be poor investments when the Money Bubble pops because of the currency risk they entail, but their prices won't fall as dramatically as those of long-term bonds.

So at a minimum, you'll want to refrain from owning long-term government bonds in the early years of the currency crisis. That means going through your 401(K) and other financial accounts and rooting out the long-term bond funds, along with "balanced," "total return," and "life cycle" funds that might contain long-term bonds.

But if you're the adventurous sort and can tolerate the possibility of being wrong for a while before being right, "shorting," or betting against, long-term bonds could be a spectacular winner over the coming decade.

There are lots of ways to sell a financial asset short. With stocks, the traditional method is simply to sell shares without first owning them. Just type in a ticker and hit "sell," and you're short. That won't work with bonds, at least for individual investors, but there are other, nearly-as-straightforward ways to get the same result. For example:

Short a Bullish Leveraged Bond ETF
Wall Street's ever-playful financial engineers have created numerous ways to place pretty much any bet. Among the

most popular of late are "leveraged" exchange traded funds (ETFs) that use derivatives to replicate the daily movement of various indices and markets. In theory they are clean, simple ways gain instant exposure to either side of a given target market. There are numerous ETFs that are designed to go up if bonds go down, sometimes 2 or even 3 times as much. On the surface, these "inverse" (so-called because their returns are the inverse, or opposite of the target market) funds sound like the ideal way to place a bearish bet on bonds.

But in reality they're among the worst funds to buy and hold because they achieve their performance by creating, for example, swaps (derivatives similar to futures contracts) that replicate and sometimes amplify the movements of an underlying market. They then rebalance periodically to maintain the same sensitivity to the movement of their market. Because the derivatives that make up the swaps tend to lose value as they mature, and these funds operate by buying relatively-expensive contracts and holding them while they depreciate and expire, the funds themselves tend to bleed value over time. So it is crucial to understand that if the market moves in the wrong direction for an extended period, these leveraged funds can lose even more than their stated multiple to the market. For this reason, they can't be held for more than a few months without their flaws completely offsetting their advantages. Figure 26.1 illustrates what happened to TBT, a popular 2X inverse Treasury bond fund, during the long stretch when interest rates were falling and Treasury bond prices were rising.

Figure 26.1: TBT Long-Term Performance 2009 – 2013

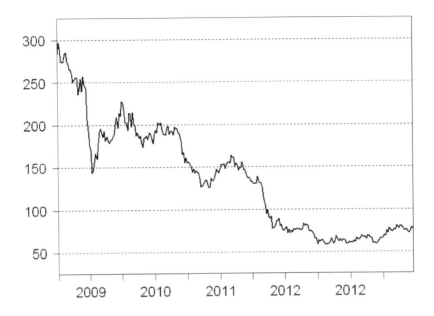

But this is not to say that leveraged funds can't be used. They can, but in a tricky way: One of the advantages of ETFs over traditional mutual funds is that they trade like stocks. This means they can be sold short like a stock, which creates an interesting opportunity for using their previously-mentioned flaws against them and to your advantage. Whereas a leveraged inverse bond ETF (one that is designed to go up if bonds go down) can only be held for short periods of time because it bleeds value, a short position in a leveraged *long* bond ETF (a fund designed to go down if bonds go down) can be held for years because its gradual loss of value works to the short seller's advantage. So to bet against bonds, ignore the inverse bond funds and short the long bond funds. (You might have to read this paragraph through a few times but we promise it will eventually make sense.) Recall the above chart of TBT. Virtually everyone who shorted it between 2008 and 2013 made money.

However, the nature of shorting creates some issues that those new to the practice should understand. When you short something, your broker goes out and borrows it from a different account before selling it and depositing the proceeds in your account. So shorting is only possible if shares are available to be borrowed, which is not always the case. And once you've successfully shorted a stock, it can still be called away from your account if your broker needs it to repay an account from which it was borrowed. This is rare but it does happen, especially during times of market turmoil. So it is possible that in shorting bonds in this way you will be right on the timing and instrument, but still lose because the broker closes the position at an inopportune time. But like we said, this is a rare occurrence. Figure 26.2 presents a list of long-term bond ETFs that can, in theory, be sold short.

Figure 26.2: Leveraged Bullish Bond ETFs

	Ticker Symbol	Leverage
Direxion Daily 30-Year Treasury Bull	TMF	3X
PowerShares DB Long 25 Year Treasury Bond ETN	LBND	3X
ProShares Ultra 20 Year Treasury	UBT	3X
Direxion Daily 10-Year Treasury Bull	TYD	3X
ProShares Ultra High Yield	UJB	3X

BUY VOLATILITY

For a sense of how an over-indebted financial system enters a catastrophic collapse, imagine a spinning top. For a while after being set in motion, the top stays in one place, spinning smoothly. But then a slight wobble creeps into its rotation, gradually becoming more pronounced until it turns violent. The unstable top then shoots off in a random direction to crash against whatever is nearby.

That's the way the financial markets will behave when the Money Bubble bursts. As this is written in late 2013 our imagined top is spinning smoothly again after a huge, near-catastrophic wobble in 2008. With US stock prices at record highs, interest rates still historically low and daily fluctuations in major markets reasonably muted, all looks well. But soon, probably in 2014 but almost certainly by 2015, the fluctuations will begin to increase until the system spins out of control.

A useful indicator of where the markets are in this process is the VIX index of volatility in the S&P 500 options market, which predicts month-ahead fluctuations in the stock market. Figure 26.3 shows how placid the US stock market, as depicted by its low volatility, was while the housing bubble was inflating in the mid-2000s. But notice what happened in 2007 and early 2008: First came some wobbles, as the early indications of a bursting housing bubble hit the markets. Then in 2008 the bubble burst and the banking system began to implode. The markets were terrified and capital was pouring in and out (mostly out) of stocks and pretty much every other financial asset class, causing wild fluctuations. The VIX soared from 20 to 80 in a matter of months.

Figure 26.3: VIX S&P 500 Volatility Index, 2005 – 2009

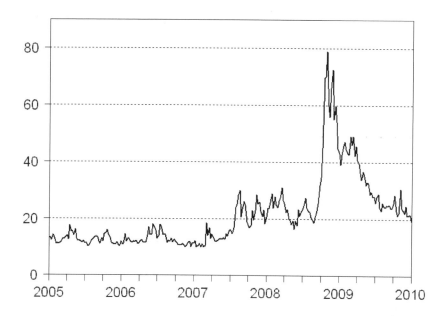

Figure 26.4 shows the VIX from 2010 to late 2013. Notice how the spasms of the financial crisis die down and a new period of calm returns – thanks to all the currency being created by the Fed and handed to the banks. The top is once again spinning smoothly. But under the surface, all the imbalances that nearly destroyed the global financial system in 2008 were not only still present, they were being amplified by governments around the world borrowing aggressively, printing, and intervening. By late 2013 the system was once again primed to start wobbling. Which means a spectacular trade is just waiting to be placed.

Figure 26.4: VIX S&P 500 Volatility Index, 2010 – 2013

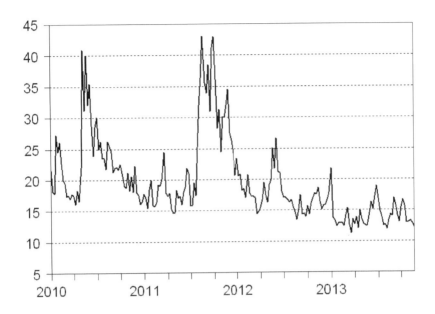

Here again, the long volatility ETFs are strictly for short-term traders, but the *inverse* volatility funds offer the same kinds of advantages for long-term short-sellers as the leveraged bullish bond ETFs. Think it through: You expect volatility to go up, so you short, or bet against, the inverse funds that want volatility to go down.

Figure 26.5: Inverse Volatility Funds

	Ticker Symbol
VelocityShares Daily Inverse VIX ST ETN	XIV
ProShares Short VIX Short-Term Futures ETF	SVXY
Path Inverse S&P 500 VIX Short-Term ETN	XXV
VelocityShares Daily Inverse VIX ETN	ZIV

SHORT (SOME OF) THE STOCK MARKET

The volatility that characterizes the next few years will be primarily to the downside for financial assets. So it follows that a bet on volatility is also a bet against the stock market or big parts thereof, and being long volatility or short the stock market will, in this case, yield the same general results. There are literally dozens of instruments available for betting against the US and other major stock markets, beginning with a plethora of bullish ETFs that in late 2013 are crying out to be shorted.

Short Vulnerable Sectors and Companies

In the environment that seems likely to prevail in 2014 and beyond, the big banks, which against all logic have grown even bigger since their near-collapse in 2008, are severely threatened by both rising interest rates and a weakening economy. Several other industries, including home builders and insurance companies, are nearly as vulnerable. So rather than focusing on broad market averages that include resource companies that might go up in a currency crisis and low-end retail and grocery chains that might hold their own when the middle class is forced to downscale, it makes sense to target one's negative bets more precisely by singling out the sectors most likely to lead the market down.

Short Individual Stocks

This is old-school shorting, and in many ways is still the best. Simply sell a stock without owning it and you've created a short position. You're responsible for dividends but otherwise can hold the position without consequence for years, if that's how long it takes. And it's more precise than any ETF: If the big banks as a group are vulnerable, then the weakest of them should be bankruptcy candidates, just as Bear Stearns and Lehman Brothers were in the 2008 crisis. So betting against them directly is more risky but potentially more lucrative.

OPTIONS: EVEN MORE LEVERAGE

Options are financial instruments that give their owners the ability, or "option" to do something with an underlying security. A call option confers the right to buy shares by calling them away from someone else at a predetermined "strike" price within a set time frame. A put option enables its holder to sell shares, or put them into another's account, again for a predetermined time and price.

Options exist for a limited time, generally less than 2 ½ years, and can be bought for a fraction of the cost of the underlying security while controlling capital equivalent to full ownership of the security. That's another way of saying options offer a lot of leverage. If you own an option that cost five percent of a stock's price, and the stock gains, say, ten percent, the value of that option will almost double. But if the price of the stock instead only equals the strike price on the day the option expires, you've lost 100 percent of your capital. So options are only for the highly risk-tolerant.

There are options on pretty much every major equity and sector ETF, with numerous expiration dates and strike prices. This variety makes possible a near-infinite range of strategies, to which a lot of very smart people devote entire careers. We advise keeping it simple, however, when trying to play something as straightforward as volatility. So consider the following:

Create Volatility Spreads

During a bubble's pre-collapse phase, when volatility begins to grow in magnitude, the disruptions don't have a dominant direction. Some days the market is way up, other days it plunges. This environment is ideal for a "volatility spread," which involves placing both bullish and bearish bets on the same security. To take a real-world example, one could buy both put and call options on the S&P 500, which is not a bet that the market goes up or down but that it fluctuates more than currently expected. If it spikes far enough in one direction, that option becomes sufficiently valuable to more than offset the loss in the other. During a time of very low volatility like mid-2013, options premiums – the extra amount the market demands over and above an option's intrinsic value – are low, making volatility spreads relatively cheap when compared to historical norms.

A variation on the volatility spread that is interesting if one anticipates a sharp market decline is the "back spread." To create this spread, sell near-the-money put options (i.e., options with a strike price just slightly higher than that of the current S&P500 or other target security) and buy a larger number of out-of-the-money puts (which will only have value if the market falls) with the same expiration date. The out-of-the money puts are cheaper, so the cash received from selling a single near-the-money put might cover the cost of two of them, making the spread cash-neutral up front.

Now, if the market just sits there or goes up, the puts will expire worthless, and you simply break even. But if the market falls dramatically, the out-of-the money puts will go up enough to make the strategy profitable. The further the market drops, the bigger the profit.

BE CAREFUL OUT THERE

Though it is possible to craft conservative strategies to profit from falling asset prices, in general these kinds of bets are just that, bets. So they should only be pursued with money that can be lost without a change in lifestyle, as part of an overall strategy that has a solid base of low-risk, highly-stable assets. But once those criteria are satisfied, the "short" side of the financial world becomes a target-rich, fascinating, potentially very profitable environment.

CHAPTER 27

PAY OFF DEBT AND INTERNATIONALIZE

"Staying a half-step ahead of a wrathful market means being early to apprehend ideas the crowd finds ridiculous today but will find obvious in retrospect."

– Michael Santoli, Barron's

The past 70 years have been a smooth stretch of highway paved by ever-increasing debt and a soaring supply of newly-printed currency. But those artificial good times have nearly run their course, and the systems built upon the expectation of their continuing will soon fail. Put another way, the next crisis will not be a garden-variety correction within a long-term up-trend. It will be a reversal of the trend itself.

The traditional way of responding to uncertainty is to pay off debt and diversify among uncorrelated asset classes. Both remain generally good ideas, though the end of the fiat currency world requires a different and more comprehensive approach. This chapter will offer some suggestions. But because everyone's situation differs, the following should be viewed as informational only. Always seek expert help before making big financial decisions.

PAY OFF DEBT

After reading the preceding 26 chapters of this book, a very reasonable conclusion might be that the best strategy is to borrow as much fiat currency as possible and use the proceeds to buy hard assets, on the assumption that the failure of that currency will wipe out your debts and leave you with a bunch of gold and farmland, owned free-and-clear. This is a seductive thought, but it rests on a flawed assumption, which is that while they're destroying the dollar, the powers-that-be will simply let debtors walk away from their obligations. They might not. Once contracts are being abrogated right and left through bank bail-ins and asset confiscations, it becomes easy to envision bankers arranging to have debt contracts re-written to their advantage by, for instance, requiring that a given debt be repaid at its fair value, not in the depreciated currency in which the debt was contracted. Thomas Jefferson (the author of the Declaration of Independence) died in poverty for, among other reasons, having to pay the debt on his father-in-law's estate twice – once in local currency that was placed with the Virginia government during the War of Independence, after which it was not accepted in payment because the currency had depreciated, and then a second time in a hard currency (British pounds, which were fully backed by gold). A good source for more on Jefferson's plight is Herbert Sloan's *Principle & Interest: Thomas Jefferson & the Problem of Debt*.

So we recommend the safe approach. Pay off as much debt as possible and convert as many financial assets as possible to hard assets. Life will be easier without those credit card bills, and you'll sleep more soundly without having to worry about the government or banks raising interest rates or otherwise changing the terms of your debts in ways that make them far more onerous.

INTERNATIONALIZE

Because the future is unknowable and unpredictable, diversification is always a good idea. Spread your assets around, so goes this line of thought, and you raise the odds of keeping most of what you have. Back in the days of a stable global financial system, this process was fairly simple: own some stocks, bonds and cash, some real estate and maybe a couple of global equity or bond mutual funds, and you were exposed to most of the major asset classes, forms of economic activity, and major currencies. If some of your holdings went down, you could be fairly certain that others would go up to compensate.

But that diversification strategy depended on three assumptions:

1) The currencies in which the various asset classes were valued would be more-or-less stable.

2) Bank and brokerage accounts had a reasonable degree of privacy and posed little financial risk to their customers.

3) Legal and financial systems would continue to function more-or-less normally, with respect for contracts and property rights and immediate, unfettered access to money in brokerage and bank accounts.

These assumptions are no longer the sure things that they once were. In a crack-up boom, for instance, the local currency can become nearly worthless in a very short time, making cash and bonds (which pay a fixed amount of currency each year) worthless as well. The collapse of Refco and Lehman Brothers and MF Global during the 2008-2009 crisis and its aftermath offer reasons to avoid excessive reliance on stock and futures brokers. Meanwhile, the coming wave of bank bail-ins and other forms of asset confiscation make bank accounts and other local assets a target of desperate governments. These events, should they come, will likely come quickly and without much warning.

The best response to this higher order of risk is a higher order of diversification. Because there's no way of knowing which kinds of crises will strike where, it is more important than ever to diversify not just among asset classes but *among countries*. Put another way, political risk is now a much bigger consideration in deciding where to keep one's capital, and no country is risk-free. Here are a few geographic diversification ideas for you and your advisor to consider:

Offshore Precious Metals Storage
Recall that during the Depression the US confiscated its citizens' gold – but only if it was stored in the United States. Going forward, gold confiscation is a lot less likely because the dollar is not on a gold standard that requires the government to have metal in storage in order to issue new currency. Also, most wealth today sits in IRAs and 401(K)s rather than precious metals. But it is possible that gold and maybe silver could be caught up in the general asset-confiscation dragnet. So storing some metal outside of one's home country and beyond the immediate reach of the local tax authorities is advisable. Singapore, Dubai, and Hong Kong, for instance, are all quite capable of resisting US pressure to turn over records and/or assets stored in their vaults. We discuss offshore precious metals storage at more length in Chapter 23, and refer readers back to that section.

Self-Directed IRA
This is a variation on the traditional individual retirement account that allows its owner to buy precious metals for offshore storage and foreign real estate, among other things. Since most Americans' savings are primarily in the form of their home (which can't be moved offshore) and their tax-advantaged retirement accounts, a self-directed

IRA might, for many, be the only way to move significant capital offshore.

A self-directed IRA enables its owner to set up an offshore trust or limited liability company (LLC) that is held by the IRA and operates overseas. But it is not a way to use retirement savings to buy a vacation condo on a Costa Rican beach. Any asset bought through a self-directed IRA is strictly an investment and has to be managed "at arm's length." That is, it must be rented out to non-related tenants and the income thus generated must flow into the account. The property can't be enjoyed by yourself, your friends or your family without jeopardizing its tax-deferred status. However, once you retire you can use it and count the use as a withdrawal from the account. This requires a bit of book-keeping, so at that point a good accountant becomes mandatory.

Also note that every country has its own rules governing foreign purchases of real estate, insurance policies and other domestic assets. An LLC that works for Latin American real estate might not be appropriate for buying a small business in Europe, for instance. So it is crucial to figure out what you want to buy before forming an entity with which to buy it.

Clearly, creating and fully utilizing a self-directed IRA requires the advice of a competent, honest advisor. A quick Internet search will turn up dozens of companies specializing in converting traditional IRAs to the self-directed variety. But investigate them thoroughly before choosing.

Second Passport

Already, in these relatively placid pre-crisis times, passports have become instruments of coercion and surveillance in many countries. For example, an American who owes back taxes or child support or any number of other things can be denied a passport. And the newest US passports are equipped with biometric identifiers and radio-frequency identity chips that enable the authorities to track their holders' travels. Similar controls are also being implemented in other countries.

So just in case, whether you're actively planning a move abroad or would simply like to travel with minimal stress, a second passport from another, less coercive and intrusive country, would be a very nice thing to have. Among the many benefits:

- It's less of a red flag. In many parts of the world, the holder of a US passport becomes a target for terrorists or criminals. A passport from a less politically controversial country gives its owner a much lower profile.

- It offers greater travel privacy. If you travel on a US passport to countries at odds with the US, re-entry can involve serious questioning. But use a passport from a different country for your travels and then re-enter the US on your American passport and there will be no travel history for you to explain.

- It serves as a backup if your primary passport is lost, stolen, or withdrawn. In such a situation you won't find yourself stranded in a foreign land with no passport.

- It makes some other countries much more hospitable. A passport from a member of the European Union, for instance, confers the right to live or work anywhere in the EU. A Dominican passport does the same for the Caribbean Community (CARICOM), which includes many of the island nations.

- It is crucial for expatriation. If you decide you want to give up your current citizenship (for instance to be able to live abroad and pay local taxes), a different passport is essential.

Now that the point of a second passport has been established, here are two possible ways to get one:

Family Connection. The country of your ancestors might offer citizenship. Ireland, for instance, offers citizenship and a passport to those with at least one Irish-born grandparent. And many countries extend the same privileges to spouses of citizens. Jews, meanwhile, are generally able to move to Israel under the Law of Return.

Long Stay or Big Investment. Many countries offer citizenship to visitors who stay for long periods of time. And many other countries offer various kinds of consideration for those willing and able to bring in large amounts of money and invest it locally. Canada offers citizenship in return for an investment that will create employment and spur economic activity. And a few countries, including Dominica and St. Kitts/Nevis will, in effect, sell a passport and citizenship in return for a hefty fee.

DO NOT TRY TO HIDE ASSETS

Beginning in 2015, the G20 countries are supposed to begin a program of automatic exchange of tax information. Even if your assets somehow slip through this net – like gold bars buried in the back garden – with the NSA monitoring all electronic communications and sharing the results with law enforcement agencies, it's a safe bet that they'll know pretty much everything, no matter what you admit to.

What's the point of internationalizing if the government knows where everything is? There are several. If, for instance, capital controls are imposed that limit domestic transactions, a foreign bank account would be free from those restrictions. Asset confiscations of most types would not apply to wealth outside the jurisdiction of the local government. And income generated in a currency that is not in the middle of a crack-up boom would become vastly more valuable.

So while trying to hide accounts or property has worked in the past, times have changed. Today the goal is to build as much flexibility into your life as possible. You'll preserve more assets this way, and in the worst case scenario will have somewhere to go and something to spend once you get there.

EPILOGUE

REBUILDING FROM THE RUBBLE

"It is impossible to grasp the meaning of sound money if one does not realize that it was devised as an instrument for the protection of civil liberties against despotic inroads on the part of governments. Ideologically it belongs in the same class with political constitutions and bills of rights."

– Ludwig von Mises

Three thousand years ago, the Greek philosopher Plato argued that the best form of government is one in which a "philosopher king" employs absolute power to create and maintain a just society. Today, this yearning for a combination of strength and wisdom at the top is as acute as ever. A strong leader gets things done, so according to this line of thought the key to success is to find the right person and turn them loose to make the system work.

But history has shown the philosopher king to be one of those intriguing ideals that, when attempted in the real world, always and everywhere falls prey to human nature. Power, it has by now been established beyond all doubt, corrupts. Good, well-meaning leaders become demagogues who put pride and ideas of 'legacy' above the welfare of citizens. Demagogues become corrupt, feathering their own nests (or foreign bank accounts) by looting their subjects' wealth. And corrupt leaders become tyrants, responding to opposition with force and turning their subjects into slaves. Initially-enlightened governments, in short, will devolve into dictatorships if allowed to.

The framers of the US Constitution, with their first-hand experience and observations of Europe's absolute monarchs, understood this weakness of human nature. So when they met in Philadelphia in 1787 to create "a more perfect Union" of sovereign states, their guiding principal was the polar opposite of Plato's: Because individuals are infinitely corruptible, governmental power should be strictly limited. They divided the federal government into three branches, delegated only 17 specific, defined powers to it, and left all other powers to the states or to the people. The hope was that each component would use its authority to keep the others in check. And – their experience with the Continental currency's hyperinflation fresh in their minds – they designated gold and silver as the only constitutionally acceptable forms of money. The explicit goal was to prevent the kind of unbridled spending that would allow the government to expand beyond its Constitutional limits.

In the 20th Century these principles got lost among the world wars and the other pressing needs that made expanded government power seem like the lesser of two evils. The result is the world described in this book, in which governments operate with nearly unchecked power, spying on and abducting citizens with impunity while borrowing, printing, and squandering impossibly large amounts of money.

That the present course is unsustainable is beyond doubt. What is in doubt is what happens after the governments and corporations that now depend on ever-increasing debt and money printing finally collapse. The world's financial powers could try to impose a new global currency, perhaps modeled on the Special Drawing Rights (SDRs) now used by the International Monetary Fund. The breakaway civilization could decide that it has feasted sufficiently on the 99 percent and impose a sound money system from above. The system could spin out of control and descend into another Great Depression. A desperate leader could use the turn-key totalitarian state he's inherited to abolish remaining civil and economic rights in the name of national security. Or a majority could coalesce around a new gold standard or other form of sound money, and force it upon reluctant politicians and bankers.

There are plenty of other possibilities, but all begin with the failure of the current system. Unsound money has had 100 years (or 42 years, depending on whether one dates its inception from the founding of the Federal Reserve in 1913 or the closing of the gold window in 1971) to corrupt the world's governments and financial system, and the process is nearly complete. Debt, government spending and the gap between rich and poor have all reached unsustainable extremes. And trust in government, corporations and other big, complex systems is eroding at an accelerating rate. The game is nearly over for fiat currency and the institutions that depend on it.

This book is about how individuals can protect themselves and perhaps profit from the massive redistribution of wealth engendered by the destruction of their countries' currencies. But in truth, the money management side of that story is fairly simple, with just a few major concepts, decisions, and actions. The transition to what comes next is vastly more complex and in many ways more interesting. Politics really didn't matter during the first 13 years of the 21st century, since both major US parties were pursuing the same objectives of bigger government, higher debt and more currency creation. But political ideas and their implementation will matter greatly when the slate is swept clean and competing visions of power and freedom become real possibilities.

And assuming the worst dystopian scenarios are avoided, money management will enter a time of near-infinite possibility. 3-D printing will bring manufacturing back from China to the US, but in a form that is nearly unrecognizable (think Star Trek rather than a traditional GM assembly line). Biotech will revolutionize medicine, ending many diseases that now stalk humanity and changing the economics of health care in ways that no one currently understands. Alternative energy will decentralize power generation and end the developed world's dependence on Middle Eastern oil, changing the political landscape (hopefully) for the better. All of these things and many more will create new fortunes for those who can see them coming and act on that prescience.

We're looking forward to a time when we can focus on the good things that are moving humanity forward rather than the bad things holding it back. So with that in mind, we'll replace the gloom-and-doom lens with one a bit more rose-colored and sketch out an optimistic – though completely feasible – scenario for the coming decade.

Years 1 - 3
The trust horizon shrinks further as governments continue to spend, borrow, print, and lie. National currencies fall from favor and a crack-up boom gains momentum. Chaos reigns in foreign exchange markets as the dollar, euro and yen fluctuate wildly versus each other and their respective governments escalate the currency war. Capital begins pouring into real assets, sending the price of precious metals, farmland, energy and some commercial real estate up dramatically. Politics become ever more contentious and fractious, with each election a "throw the bums out" catharsis followed by near-instant disillusionment with the new leaders. Catastrophic collapse appears imminent.

Years 4 – 6

While the above is going on, a debate is raging online and in the media. Bitcoin and other, newer forms of crypto-currency are gaining adherents, and the idea is spreading that monopoly national currencies that had seemed so inviolate were actually part of the old dysfunctional order and thus dispensable. Gold's soaring exchange rate leads a growing number of reporters and pundits to investigate the nature of money and conclude that precious metals are "real" money while paper is an inferior fake. Pressure begins to build both in the market – as people swap fiat currencies for cyber-currency or gold – and the political/media realm, as more people begin echoing Ron Paul's call for the audit/closure of the Federal Reserve and a return to some form of sound-money regime. Just as faith in the dollar is about to evaporate, a charismatic legislator calls for a new gold standard that defines the dollar as $1/10,000^{th}$ of an ounce of gold (so that dollar bills once again become warehouse receipts for gold), bans fractional reserve banking and legitimizes competing currencies in a "monetary free market." And just like that, faith in the dollar is restored. Price levels – after a quick jump to account for the dollar's devaluation versus gold – stop rising and stability returns to the currency market. The economy starts growing again, at rates not seen for years. Seeing that sound money works, Europe and other nations begin to emulate the US.

Years 7 - 10

The global financial system and economy adjust, sometimes quite painfully, sometimes smoothly, to monetary stability and strict limits on the size of government. The US ends its global military empire, closing overseas bases and calling home its soldiers, and institutes a new "Monroe Doctrine" calling for military non-interference. It then extends this concept to financial markets by banning government and central bank intervention. Other countries, accustomed to relaxing and/or chafing under US protection, adjust their military budgets and alliances to become more self-reliant. There are conflicts and even a few wars, but overall the level of violence is lower than during the decades of US dominance.

Those who held fiat currency savings are much poorer for having trusted their governments, but what capital they have left – mainly tangible assets like houses and farmland – is safe and now earns a decent return or otherwise enables them to live a comfortable, productive life. Borrowers who were able to make their payments have had their debts all-but-eliminated by the dollar's devaluation, though a much larger number failed to make their payments and lost everything.

Big banks are much smaller and small banks much healthier. Finance's dominant role in the economy and politics ends. The treasury secretary in 2020 is from a manufacturing company that earns more than Goldman Sachs and JP Morgan Chase combined. The focus has shifted from making money by shuffling paper to making money by building useful things. Technology is the main topic of discussion in the financial markets rather than interest rates or the latest Fed statement. Speaking of the Fed, it still exists but is now limited to exchanging gold coins for pieces of paper at the request of free, peaceful and increasingly rich citizens. And historians, looking back on the previous century, characterize it as the last gasp of the all-powerful nation-state, which was destined to end in a frenzy of debt, paper money and broken promises.

"We all want progress, but if you're on the wrong road, progress means doing an about-turn and walking back to the right road.

– C. S. Lewis

APPENDIX

HOW DO YOU MANIPULATE THE GOLD MARKET?

In Chapter 21 we note that gold's exchange rate is being manipulated and that for much of 2013 gold was in backwardation. These two events are directly linked, and together point to a very significant turning point in the year ahead. Because most people don't find such things as fascinating as we do, we kept our original discussion as simple as possible. But there's more to be understood, so for readers interested in a more complete explanation, we offer the following:

Because gold is money, its manipulation begins with interest rates. This point was clearly demonstrated by Reg Howe in 2001 with his essay: *Gibson's Paradox Revisited: Professor Summers Analyzes Gold Prices*, now posted on GoldenSextant.com. Howe examined a 1985 paper written by Lawrence H. Summers (before he joined the Clinton Administration and eventually became Treasury Secretary) and Robert B. Barsky.

To understand the importance of Summers' and Barsky's findings, we begin with John Maynard Keynes, who did much of his best work in the years following World War I. He noted that the empirical evidence from the 19th century during the classical gold standard showed that interest rates did not rise when the general price level fell, contradicting economic theory of the time. The prevailing thinking was that slower money supply growth – leading to lower prices – would cause interest rates to rise because less money would be available than in a higher growth situation, which it was believed would lower interest rates because a more rapid growth would mean more money was available. Hence the 'paradox,' which Keynes named after British economist Alfred Gibson, who first noted that the empirical evidence did not support prevailing theory.

But the empirical evidence began to change around 1995 because the general price level (at both the wholesale and consumer level) was rising but bond interest rates were not. Howe observed:

"The historical evidence adduced by Barsky and Summers leaves but one explanation for this breakdown in the operation of Gibson's paradox: what they call "government pegging operations" working on the price of gold. What is more, this same evidence also demonstrates that absent this governmental interference in the free market for gold, falling real rates would have led to rising gold prices which, in today's world of unlimited fiat money, would have been taken as a warning of future inflation and likely triggered an early reversal of the decline in real long-term rates."

Howe concludes: "By demonstrating that falling real long-term rates [an event evidencing rising inflationary pressures and prices] will lead to rising gold prices absent government interference in the gold market, Barsky and Summers underscore the futility of trying to control the former without also controlling the latter." In other words, to successfully depress interest rates, a government must also actively depress gold.

Howe's paper is one of the seminal works explaining why governments intervene in the gold market to suppress its exchange rate. Though it was written twelve years ago, well before the 2008 financial crisis, Quantitative Easing and in particular, the Zero Interest Rate Policy (ZIRP) central banks have forced on the financial markets, the principle Howe explains highlights the significance of the recent, prolonged occurrences of backwardation in gold.

Since 2008 and the introduction of ZIRP, gold borrowing rates for up to one year have been at or below zero percent. Anything below zero percent is contrary to normal market behavior because the lender of gold is paying the borrower, rather than the other way around. In fact, gold's interest rates have never before been below zero. Why is it happening now? Clearly, the reason is government intervention.

There are two points to consider here. First, for large institutions, gold lending is not a free-market activity. The rates posted by the trading members of the London Bullion Market Association provide the general reference point (much like Libor is the reference for interbank dollar interest rates) and cover the lending of (generally 400-ounce) bars that meet the LBMA standard. In this market, a round lot is 80 bars (approximately one metric tonne or 32,150 ounces – about $42 million). Odd lot transactions under 25 bars (presently about $13 million) are rare. So for all practical purposes, this market is dominated/controlled by central banks. In other words, gold's interest rates are whatever the central banks want them to be, and even those few large private sector institutions that participate in this market by lending their gold have to take what the central banks give them. After all, if you are an institution and want to lend your gold to a triple-A credit at 1 percent but central banks are willing to lend at 0.5 percent, you are not going to locate a borrower.

This central bank control of gold's interest rates leads to the second point: If the central banks are going to achieve a ZIRP for dollars and euros, they must also achieve a ZIRP or even less than ZIRP for gold, i.e., negative gold interest rates in which central banks pay you to borrow their gold. If central banks did not control gold interest rates in this way, they would be higher than dollar interest rates with the result that gold would move into backwardation, which is the greatest fear of central bankers whose principal aim is to perpetuate the existing fiat currency system.

Backwardation or its mirror opposite, contango, arises simply from math when measuring the time value of money using the interest rates of a currency pair (i.e., the exchange rate of one currency to another). If the interest rate for both currencies is identical regardless of the tenor, their future (often call "forward") exchange rate is always the same. But if there is any difference in their interest rates, the future exchange rate of every currency pair is either in backwardation or contango. For example, Indian rupee interest rates are higher than dollar interest rates, so the dollar is in contango against the rupee, and the rupee is in backwardation against the dollar. The 'sounder' money of the pair – i.e., the one with the lower inflation and therefore lower interest rates, which are conditions that market participants assume will prevail in the future – will always be in contango against the other currency. Consequently, gold is normally in contango against the dollar.

Gold backwardation creates an opportunity to profit from an arbitrage. A holder of physical metal can sell today and buy it back at a lower price in the future, which is just one part of the profit earned by the arbitrageur. The others are that he avoids storage costs on his metal, plus he has the proceeds from the sale which can be used to generate income until he needs the proceeds to buy back his metal in the future. But the downside is that this transaction involves counterparty risk. You might not receive your gold back in the future because of the risk of default by the counterparty.

Now you might be thinking, because the rupee is backwardated against the dollar, does the same arbitrage opportunity exist? The short answer is *no*, because dollars and rupees on the one hand and gold on the other are inherently different. In contrast to all national currencies, gold does not have any counterparty risk because it is a tangible asset.

If gold is in prolonged backwardation because no one wants to take the arbitrage, one can only conclude either or both of the following:

(1) Physical gold in the vault is more attractive to its owner than the alternative of holding dollars, euros or other fiat currencies. The potential profit to gold owners from the arbitrage is not worth the counterparty risk.

(2) The vaults of those central bankers willing to lend metal are nearly empty, or they have reached the point where they no longer want to take the risk of lending whatever metal they have left. Otherwise these central banks would lend gold – even if they needed to pay the borrower instead of receiving interest income from the borrower – to lower gold's exchange rate and thereby eliminate the backwardation. Borrowed gold is sold, which depresses its exchange rate.

This point in turn leads to an important monetary principle: Money is debased when its supply increases at a rate greater than demand for it. The debasement of fiat currency is manifested by rising prices, i.e., lower purchasing power of the fiat currency. Because goods and services in the economy are priced in fiat currency, the debasement of gold arises differently. The result is the same – i.e., lower purchasing power – but this result comes about from gold's exchange rate falling to a lower level, meaning it purchases less goods and services.

It is interesting to note that since May 2013 gold interest rates have been climbing along with those for national currencies, signaling that central banks are not only losing control of dollar and other currency's interest rates, but gold interest rates too.

Regardless what gold's current exchange rate may make it appear to be, gold is really undervalued at these levels, just like it was when it briefly backwardated in 1999 and then again in 2008 – both of which marked important low points in gold's exchange rate. The purchasing power of the dollar has been substantially eroded over the years, so gold's undervaluation becomes clear when it is properly inflation-and-debasement adjusted to accurately make a comparison (see Chapter 22). Another reason is that those central banks willing to lend gold to manipulate its price have less gold in their vault than when the previous backwardations occurred. If they have less ammo (physical gold), price manipulation will be that much more difficult for them. The manipulators can still operate in the paper market in attempts to drive the gold price lower (or keep it from rising – and these interventions have occurred repeatedly this year), but eventually their credibility will erode if they are asked to deliver metal against their short positions, and they instead resort to offering cash settlement.

What the above describes of course is a scheme aimed at suppressing gold's exchange rate, which is so well documented by GATA. Dollar interest rates cannot be manipulated without also simultaneously manipulating gold interest rates to prevent backwardation, which should be easy for central banks to do because they dominate/control the gold lending market. But the frequent backwardations this year are evidence that the manipulation of the gold market is nearing its end.

When the manipulation of gold in the 1960s ended with the collapse of the central bank cartel called the London Gold Pool, gold began rising because its contrived undervaluation ended. There is every reason to expect a similar result when the current central bank gold manipulation ends, which may not be too far in the future given some important news breaking as we conclude our book.

Following on the heels of Libor and foreign exchange market rigging, regulators are now beginning to look at activity in the gold market. On November 19, 2013, Bloomberg reported: "The U.K. Financial Conduct Authority is reviewing gold benchmarks as part of its wider probe of how global [interest] rates are set, a person with knowledge of the matter said."

This news is a positive development for advocates of transparent and free-markets, but it remains to be seen just how far the regulators are willing to probe in any investigation as well as release their findings. After all, the truth about gold interest rates might be the pin that finally pops the Money Bubble.

ABOUT THE AUTHORS

James Turk and John Rubino are the co-authors of *The Coming Collapse of the Dollar and How To Profit From It: Make a Fortune by Investing in Gold and Other Hard Assets* (Doubleday, 2004).

James Turk is the founder and a director of GoldMoney, a Jersey, Channel Islands company and a leader in online gold trading. He is also a director of the GoldMoney Foundation, a not-for-profit educational organization dedicated to providing information on sound money. He has specialized in international banking, finance and investments since graduating in 1969 from George Washington University with a B.A. degree in International Economics. Beginning his business career with The Chase Manhattan Bank (now JP Morgan Chase), he later managed the Commodity Department of the Abu Dhabi Investment Authority, that country's sovereign wealth fund. He is the author of several monographs and numerous articles on money and banking. He and his wife live in London, England.

John Rubino runs DollarCollapse.com, a popular financial website, and contributes regularly to CFA Magazine. His books include *Clean Money: Picking Winners in the Green-Tech Boom* (Wiley, 2008), *How to Profit from the Coming Real Estate Bust* (Rodale, 2003) and *Main Street, Not Wall Street* (Morrow, 1998). After earning a Finance MBA from New York University, he spent the 1980s on Wall Street, as a Eurodollar trader, equity analyst and junk bond analyst. During the 1990s he was a featured columnist with TheStreet.com and a frequent contributor to Individual

Investor, Online Investor, and Consumers Digest, among many other publications. He lives in Idaho with his wife and two sons.

INDEX

D

E

F

G

N

O

P

Q

T

U

V

Articles by James Turk can be found on his company's
website:
www.goldmoney.com

Articles by John Rubino can be found on his website:

www.dollarcollapse.com

34087443R00199

Made in the USA
Lexington, KY
22 July 2014